J

The History of
Movie
Photography

The History of
Movie
Photography

BRIAN COE

Eastview Editions
Westfield, NJ

323263

Eastview Editions
PO Box 783
Westfield
NJ 07091

Text © Brian Coe 1981
Compilation and design © Ash & Grant 1981

First published in the USA by Eastview
Editions 1981

Cataloging in Publication Data

Coe, Brian, *b. 1930*
    The history of movie photography.
    1.   Moving-picture cameras – History
    I.   Title
    778.5'3'0934   TR848

    ISBN 0–89860–067–7

    Printed in Hong Kong

Contents

PAGE 1 A Zoetrope

PAGE 2 ABOVE A lever slide of the 1880s
BELOW A frame from a film made by the
Lumière brothers in 1895

PAGE 4 LEFT Rudge's magic lantern
CENTRE American Film Co. studio, 1916
RIGHT Poster for *The Jazz Singer*, 1927

ABOVE Frame of
Multicolor film, 1929
ABOVE RIGHT Filming *Scott of the
Antarctic*. Note the Technicolor camera
on the right and the 1910 camera seen
in the film on the left
BELOW LEFT Still from *King of Kings*
BELOW RIGHT Univex Straight 8
camera, c. 1936

Introduction

The popularity of the cinema has led to the appearance over the years of many books dealing with the development of the medium. Most have concentrated on the work of the directors, artists and writers. The practical developments which made the cinema possible, and which have led to the advanced technical accomplishments of today, are less often dealt with. The vexed question of the invention of cinematography has been much discussed in the past, with often unsupported claims being made on behalf of individuals and nationalism frequently being substituted for impartial research. Who invented cinematography? No one person was responsible, and no country can be given sole credit for being the birthplace of the movies. This book sets out to try to put the story into perspective and to show how the main streams of development which produced the motion picture came together at the end of the last century. To try to follow in detail the technical developments in the business of cinematography during the last eighty years would not be possible in a book of this size, but the main lines of technical advance are followed to the present day. For further information, the reader is referred to the bibliography. In addition, the following organisations, among others, have permanent displays relating to the history of the motion picture:

England:	The Science Museum, London
	The Kodak Museum, Harrow
	The Barnes Museum of Cinematography, St. Ives, Cornwall
France:	The Cinématheque Francaise, Paris
Germany:	Deutsches Museum, Munich
Czechoslovakia:	Narodny Technische Muzeum, Prague
America:	International Museum of Photography at George Eastman House, Rochester, New York

Where prices are given, they are in the currency of the day. In pre-decimal British coinage, there were 12 pence to the shilling and 20 shillings to the pound. Thus, the shilling was the equivalent of five pence today. The guinea was 21 shillings, or £1.05 in today's money. However, inflation during the last sixty years has greatly altered the value of money. Wages for a working man in the last century rarely exceeded £1 a week; even a very skilled worker would do no better than two or three pounds a week. This must be borne in mind when trying to compare prices with those of today.

1
Shadows on a sheet

Shadow plays have been a feature of oriental life for, it is believed, several thousand years. It is impossible to know whether they originated in India or Java, but the shadow puppets used throughout the Far East had, and still have, a basically similar construction. Often they were made from thin, stiff leather as in, for example, the Javanese Wayang Purwa shadow shows. The figures, derived from characters in religion and folk lore, are usually intricately perforated and painted and gilded on the surface. Each figure is supported by a split cane rod, bent to follow the shape of the subject and the arms are jointed at the shoulder and elbow. This articulation allows them to be moved by thin rods attached to the wrists of the figure. The puppet is operated immediately in front of a translucent sheet, with a lamp placed at some distance from it. The operators speak dialogue and an orchestra provides a musical accompaniment. By tradition, the men in the audience sit on the lamp side of the screen where the figures are seen in their colours against a white background, while the women sit behind the screen seeing the presentation as moving shadows.

The shadow plays had spread to Europe via the Middle East by the late Middle Ages and enjoyed a considerable success during the latter part of the eighteenth century. A shadow play theatre was opened by Séraphin at Versailles in 1776 and he opened another in Paris at the Palais Royal in 1784. Both were popular and successful and, with some change of content, survived the Revolution. They continued to operate until the late 1850s. Other versions of the so-called 'Ombres Chinoises' remained popular throughout the century, notably the shows at the Théâtre des Ombres du Chat Noir in Paris. These European shadow shows used elaborately articulated figures, usually of metal which allowed more complex movements than their oriental predecessors, and small but powerful lamps which gave much more distinct shadows.

The use of optical devices, as opposed to the casting of shadows, to produce an image on a flat surface began with the development of the camera obscura (see panel above).

In Battista della Porta's application of the camera obscura (which later evolved into the photographic camera) the essential components of the optical projector were present – a light source, subject, projection lens and a screen – used; however, in a rather inflexible form. At some point, by a rearrangement of these elements the light source, subject and lens were brought close together and the magic lantern was born. When this was first achieved, and who did it, is in some doubt. The Jesuit Athanasius Kircher, in the first edition of

Camera Obscura

From ancient times it had been observed that a small hole in the wall or window of a darkened room produced an inverted image of the outside scene on the opposite wall. The earliest illustration of the camera obscura (literally 'dark room') was printed in a book by Gemma Frisius, a Dutchman, in 1545. The Italian Battista della Porta gave details of several forms of this device in his book *Magia Naturalis*, first published in 1558. He described the use of both lenses and concave mirrors to make the image clearer and upright. He proposed that these optical devices could be used to 'project' into a darkened room tableaux and scenes of action in a sunlit exterior. During the next three centuries versions of the camera obscura were used by artists as an aid to drawing. Transportable versions like sedan chairs were used by 17th-century artists, as were smaller versions constructed as small tents which collapsed for easy transportation. In the same century, an important development of the camera obscura came with the introduction of small, portable models in the form of one wooden box sliding within another, containing a mirror which reflected the image from the lens onto a translucent screen set in the

Portable camera obscura

top. This primitive reflex camera design was the source of inspiration for the early experimenters in photography at the beginning of the 19th century.

his book *Ars Magna Lucis et Umbrae*, published in 1646, discussed various ways of projecting images, using variations of the ancient technique of mirror writing – if opaque letters are set on the surface of a plane or concave mirror, they will be seen as diffuse silhouettes when the mirror reflects a small light source, such as the sun, onto a surface. Kircher demonstrated that by placing a lens between the mirror and a screen, a sharp but inverted image of the writing would appear on the screen. By using a spherical water-filled flask as a condenser to concentrate the light, Kircher found that texts painted on its surface could be projected by light from a candle after dark. It is possible that in 1653 or 1654 Andreas Tacquet, another Jesuit, presented projected pictures using Kircher's methods to accompany a lecture by a colleague, Martin Martini, about his trip to China. The story is related by Kaspar Schott in *Magia Optica* (1657).

BELOW Athanasius Kircher, who described forerunners of the magic lantern in his book *Ars Magna Lucis et Umbrae*, 1646. BELOW LEFT A primitive form of projector illustrated by Kircher in the second edition of his book, 1671

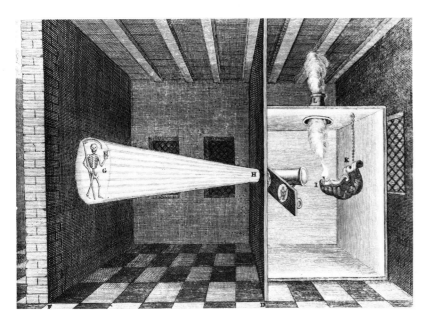

The Javanese shadow puppets are made from thin leather, painted, gilded and perforated. ABOVE An intricate shadow cast by a shadow puppet

An early magic lantern, in which a candle was used as the light source

Kircher's experiments involved the separate use of the basic elements of a projector, but they were not properly integrated into one convenient device. It seems likely that this integration was achieved by the Dutch scientist Christiaen Huygens. In his notes for 1659 Huygens sketched nine skeletons in various poses, four of them drawn inside circles, describing them as 'for representation by means of convex lenses and a lamp'. From later correspondence with a Parisian, P. Petit, it seems that Huygens had constructed and used a projector at this time, perhaps of the type illustrated in his notes for 1694, where there is a drawing of the optical system of a 'laterna magica' with a concave mirror concentrating the light from a candle onto a condensing lens, through a transparent picture and a projection lens, onto a screen. It is also probable that the Danish scientist Thomas Rasmussen Walgenstein had made and used a magic lantern by 1664.

In the second edition of Kircher's book, published in 1671, there is a description and illustration of a form of projector, but the absence of a projection lens in front of the picture suggests that Kircher did not fully understand the proper requirements of such a device. It may have been nothing more than a shadow projector, a development from his mirror writing experiments. Samuel Pepys, the English diarist, noted in his entry for 19 August 1666, 'Comes by agreement Mr. Reeves, [bringing] a lanthorn, with pictures in glasse, to make strange things to appear on a wall, very pretty'.

So impressed was Pepys that he soon purchased the lantern together with two telescopes for £9.5s.

It is obvious that the magic lantern had come into widespread use towards the end of the seventeenth century. Professor C. Sturm of Altdorf described the use of the lantern in a book published in 1676, and illustrated a slide of the head of Bacchus. A book by William Molyneaux of Dublin published in 1692 described several models of magic lantern and carried an advertisement by John Yarwell for all the instruments described, to be had 'at the Archimedes and Three Golden Prospects, near the Great North Door in St Paul's Church-Yard'.

During most of the eighteenth century the use of the magic lantern was restricted by the inefficiency of the light sources available. A candle, or an animal fat or oil lamp flame permitted only a dimly lit picture, if anything other than a very small picture was wanted. The Argand pot lamp, developed around 1780, improved the brightness of the flame by using a circular wick which supplied oxygen to the centre of the flame and by the use of a chimney which gave a strong up-draught. The lamp burnt tallow, or a thick oil, which had to be pre-heated before the lamp would burn. The development of the magic lantern from a mere toy to an instrument of large-scale entertainment was made possible by the development of brilliant light sources.

The most important of these was the lime light. In 1801 Professor Robert Hare invented the oxy-hydrogen blowlamp, in which a stream of oxygen was blown through the flame of burning hydrogen to produce an intensely hot flame. He found that if this flame was played upon a refractory substance a brilliant light was produced. His discovery was described in the *Philosophical Magazine* in 1802. In demonstrations with a projection microscope at the London Mechanical Institute in the early 1820s, Dr G. Birkbeck used an oxy-hydrogen lamp devised by Goldworthy Gurney in which a piece of lime

An engraving by Rowlandson, 1799, showing a magic lantern show. It was printed as a paper transparency for a peep-show box

Magic lantern slides dating from around 1775. Slides of this age are rare

Lime light jets for the magic lantern:
ABOVE A blow-through jet; BELOW A
mixing jet

(calcium oxide) was made incandescent. The lime light came into
prominence with the publication in 1826 of details of a signal light,
invented by Lieutenant Thomas Drummond, in which a ball of lime
was held in a spirit or hydrogen flame through which a jet of oxygen
was passed. From this time the Drummond, or lime, light came into
use for the magic lantern, permitting much bigger pictures on the
screen. By the middle of the century, it had become the principal
light source for all lanterns other than those for domestic use.

Various forms of burner were introduced, known as jets. The two
principal forms were the blow-through jet, where the oxygen was
blown from one jet through a hydrogen flame burning at an adjacent
jet, and the mixing jet, where the two gases were mixed together in
a chamber just below the single jet. The lime, usually in the form of
a cylinder, was carried on a peg which allowed it to be rotated to
bring a fresh surface into the flame when required. The mixture of
the two gases was highly explosive and catastrophes were not
unknown, when careless operators tried to fill with one gas a bag
containing a little of the other.

After the invention of the incandescent electric light bulb in 1878,
an increasing number of public buildings were wired for electricity
and the electric arc lamp, rivalling the lime light in its brilliance,
came into wider and wider use. Although it had its own problems of
safety and, some thought, gave a harsher light than that of the lime
light, it was more convenient and by the early years of this century
had begun to replace its rival. For domestic projection, paraffin oil
lamps replaced the earlier Argand burners in the second half of the
last century. Marcy's Sciopticon lantern, developed in America in
1872, used a two-wick burner of special design which gave a very
white light. An improved lamp, invented by the London manufacturer Frederic Newton in 1876, used a two-wick burner with a very
tall chimney; later, variations using three, four and even five wicks
were introduced. These lamps gave enough light for a reasonably
bright picture in a small hall, although they came nowhere near the
brightness of the lime light or the arc lamp. In the home, incandescent gas mantle burners could be operated from the house supply
and by the end of the century the new electric lamp bulbs were
becoming efficient enough to give an adequate light for home use.

The discovery in the 1890s of an inexpensive method of producing
acetylene, an inflammable gas easily generated by dripping water
onto calcium carbide in a pressure container, led to the use of lamps
with two, three or four burners. One of the most dangerous lantern
lamps, at least if wrongly handled, was the ether saturator. Ether,
a highly volatile and very inflammable liquid, was placed in a
reservoir filled with an absorbent material through which a stream
of oxygen was passed. The ether-oxygen mixture was burnt at a jet
to heat a lime cylinder to incandescence. The simplest light source
of all, and the oldest, as we have seen, was a candle flame, and toy
lanterns, widely sold at the end of the last century and the beginning
of this, often made use of it. It would produce only a yellow, flickering
picture a few inches across, but toy lanterns delighted several
generations of children.

The form of lantern slide used in the early magic lanterns in the
eighteenth century was a long strip of glass painted with several
subjects and set in a wooden frame, which was passed through the
lantern. The colour used on early slides was not very transparent and
the light sources not very bright so that the figures, painted on clear
glass, were seen as little more than silhouettes. From the early nine-

Robertson's Phantasmagoria show, 1798, used macabre figures rear-projected on translucent screens

teenth century, the slides were painted in more transparent colour and figures were often surrounded by opaque black paint to enhance their brilliance and colour on the screen. At first it was the custom to paint several figures or subjects on one glass slide, or slider as it was then generally called, which naturally slid through the lantern to show each subject in succession. By the middle of the last century, however, the general practice was to have smaller, single subject slides, except for those used for special effects.

The first spectacular application of the magic lantern was devised by a Belgian, Étienne Gaspard Robert, known as Robertson. He created a remarkable show using a magic lantern of his own devising called the Phantascope. Mounted on a wheeled carriage, it could be moved towards or away from a translucent screen, while the lens was adjusted to maintain correct focus. The audience, on the other side of the screen, saw grotesque and macabre images enlarging and diminishing, while a shutter device on the lens allowed the images to appear or disappear gradually or suddenly. His Phantasmagoria show was presented in March and April 1798 at the Pavilion de l'Échiquier in Paris, and later in the chapel of the old Couvent des Capuchins near the Place Vendôme, where, to increase the mystery, images were projected onto smoke as well as on a conventional screen. In his book *Letters on Natural Magic*, published in 1834, Sir David Brewster described a similar show

'brought out by M. Philipstal [sic] in 1802, under the name of the *Phantasmagoria*, and when it was shown in London and Edinburgh it produced the most impressive effects upon the spectators. The small theatre of exhibition was lighted only by one hanging lamp, the flame of which was drawn up into an opaque chimney or shade

13

when the performance began. In this "darkness visible" the curtain rose and displayed a cave with skeletons and other terrific figures in relief upon its walls. The flickering light was then drawn up beneath its shroud, and the spectators in total darkness found themselves in the middle of thunder and lightning. A thin transparent screen had, unknown to the spectators, been let down after the disappearance of the light, and upon it the flashes of lightning and all the subsequent appearances were represented. This screen being half-way between the spectators and the cave which was first shown, and being itself invisible, prevented the observers from having any idea of the real distance of the figures, and gave them the entire character of aerial pictures. The thunder and lightning were followed by the figures of ghosts, skeletons, and known individuals, whose eyes and mouth were made to move by the shifting of combined sliders. After the first figure had been exhibited for a short time, it began to grow less and less, as if removed to a great distance, and at last vanished in a small cloud of light. Out of this same cloud the germ of another figure began to appear, and gradually grew larger and larger, and approached the spectators, till it attained its perfect development. In this manner the head of Dr. Franklin was transformed into a skull; figures which retired with the freshness of life came back in the form of skeletons, and the retiring skeletons returned in the drapery of flesh and blood.

The exhibition of these transmutations was followed by spectres, skeletons, and terrific figures, which, instead of receding and vanishing as before, suddenly advanced upon the spectators, becoming larger as they approached them, and finally vanished by appearing to sink into the ground. The effect of this part of the exhibition was naturally the most impressive. The spectators were not only surprised but agitated, and many of them were of the opinion that they could have touched the figures.'

In the early years of the last century Henry Langdon Childe developed a new projection technique which greatly widened the scope of the magic lantern. Childe's 'dissolvent views' were shown by using two lanterns side by side, both aligned so as to project on

ABOVE LEFT The large lantern slides painted for the shows at the Royal Polytechnic Institution were of remarkable quality. This example is from the story of Baron Munchausen

ABOVE A dissolving view series showing the transformation of flowers from bud to full bloom and then to decay. The effect of this beautiful series is enhanced by the superimposition of a moving butterfly

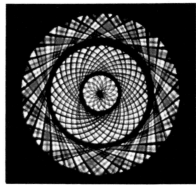

TOP The highly popular 'Man eating rats' slide. The sleeper's jaw can be moved up by operating a lever; the rats, in an endless procession, run into his mouth when the handle is turned. This subject could cost ten shillings in the 1880s, perhaps half a week's wages

FAR LEFT A dissolving view series in which the scene can be made to change from summer to winter and then to night-time

LEFT Three Chromatrope slides, which produce kaleidoscopic patterns on the screen

ABOVE A variant of the lever slide, introducing a realistic movement to the girl on the swing

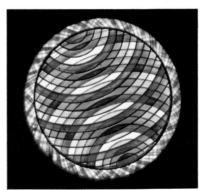

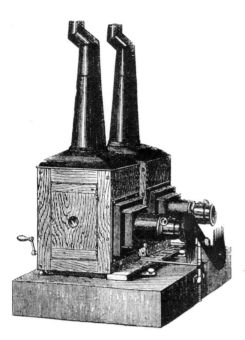

A dissolving view lantern set sold by Newton in the 1870s. The comb-like dissolvers alternately cover and uncover each lens. They are operated by a handle at the rear

A mid-Victorian magic lantern show

the same portion of the screen. Two toothed or comb-like plates could be moved simultaneously in front of the lenses, so that as one was covered up, the other was uncovered. On the screen, one image was thus made to dissolve into the next, with no interruption in the picture. Not only did this method give a smooth transition between pictures and avoid a sideways movement of the picture when changed, but it also allowed the production of transitional changes and moving effects on the screen. Daytime could change to nighttime by dissolving between two slides identical in form, but painted with different lighting effects. Parts of a scene could be made to change or move in the same way. Many similar and even more spectacular effects to those of the Phantasmagoria could be produced, without the mechanical complications of the latter show.

Childe's 'dissolvent views', brought before the public in the 1830s, used two ordinary lanterns placed side by side with a mechanical dissolver in front of the lenses, a technique which has been revived in recent years in modern slide shows. By the middle of the last century, an alternative form, the biunial lantern, was in use. The biunial lantern consisted of two lanterns, one on top of the other. The dissolving effect could be produced by a vertically moving shutter, but was more often carried out by turning down the lamp in one projector while turning up that in the other. The lime light, requiring two gases to be fed to it, was not easy to control, but John Benjamin Dancer, an optician from Manchester, was one of the first to devise a tap which would turn the lime light down without turning it out. He supplied the Manchester Mechanic's Institute with his device, which was used to present dissolving view shows there with great success in the late 1850s. In 1864 Michael Noton invented a single tap which controlled two lime lights, turning one up and one down simultaneously and variations and improvements on the 'single plug or star dissolver' remained in use until the lime light fell from favour.

The first lantern fitted with three lenses seems to have been that shown by the Reverend Canon Beechey at the Great Exhibition in London in 1851. His spherical lantern had a single lime ball lamp,

C. GOODWIN NORTON & SON.

Animated Photographers.
LANTERN ENTERTAINMENTS AND EXHIBITIONS
Of the Highest Class.
◂ Prospectus on application. ▸

Goodwin Norton, a well-known lanternist, with his triunial, or triple, lantern

with three lens systems fitted with prisms so that they could be converged onto the same screen. The usual pattern of triunial, or triple, lantern was produced by putting a third lantern on top of a biunial model. Sometimes, the three lanterns were made all of a piece, but more usually the top one was detachable so that it could be used as a single lantern if required. Triunial lanterns were normally fitted with lime lights controlled by dissolving taps. Both biunial and triunial lenses were often fitted with 'flashers', hinged flaps on the front which could be operated to give momentary effects on the screen – a flash of light, for instance. Slots in the ends of the lens tubes could be used to insert 'tinters', coloured transparent sheets which gave a wash of colour to the slide on the screen. The third lens of a triunial lantern could be used to superimpose effects on dissolving view scenes produced by the bottom pair. The effects of falling snow, rising moon, lamps lighting in a house and so on could be added to a picture in this way. One operator, D. Noakes, created a quadrunial lantern with four lenses one above the other, capable of producing the most complex effects on the screen. Noakes gave regular presentation of his dissolving view shows on a huge screen in the Royal Albert Hall in London.

The following description, from Lewis Wright's book, *Optical*

A biunial lantern by Hoare, c. 1890, for the presentation of dissolving views and superimpositions

Mechanical slides

Rotary or gear slides were fitted with circular glasses, one of which was usually fixed and carried the main part of the picture, while another was free to rotate, carrying the moving detail of the scene. In the early slides the moving glass was sometimes rotated by a belt and pulley drive.

More often the moving glass was set in a toothed brass rim, engaged by a pinion wheel turned by a handle at the side of the slide. The effects ranged from the turning of windmill sails to the 'man eating rats' where an endless succession of rats, painted on the turning glass, appear to run into

the open mouth of a sleeping man.

Sometimes more elaborate effects were produced by using two counter-rotating glasses as well as a fixed one. Such slides might show swarms of bees round a hive, or water pouring from a fountain. The spectacular Chromatrope used two counter-rotating discs with coloured geometric patterns, which produced dazzling, almost hypnotic changing patterns of colour and form. The Eidotrope used discs of perforated metal instead of glasses, giving a swirling pattern of brilliant white dots on the screen. Coloured 'tinters' placed in front of the lens could add colour to the effect.

Lever slides used a moving disc turned through part of a circle by

LEFT *Belt and pulley rotary slide*
BELOW LEFT *Astronomical gear slide*
BELOW *Double lever slide*

Projection (1891), gives some idea of the effects that an expert lanternist could achieve with the triple lantern:

'Let us suppose, then, an English landscape, with a wind-mill, and mill-pond in front. It may be first thrown on the screen in the fresh green of an English spring. Presently the mill turns round, then the scene dissolves (without appearing to change) into the warmer hues of autumn, and one or two swans glide gently over the glassy lake. The scene dissolves again into a tempestuous night, the sky covered with clouds, and little light getting through from the partly turned-down lantern. Flash after flash of lightning breaks across the dark sky, followed by peals of thunder (provided by shaking a square of sheet-iron), and finally a 'rain-slide' is thrown upon the scene, the sound of the storm being well represented by pouring some barley into an appropriate vessel, and a

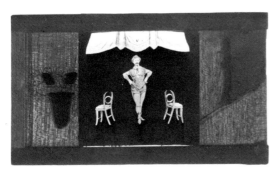 

A slipping slide

a lever protruding from the side of the slide. Two or even three glasses might be moved in this way. For example, in *Paddy teaching the dog to smoke*, the scene is an Irish kitchen. The dog sits up, begging, its lower jaw moved by one lever. Paddy lowers his arm, with a pipe in his hand, moved by two levers operated together. When the pipe is put in the dog's mouth, Paddy's arm is raised again, by working one lever, leaving the pipe behind.

The slipping slide used one glass sliding over another, fixed, glass. In its most common form, the fixed glass was painted with two phases of some simple movement. Black painted patches on the slipping glass alternately covered and uncovered the two phases as the glass was slid to and fro. The slipping glass construction was used in conundrum slides where a question was posed in written or pictorial form, and the answer, often an excruciating pun, was

uncovered by the slipping glass.

The remarkable Cycloidotrope used a disc of smoked glass rotated in the slide, while a stylus carried on a pivoted arm traced a pattern on it. On the screen this produced a brilliant white line which traced a complex regular pattern, the form of which could be varied by adjusting the series of pivots which controlled the movement of the tracing arm.

ABOVE *The Cycloidotrope*

BELOW *Articulated slide*

flash or two of lightning being still continued. Finally these effects are changed for one showing the moon emerging from behind a cloud. This must be done *very gradually*, and while the moon-slide is thus worked the scene is gradually dissolved into a bright moon-light scene, with the light effect upon the water. After a few moments a 'snow-slide' is put in, and when this has fallen for a few seconds the landscape is again dissolved into a winter scene, with snow upon the landscape and ice upon the pond, on which skaters execute their gliding movements; or this last may be done when the scene is again changed to a night and bonfire effect, with lights in the mill windows.

Such is an example of what may be called high-class dioramic lantern exhibition; and if the different slides match the register *exactly*, the effect is indescribably beautiful. All depends upon that, and also upon having an adequate staff of assistants, for one alone

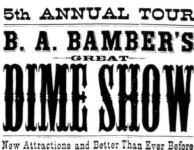

5th ANNUAL TOUR
B. A. BAMBER'S
GREAT
DIME SHOW
New Attractions and Better Than Ever Before

TRAVELS,   ASTRONOMY,

ART,   FUN,

HISTORY.   ELECTRICITY.

B. A. BAMBER.

GRAND STEREOPTICAL
DISSOLVING VIEWS
SCENES IN MANY LANDS
FROM GREENLAND'S ICY MOUNT. TO INDIA'S CORAL STRAND.

THE WONDERS OF THE WORLD.   THE BEAUTIES OF THE WORLD.

Read Carefully Every Word of the Following Programme
PART I.
THE PLANETARIUM
Will be exhibited and explained. This is an instrument lately invented for showing the Planets of the Solar System in their annual motion around the Sun; it also shows their relative size and distance from the Sun, the cause of Tides, Eclipses, Change of Seasons and Signs of the Zodiac. This part will be a lasting benefit to all who desire to know more about the wandering stars that reflect the sun's light upon us by night. After this instrument has been exhibited Telescopic Views of the larger Planets will be reflected upon the canvas.

PART II.
NATURAL SCENERY
Comprises Views of some of the most Prominent Objects of Interest in both the Old and New World. All cannot travel and see these places, but whoever attends this Entertainment will see them reflected on canvas with a glow of beauty never to be forgotten.

PART III.
THE ILL-FATED SHIP
Comprises a series of Paintings, showing the sunshine and shadow of a Sailor's life.
SCENE 1.—Ship at dock in Liverpool Harbor, passengers leaving their native country.
SCENE 2.—Just out of the harbor, sailing on the blue waters of the Irish Sea.
SCENE 3.—A Storm arises, which rapidly increases; the furling and reefing of sails.
SCENE 4.—Height of the Storm, rolling on the boundless deep and struck by lightning.
SCENE 5.—Horrible calamity at sea; ship on fire, most on board perish in the flames.
SCENE 6.—The few who make their escape on a raft are now afloat on the wide Ocean.

PART IV.
The Highland Lover's Courtship for Marriage
Showing how it is done, also the result which usually follows; a caution to those about to embark in this kind of a ship.

PART V.
STATUARY
A Magnificent Collection of Statuary from the Centennial Art Gallery will be exhibited, besides other noted works of Sculpture, the beauty of which cannot be described; they must be seen to form any idea of their real beauty and grandeur. Among the many we mention "Flight of Mercury," "Ophelia," "Evening," "Forced Prayer," "Council of War," &c., &c.

PART VI.
MISCELLANEOUS
These embrace a large collection of Paintings, Artistic Gems, Dissolving Views and Transformation Scenes, which have been procured at great expense, and for faithfulness in perspective and beauty of design they stand unrivaled. The whole will be enlivened with
NUMEROUS COMIC SCENES
Electricity Without Extra Charge
A very fine Galvanic Battery is provided for any who may wish to try it. This is an excellent remedy for Rheumatism, Neuralgia and Headache. Be sure to come before the show begins if you want to try it.

Positively Everything Advertised on this Bill will be Shown
REMEMBER, THE PRICE OF ADMISSION IS
ONLY 10 CENTS FOR ANYBODY AND EVERYBODY
Doors Open at 7 o'clock.   Begins at 8 o'clock.

could not possibly conduct all the various operations described. Two would often be required at the lantern, irrespective of any acoustic effects; and in some cases the work would be better done with four lanterns than even three.'

The Royal Polytechnic Institution in Regent Street produced very complex visual effects in its magic lantern shows, which employed as many as six huge lanterns projecting hand painted slides 8 × 5 inches (203 × 127mm) in size. In one of their popular presentations, *The Siege of Delhi*, artillery fire, shells bursting and so on were shown by the use of several lanterns at once, and Professor Pepper reported,

'The optical effects were assisted by various sounds in imitation of war's alarms, for the production of which more *volunteers* than were absolutely required would occasionally trespass behind the scenes, and produce those terrific sounds that some persons of a nervous temperament said were really *stunning*.'

Until the Royal Polytechnic Institution was sold in 1881, its lantern shows were held to be the peak of achievement of the lanternist's art.

The early lantern slides were painted by hand onto glass. When well done, as at the Polytechnic, the results could be remarkably good. Often, the painting was rather poorly done. Sir David Brewster remarked in 1834,

'The magic lantern is susceptible of great improvement in the painting of the figures, and in the mechanism and combination of the sliders. A painted figure which appears well executed to the unassisted eye, becomes a mere daub when magnified 50 or 100 times; and when we consider what kind of artists are employed in their execution, we need not wonder that this optical instrument has degenerated into a mere toy for the amusement of the young. Unless for public exhibition, the expense of exceedingly minute and spirited drawings could not be afforded; but I have no doubt that if such drawings were executed, a great part of the expense might be saved by engraving them on wood, and, transferring their outlines to the glass sliders.'

This idea had already been adopted by the lantern slide maker Phillip Carpenter around 1823, introducing 'copperplate' slides that had been produced by transferring the outlines of the pictures from engraved copper plates to glass as a guide to the colourists.

Because of the work involved, hand-painted slides were inevitably expensive. For less demanding purposes, an inexpensive method of producing slides in quantity was patented by S. Solomon on 1 November 1865. The designs were printed in colour by chromolithographic printing onto a gelatin-coated paper from which they could be transferred to a glass slide. This method of transfer printing was widely used to produce miniature slides for toy lanterns and cheap slide sets in the standard size for domestic lanterns. A set of twelve could cost as little as one shilling.

The realism of the projected image was greatly improved by the adoption of photographic reproduction. In 1847 Abel Niépce de Saint-Victor described the first practical method for producing negatives on glass, using a thin film of albumen (egg-white) coated on a glass plate and made sensitive to light. The Langenheim brothers, Frederick and William, were granted an American patent in 1850 for a process of making positive transparencies on glass using the albumen process. They displayed examples of their 'Hyalotypes' at the Great Exhibition in London in 1851, and the process was soon widely used for the production of lantern slides and stereoscopic transparencies. What was to become, in Europe, the standard lantern slide size, $3\frac{1}{4} \times 3\frac{1}{4}$ inches (82.6mm × 82.6mm), was derived from the closely similar size of stereoscopic negative.

The first commercial photographic lantern slides in England were sold by Negretti and Zambra, who imported most of them from their French counterparts Ferrier and Soulier. The monochrome photographic slide could be, and frequently was, embellished by colouring with transparent colours applied by hand. By 1865 a writer was able to note 'photographic transparencies are now steadily taking the place of the old class of painted slide for the magic lantern', although the latter continued to be offered for sale well into this century. Commercial hand-coloured photographic slides remained on the market for much longer, although the magic lantern went into slow decline as an entertainment after the First World War, by which time the cinema had become established. Even so, in the 1920s Newton and Company, a long established and leading firm of lantern suppliers in England, were producing 2,000 slides a week, with a stock of 200,000 titles.

So far, we have considered only those slides which produced a static image on the screen, although the Phantasmagoria and dissolving view shows could introduce elements of movement or change on the screen. Slides which incorporated mechanisms for moving part or the whole of the image on the screen were introduced very early on in the history of the magic lantern. Kircher's experiments included the use of a jointed cardboard figure manipulated in the 'mirror writing' projection arrangement to give a moving shadow on the screen. The Dutchman Petrus van Musschenbroek in his book *Beginselen der Naturkunde* (1736) mentioned and illustrated mechanical slides he had constructed for the lantern. They included a windmill whose sails, painted on a separate glass disc, could be turned by a belt and pulley drive, a man who drank from a goblet when a lever was operated and a tight-rope walker who moved along a rope when one glass was slipped over another. These three examples incorporated the fundamental principles used in the mechanisms of the mechanical slides which became especially popular in the first half of the last century and which delighted subsequent generations of children (see panel on previous page).

By the time that the first movie films appeared at the end of the last century, the magic lantern was capable of very advanced, beautiful, even realistic effects. For some of those who saw the early films, with their jumpy, dim, black and white images, they seemed no advance at all. Yet, through a marriage of the magic lantern and devices exploiting a curious optical phenomenon called persistence of vision, a medium was born which was ultimately to destroy the magic lantern show as a form of public entertainment.

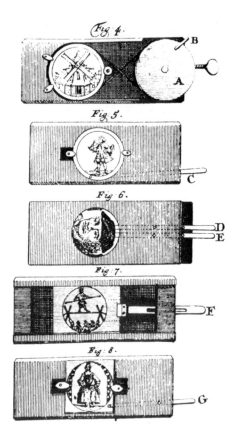

Van Musschenbroek illustrated a variety of mechanical slides in his book of 1736. They included rotary slides (Fig. 4), slipping slides (Fig. 7) and lever slides

OPPOSITE PAGE An advertisement for an American magic lantern show, c. 1880

21

2
Illusions of reality

At the end of the eighteenth century there was a growing interest in entertainments in which optical and other devices were used to give an enhanced illusion of reality to pictures. We have already seen how this was so with the development of the Phantasmagoria and dissolving view lantern shows. Another popular presentation which used a different principle was the Panorama, devised by a painter, Robert Barker, and patented by him in June 1787. The Panorama, first demonstrated in Edinburgh in 1788, consisted of a huge scenic painting on a canvas fitted around the walls of a cylindrical building. Illuminating the painting strongly from above created for the spectators standing in the middle of the room the illusion that they were viewing a real scene. The first show in Edinburgh was a panorama of that city. Barker built The Panorama in Leicester Square, London, in 1793, and opened it the following year with a painting of the Grand Fleet at Spithead. The painting was nearly 300 feet long; a smaller panorama could be shown in an upper gallery. Another Panorama building opened in the Strand in 1802. The engineer Robert Fulton patented the Panorama in France in 1799 but sold the rights to James Thayer and his wife who presented it in a building of a similar size to that in Leicester Square on the Boulevard Montmartre, in Paris. The popularity of this entertainment is reflected in the widespread production of smaller paper panoramas, printed with scenes of landscapes, processions and so on, for use in the home. Some, scroll-like, were wound on rollers and were of considerable length. For example, *A Roman Triumph*, published by W. Sams, Bookseller, of London in 1822 depicted a Roman procession in a roll nearly 16 feet (4.8 metres) long and $6\frac{1}{2}$ inches (16.5cm) high. The popularity of the Panoramas declined after the middle of the last century, but several nineteenth-century panoramas survive in Eastern Europe and are still open to the public. For example the Maroldovo Panorama is in the J. Fucik Culture Park in Prague and illustrates the Battle of Lipan. It was painted for the Architectural and Engineering Exhibition in 1898 and was moved to its present site in 1908. A foreground of three-dimensional objects blends effectively into the cylindrical painted canvas, which is 95 feet (30 metres) in diameter and 36 feet (11 metres) high.

Another entertainment which used large paintings, but one capable of producing more elaborate effects, was the Diorama, invented by Louis Jacques Mandé Daguerre, the inventor of the Daguerreotype photographic process, and Charles Marie Bouton, the painter. The Diorama used large translucent paintings, which, by the manipulation of shutters and screens, could be partially or wholly lit from the front or behind, to produce various effects of transformation. The audience sat on a revolving stage so that several paintings could be exhibited. The mechanisms for varying the lighting made it impractical to move the paintings which were about 72 × 46 feet (22 × 14 metres) in size.

The first Diorama opened in Paris on 11 July 1822. Two pictures were shown, *The Valley of Sarnen* by Daguerre and *The Interior of Trinity Chapel, Canterbury Cathedral* by Bouton. When the London Diorama opened in London in September 1823 (in a building built by A. L. Pugin) these two paintings were moved over from Paris. Later, Daguerre, with Hippolyte Sebron, produced a more elaborate effect by painting on both sides of the canvas, so that by changing the lighting from the front to the back a complete transformation could take place – from daytime to nighttime, for example, an effect perhaps inspired by the dissolving views of the magic lantern. The first painting to use this technique was *The Central Basin of Commerce at Ghent*, shown in March 1834 at the Paris Diorama.

The Diorama was clearly a remarkable show. A report in *The Times* describing *The Valley of Sarnen* in October 1823 said,

'The most striking effect is the change of light. From a calm, soft, delicious, serene day in summer, the horizon gradually changes, becoming more and more overcast, until a darkness, not the effect of night, but evidently of approaching storm – a murky, tempestuous blackness – discolours every object, making us listen almost for the thunder which is to growl in the distance, or fancy we feel the large drops, the *avant-couriers* of the shower. This change of light upon the lake (which occupies a considerable portion of the picture) is very beautifully contrived. The warm reflection of the sunny sky recedes by degrees, and the advancing dark shadow runs across the water – chasing, as it were, the former bright effect before it. At the same time, the small rivulets show with a glassy black effect among the underwood; new pools appear, which, in the sunshine were not visible; and the snow mountains in the distance are seen more distinctly in the gloom. The whole thing is nature itself . . . The whole field is peopled: a house, at which you really expect to see persons look out of the window every moment – a rill, actually moving, all these things (realities) before you . . .'

A beach camera obscura, c. 1900. The hut presented a view of the beach and sea front projected on a white table inside the dark interior by a lens and reflector set in the roof

An advertising brochure for Poole's Myriorama in the early 1900s. It presented huge paintings wound on rollers past the spectators, with special effects introduced by changing lighting

The Mareorama, shown at the Paris Exposition of 1900, like Poole's Myriorama used huge painted panoramas, but with the added effect of movement given by hydraulic rams to the observer's platform, which was shaped like a ship. Two panoramic pictures, one on each side of the 'ship', were used, 40 feet (12.2m) high and 2,500 feet (762m) long

For audiences who had never seen a movie film, or even a dissolving view lantern show, the effect must have been astonishing. They had to pay for the experience. In 1825 the Diorama in Bold Street, Liverpool charged two shillings for admission and half price for children, a substantial sum of money at that time. The presentation of each picture took from 10 to 15 minutes.

Daguerre's Diorama in Paris was burnt out on 3 March 1839, when a workman brought a lighted taper too near a recently varnished canvas. It was subsequently rebuilt and Daguerre and other operators in France, England, Germany, America and elsewhere continued to run Diorama shows. After the middle of the century their popularity waned, perhaps as the result of the competition from dissolving view lantern shows which could produce similar effects without the need for special buildings. The London Diorama was closed after January 1851.

Joseph Poole revived the Diorama principle in his 'New and Colossal Myriorama' show which toured England at the beginning of this century. Scenes from around the world were painted by a team of artists, working from sketches and photographs, on a canvas which Poole's brochure claimed was 'about a mile in length and fifteen feet deep'. The canvas was fitted on a framework which allowed it to be wound past a proscenium, through which it 'glides past the spectator with an almost imperceptible motion and entirely free from noise or friction'. The canvas was lit by gas lamps from the front and from behind, controlled by one operator only who worked the 'startling and wonderful changes'. Poole stated 'A gentleman possessing the necessary elocutional and educational requirements is retained to describe the main features of the various scenes', and an orchestra played 'national and appropriate airs'. 'Artistes of special ability and refinement' performed songs and dances during the presentation. In a typical show, 45 scenes were presented, including such special effects as the blowing up of an ammunition wagon and the demolition of a bridge during scenes of the Boer War. Six 'Mammoth Myrioramas' toured the British Isles, each with a different programme.

As with the Panorama, the success of the Diorama led to the production of miniature versions for the home. The simplest form was the Protean View, which was popular in the 1820s and 1830s. The Polyorama Panoptique was a miniature form of Diorama

Protean views

The popularity of the Diorama, in which dramatic transformations were created by changes of lighting on large paintings, led to the appearance of toys in which similar effects could be created in miniature. Thin paper transparencies were printed with scenes which changed when held to the light. Extra details, or colours, or completely different scenes were printed on the back. Scenes changed from day to night; figures appeared or disappeared. In some, two phases

Protean View front-lit (left) and back-lit (right)

of movement were printed on the back and front so that an illusion of movement could be produced by a rapid change of lighting from front to back. Viewing boxes were sold with hinged lids and backs connected by a link so that as one was closed the other opened, giving a smooth transition of lighting. The Polyrama Panoptique was a typical example, popular in the middle of the 19th century. It took paper

transparencies mounted in wooden frames, capable of a variety of transformations. Similar techniques were used to prepare paper transparencies for the stereoscope, popular in the 1850s and 1860s. The pairs of photographs were coloured on the back and were often pierced where candle flames or other lights were shown. Changing the lighting from front to back revealed the effects.

Polyrama Panoptique

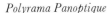

introduced in the middle of the last century in France, and widely sold in Europe (see panel above). In its most common form, it consisted of a paper-covered wooden box with a single lens eyepiece connected to it by paper bellows. Hinged shutters on the top and at the back were linked by a wire strut, so that as one was closed the other opened, altering the lighting smoothly from front to back. The paper transparencies were set in wooden frames; they consisted of several tissues sandwiched together, the front one carrying the main picture, and those in the rear printed with extra details, alternative subjects and colours. Frequently, the tissues were pierced to produce points of lights when lamps were shown in the scene. Operating the hinged shutters produced a variety of transformations – night to day, winter to summer, or streets with and without people. The moon could appear in the sky, or lamps come alight. The same principles were applied to the production of paper transparencies for the stereoscope.

The principle of the stereoscope had been proposed by Sir Charles Wheatstone in 1832. Starting from the fact that our two eyes observe the world from two different points of view, and yet we see a single view in depth, Wheatstone reasoned that if each eye could be presented with a picture appropriate to it, differing slightly from that seen by the other eye, the brain would combine these dissimilar views to give an illusion of depth in the picture. In 1832, only drawings were available for the stereoscope, and the difficulty of producing anything more than very simple geometric figures for the viewer limited the application of his idea. Wheatstone had suggested devices with lenses to combine the drawings, but preferred to use a pair of mirrors at right angles, reflecting to each eye a picture placed at each end of the stereoscope. Such a method allowed large pictures to be viewed. With the introduction of practical photographic processes in 1839, the possibility of producing stereoscopic images from life arose, and in the early 1840s William Henry Fox Talbot, the inventor of the first process for negative-positive photography, made some stereoscopic pairs of photographs of sculpture and buildings. At least one stereoscopic portrait, of the mathematician Charles Babbage, was made by the painter and photographer Henry Collen. Little progress was made, however, until 1849, when Sir David Brewster revived the idea of a stereoscope using lenses. He fitted two lenses in a tapering box and by viewing small photographs taken at a separation of two to three inches saw an image with remarkable depth. No-one in England could be interested in the possibilities of manufacturing such a device, so Sir David put it in the hands of the Parisian optician Jules Duboscq. Duboscq displayed his stereoscope at the Great Exhibition in London in 1851 and it was an immediate success, especially after it attracted the favourable attention of Queen Victoria. So great was the public enthusiasm that it has been claimed, with what truth it is hard to say, that 250,000 stereoscopes were sold in London and Paris in the three months after its first display at the Crystal Palace. This figure is more likely to be that of the stereoscopic photographs sold – but even so, it indicates a huge public demand.

Sir David Brewster, who popularised the lenticular stereoscope in the early 1850s

Stereo-Daguerreotypes, cards with stereoscopic paper prints and stereo-transparencies on glass were supplied by photographers and manufacturers. When viewed in one of the increasingly wide range of stereoscopes these photographs gave an amazing illusion of depth and reality (albeit somewhat frozen in appearance). Paper stereographs, similar in structure to the slides for the Polyorama Panoptique, could be used for similar transformations, but with the added effect of three dimensions to give extra realism to the illusion. The enclosed box-form stereoscopes based on Brewster's original design usually had hinged lids with reflectors to light the front of the stereograph. By closing the lid and holding the viewer to the light the transformation would take place.

The principle of viewing photographs through an optical system intended to enhance the realism of the picture was based on a method which had been introduced in the early part of the eighteenth century for viewing engravings. The Zogroscope was fitted with a large diameter convex lens mounted vertically in a frame fitted to a telescopic stand by which it could be moved up and down. Behind and above the lens a mirror was hinged, so it could be adjusted to reflect through the lens a view of an engraving laid at the base of the instrument. The engraving, or *vue d'optique*, was usually printed in reverse to allow for the effect of the mirror and was viewed with both eyes through the lens. The enlargement of the print and aberrations introduced by the lens gave an enhanced effect of perspective in the print. Sometimes the optical system was entirely enclosed in a box; such show boxes were in use from around 1730. Some took single prints, others could also accept series of prints stuck together on rolls so that they could be wound through in succession. By cutting off some of the extraneous light, the show box version of the Zogroscope further enhanced the illusion. With the rapid development of photo-

The Zogroscope, an 18th-century viewer for engravings. A 'vue d'optique', usually laterally reversed in printing, was laid at the base and viewed reflected in a mirror through a large lens. An enhanced effect of perspective was introduced. ABOVE A 'vue d'optique' engraving of Fenchurch Street, London

graphy, after the introduction of the wet collodion process in 1851 had made possible the production of finely detailed paper photographic prints, the show box principle was applied to the viewing of photographs.

The English photographer Francis Frith devised the Cosmoscope in the early 1860s. It was a form of table viewer in which photographs, printed on the customary thin albumen paper and coloured from behind like the paper stereographs, were mounted in cardboard frames so that they could be inserted in a groove at the back of the instrument. By viewing the photograph by reflected or transmitted light at the end of a dark tunnel, a striking effect was produced. Carlo Ponti, an Italian photographer, patented a similar viewer which won a medal at the International Exhibition at the Crystal Palace in 1862. It was built on a very grand scale, as its name, Megalethoscope, implied and it consisted of a free-standing viewer in which big photographic prints were viewed through a single large lens. The Graphoscope, a viewer which became popular after Charles Rowsell filed a provisional patent for the design in February 1864, also used the principle of a large lens, set on a hinged frame at one end of a board. At the other end, a sliding easel supported a large photographic print. As with the Zogroscope of a century before, the use of a large lens permitting both eyes at once to view the print produced an enhancement of realism.

Many of the optical toys popular in the last century made use of effects of movement or change. The Kaleidoscope, invented by Sir David Brewster and patented in 1817, used two mirrors placed at a

Knight's Cosmorama, 1854. A stereoscope fitted with hinged flaps at the top and back, linked so that transformations could be made with paper transparencies

ABOVE Rousell's Graphoscope, 1864, used a large lens for the viewing of photographs placed on a sliding easel. A pair of lenses in a hinged frame could be brought into position for viewing stereoscopic transparencies

RIGHT Ponti's Megalethoscope, c. 1862, allowed large photographic prints to be viewed through a large magnifying lens. A variety of models were made, all more or less elaborate in design

critical angle. When the eye was placed to look along the angle formed by the mirrors, the effect of multiple reflection produced a regular complex pattern of anything placed at the base of the mirrors. By placing pieces of coloured glass, fragments of cloth or other material in the base of the instrument and turning it, a changing geometric pattern was produced. J. Darker, a London optician, succeeded in adapting the principle for the magic lantern in the 1860s. His projection Kaleidoscope produced a remarkable effect when used to fill a large screen with a colourful, constantly changing pattern.

Another device which multiplied images was on sale in the second quarter of the last century. The Polyscope used a magnifying lens, the surface of which was cut into a number of facets, so that any object viewed through the lens was multiplied. In one version the lens was fitted at the end of a narrow box, at the other end of which small glass transparencies could be placed. Seen through the lens, a central image was surrounded by as many identical images as there were facets on the lens. If the lens was rotated the outer images appeared to move around the stationary central image. This principle has been reintroduced recently as an accessory for still and movie camera lenses.

The phenomenon of the persistence of vision – the ability of the eye to retain a momentary impression of a stimulus after the source has disappeared or moved on – was observed in ancient times. A firebrand whirled in the dark seems to leave a continuous trace rather than being seen as a moving point. One of the first scientific studies of the effect was carried out by Chevalier d'Arcy, who described his experiments in a memoir to the French Académie des Sciences in 1765. He attached a burning coal to a wheel which he rotated until the point of light appeared to form a complete circle. Since he was able to establish the speed of rotation of the wheel he deduced that the duration of the persistence of vision was about 1/10 second. The *Quarterly Journal of Science* for January 1821 published a note over the initials J. M. (probably the editor, John

Murray) calling attention to the strange effect to be observed when the spokes of a rapidly moving wheel were seen through a fence or other regular vertical grille. The writer requested an explanation from one of the mathematicians among the readers. His request was taken up by Peter Mark Roget, a doctor, the son of a Swiss father and an English mother. In a paper presented to the Royal Society on 9 December 1824 he discussed the phenomenon:

'A curious optical deception takes place when a carriage wheel, rolling along the ground, is viewed through the intervals of a series of vertical bars, such as those of a palisade, or of a Venetian window-blind. Under these circumstances the spokes of the wheel, instead of appearing straight, as they would naturally do if no bars intervened, seem to have a considerable degree of curvature ... the illusion is irresistible, and, from the difficulty of detecting its real cause, is exceedingly striking.'

Roget established that the effect was due to the persistence of vision, and also observed that if the wheel was viewed intermittently, it would appear to be stationary. Roget, who is perhaps best known for his compilation of the *Thesaurus of English Words and Phrases*, written after he retired from medicine in 1840, provided the stimulus to a number of scientists in several countries to investigate the process of the persistence of vision and its effects.

In 1826 Dr John Ayrton Paris, a London physician, put on sale a device he called the Thaumatrope. It was a disc of card bearing pictures on both sides – a bird on one side, a cage on the other, or a horse and rider, and so on. The card could be spun by twisting a thread attached along its diameter. As the card spun, through persistence of vision the eye retained an impression of the image on one side for long enough for the other side to be revealed. The result was that the two images were superimposed – the bird was in the cage, the rider on the horse. Writing in 1864, the mathematician Babbage claimed that the principle of the Thaumatrope had been demonstrated by Sir John Herschel, the astronomer, at a dinner party in 1826. He is said to have shown that both the head and reverse of a coin could be seen at the same time by spinning it. Babbage claimed that he had told W. H. Fitton of the trick and that Fitton had produced and demonstrated a picture disc several months before Paris put his Thaumatrope on sale. Unfortunately, Babbage's account is unreliable on several counts, not the least error being the

Two Thaumatropes, cards spun on twisted thread, giving a 'persistence of vision' effect

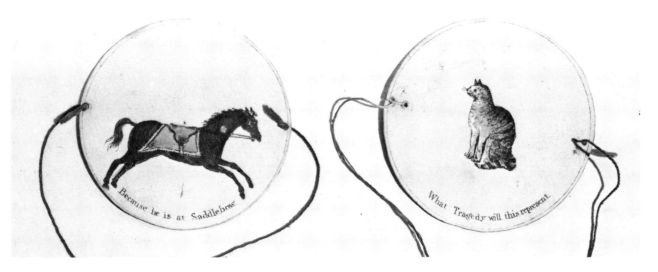

Because he is at Saddlebow

What Tragedy will this represent

Joseph Antoine Ferdinand Plateau (1801-1883), the Belgian physicist who invented the first moving picture device, the Phenakistoscope, in 1832

Michael Faraday (1791-1867)

statement that Sir Joseph Banks presided over the dinner when Fitton demonstrated his toy, when in fact Banks had died in 1820! Whatever the inspiration, it was Dr Paris who introduced to the public the first toy to make use of the persistence of vision effect. In another version of the device, Paris proposed the use of elastic threads so arranged that the card was also twisted while it was rotating. This could give illusions of movement – a man drinking, or a juggler performing and so on.

The first application of the persistence of vision effect to create the illusion of continuous movement was made by the Belgian physicist Joseph Antoine Ferdinand Plateau. He began a study based on the work of the Chevalier d'Arcy, repeating his experiments, and established in 1827 that the duration of persistence of vision varied with the colour of the stimulus. In his early experiments he had observed that if a series of pegs were placed perpendicular to, and equally spaced around, the circumference of a wheel, when the wheel was rotated and viewed through the pegs on the edge, the wheel appeared to be stationary. He established that if two rapidly, counter-rotating wheels on a common axis were viewed one through the other, one wheel appeared to be stationary. These and other observations he described in a letter to *Correspondance Mathématique et Physique*, dated 20 November 1828. He then read of the earlier observations of Roget and carried out further experiments on which he based his dissertation for the degree of Doctor of Physics, delivered on 3 June 1829, in a paper entitled *Certain Properties of the Impression Produced by Light on the Organ of Sight*.

The English scientist Michael Faraday, unaware of Plateau's work, was at the same time investigating persistence of vision phenomena. In a paper entitled *On a Peculiar Class of Optical Deception*, dated 10 December 1830, and published in the *Journals of the Royal Institution* in February 1831, Faraday, after referring to Roget's earlier paper, gave an account of how his attention had been drawn to the curious effect by a miller, who showed him two toothed wheels turning at speed in opposite directions. When one was viewed through the other, a rather blurred impression of a single stationary wheel was given. The engineer Isambard Kingdom Brunel had also noticed the same effect whilst watching gear wheels. Faraday built a device in which two toothed wheels, mounted on the same axis, could be rotated in opposite directions. One, deeply cut, was used to observe the other. By adjusting the relative speeds of the two wheels, or the number of teeth on the observed wheel, Faraday showed that the observed wheel could be made to appear stationary, or to revolve slowly in either direction. By making rings of equally spaced holes on a toothed disc, and viewing it in a mirror, the same effects could be observed. When there were more holes than teeth, they appeared to rotate slowly in the direction of rotation of the disc; when there were fewer holes, they appeared to move in the opposite direction.

When Plateau read of Faraday's work he was at first distressed that his priority of observation had not been acknowledged but later Faraday wrote to him, recognising his prior publication. In his turn, Plateau realised that Faraday had made an important advance. Taking Faraday's wheel, Plateau created from it the Phenakistoscope. (In the literature there are at least four different spellings of this name: Phenakistoscope, Phenakistiscope, Phenakistascope, and Phenakisticope. The latter is almost certainly a misprint which, occurring on an early commercial example of the device, has been repeated over the years. The first is the preferred spelling in England.

The Phenakistoscope was held before a mirror and the figures were viewed in motion by reflection when seen through the slotted edge of the disc as it rotated

The name is based on two Greek roots: *phenax* – deceiver, and *scopein* – to see.) Plateau replaced the holes on Faraday's disc with 16 drawings of a figure, equal in number to the slots in the edge. Each of the equally spaced figures differed slightly from the next, representing phases of a movement. When the disc was rotated on a spindle and held before a mirror, in the reflection seen through the slotted edge the figures appeared to move. As each slot passed in front of the eye, the very brief glimpse of the reflection showed the disc as virtually stationary; then the next segment covered the eye until the next slot reached it, giving another glimpse of the reflection. This time, each figure on the disc was in the position of its predecessor on the previous occasion. If the disc turned fast enough, all these impressions blended and, through persistence of vision, gave the illusion that the drawings were in movement. Plateau described his invention in *Correspondance Mathématique et Physique* in a letter dated 20 January 1833 and accompanied the description with a drawing of a disc showing a dancer performing a pirouette. The Phenakistoscope was on sale in England in the early months of 1833. For the English version, Plateau had suggested the name Phantasmascope, which was contracted by the publisher to Phantascope (or Fantascope). Many imitations, often of inferior quality, were produced by other publishers but the novelty soon wore off and after a few years demand for the toy dropped to a low level.

By a strange coincidence, Simon Stampfer, an Austrian scientist who may also have been stimulated by Faraday's publication, independently invented an identical device as a result of experiments begun in December 1832. Stampfer did not publish his results directly but put in hand the manufacture of a set of six double-sided discs which were printed in February 1833. He applied for a patent, which was granted on 7 May 1833. The first edition of discs having sold out in a month, a second set of 16 subjects was prepared and published in July 1833. In the first set of discs Stampfer had used round holes; in the second set the discs were slotted. Stampfer named his device the Stroboscope. He also suggested, but does not appear to have produced, a form in which the pictures were printed on a

The Zoetrope

The idea that a sequence of drawings should be made on a band of paper to be viewed in a rotating slotted cylinder was first suggested by Simon Stampfer in 1833. In the following year, William George Horner described a similar arrangement, involving a series of drawings made between equally spaced holes pierced in a cylinder which could be

'placed cylindrically round the edge of a revolving disc. Any drawings which are made on the interior surface in the intervals of the apertures will be visible through the opposite apertures, and if executed on the same principle of graduated action, will produce the same surprising play of relative motions as the common *magic disk* does when spun before a mirror . . . the phenomenon may be displayed with full effect to a numerous audience. I have given the name of *Daedaleum* as imitating the practice which the celebrated artist of antiquity was fabled to have invented, of creating figures of men and animals endued with motion. . . . I have . . . communicated every needful part of the detail, some weeks ago, to a respectable optician of Bristol, Mr. King, jun.'

The London and Edinburgh Philosophical Magazine, January 1834

Little came of the invention at the time, but the idea was resurrected in several patents in the 1860s and the Zoetrope appeared on the market. It remained a popular parlour toy for the rest of the century.

Zoetrope

Zoetrope picture bands

strip of paper to be placed inside a cylinder with slotted walls.

In *The London and Edinburgh Philosophical Magazine* in January 1834 William George Horner proposed an improvement on the Phenakistoscope disc, which he called the Daedalum (see panel above). Like Stampfer, Horner suggested that the sequence of pictures be drawn between equally spaced holes pierced in a cylinder, but he appears to have done nothing more about the invention and the idea was resurrected once again in an English patent by Peter H. Desvignes filed on 27 February 1860. Desvignes proposed several devices in his patent, including a slotted drum with bands of pictures, but there seems to have been no commercial exploitation until after the filing of virtually identical patents in 1867 by M. Bradley in England, on 6 March, and William E. Lincoln in America on 23 April. Lincoln called his device the Zoetrope; it consisted of a metal cylinder which rotated freely on a spindle. A band of paper with 13 equally spaced drawings of phases of an action was placed around the bottom of the inside of the cylinder, and was viewed through a series of 13 slots in the upper part of the cylinder as the whole drum was rotated. The Zoetrope had several advantages over the disc viewer. As Horner had pointed out, a number of people at once could view the pictures, instead of only one with the Phenakistoscope. The paper bands were easier and cheaper to produce, and the drum rotated more evenly, and for a longer time than the disc. The Zoetrope remained a popular parlour toy for the rest of the century; the bands of subjects, often rather grotesque, could be bought for sixpence each, and circular discs to lay on the bottom of the drum were also available.

The application to methods of projection of the principles behind these first moving picture devices took the story a step further towards cinematography. The first published attempt to couple a persistence of vision device with the magic lantern was made by an Austrian soldier, Franz von Uchatius. He began experiments in 1845 to make a projection version of Stampfer's Stroboscope and by 1853 he had produced two projection devices, described in the Annals of the Academy at Vienna in April of that year. The first model was an exact translation of the Stroboscope to a projection device. A series of twelve pictures painted on pieces of glass was set around the edge of a wooden disc which could be rotated in front of an oil lamp. A second disc, carried on the same shaft as the first but rotating in the opposite direction, was pierced with a series of 12 apertures each of which passed in front of a picture as it passed the lamp. A single projection lens threw the images in rapid succession onto the screen. Although this machine worked, it gave a very dim picture of small size. Uchatius' second model used a fixed disc with 12 transparent pictures, each with a separate lens. The 12 lenses were arranged to converge on the screen. A lime light carried on a rotating arm moved behind each picture in turn when a handle was operated. The transition between one picture and the next on the screen was more gradual, rather as in a dissolving view projection, and the picture was very bright. Uchatius' lantern was manufactured for a time by Proketsch of Vienna.

In England, T. Ross applied for two patents for projection Phenakistoscopes. The first patent, applied for on 6 March 1869, was for a slide for the magic lantern, incorporating a rotating, transparent, 13-picture disc, with a 13-slot counter-rotating shutter disc. In principle, this was identical to Uchatius' first design and suffered from the same defects. The second patent, filed on 10 October 1871, was more efficient mechanically and was manufactured and sold by Pumphrey Brothers of Birmingham under the name 'The Wheel of life'. Again in lantern slide form, this device contained a transparent disc of glass or mica, with 13 phases of movement; in front of it was carried a thin metal disc with a single slot, rotating at 13 times the speed of the picture disc, so that it made one revolution in the time that the picture disc took to move from one image to the next. The two discs were turned by a belt and pulley driving system. The French optician Molteni sold an identical device in 1882.

Two versions of Ross's 'Wheel of Life', a projection version of the Phenakistoscope which gave animated pictures on the magic lantern screen

The problem with such projection devices is that, in order to retain some degree of sharpness in the perceived image, the slot in the shutter disc must be very narrow. Thus, for most of the time of projection, no light is reaching the screen and the picture tends to be rather dim. If a mechanism were used to stop each picture in turn in front of the light for a short time, the shutter slot could be wider and the picture consequently brighter and sharper, with no blurring due to the continuous movement of the pictures. The first projection device to use such an intermittent movement, a fundamental principle of the movie film, was made by the London optician L. S. Beale. In 1866 he devised the Choreutoscope, a special slide for the magic lantern. The Choreutoscope used a picture strip showing six figures of a skeleton in various poses. This transparent slide was fitted to a notched wooden strip which was moved on intermittently by turning a rotating disc fitted with a protruding pin which, once per turn, engaged in a notch on the wooden strip and moved it on one step. As the strip moved, a shutter, also worked from the rotating shaft, was raised to cover the picture. When the device was fitted in a lantern and the handle turned quickly, the six pictures were seen in rapid succession, each one quite still and bright. Persistence of vision combined them into the illusion of a dancing skeleton. Beale had used, in a modified form, the mechanism of the Maltese Cross, or Geneva stop mechanism, which watchmakers had for many years employed to prevent overwinding of a watch-spring. As we shall see, this mechanism was to be of great importance in the development of cinematography.

A similar although more elaborate device was patented in America by A. B. Brown in 1869. In Brown's lantern, a form of Maltese Cross movement drove a transparent picture disc intermittently and a two-sector disc shutter covered the pictures while they were changing. The London lantern manufacturer William Charles Hughes revived the Choreutoscope idea in a patent filed on 9 October 1884. His apparatus was almost identical to that of Beale but enjoyed rather more commercial success. Soon after, Molteni of Paris produced versions of the Choreutoscope using a six-picture transparent disc rotated intermittently by a modified Maltese Cross mechanism.

Beale's Choreutoscope, 1860, used a simple intermittent mechanism to project six still pictures in rapid succession in the magic lantern

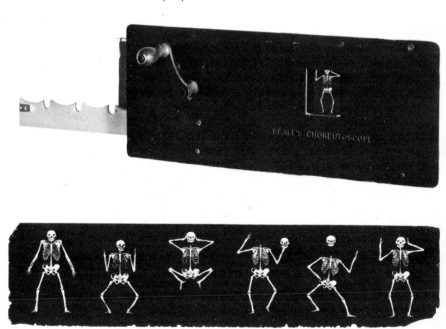

These lantern projection devices incorporated important principles, such as the intermittent movement of a picture strip and the use of a shutter to cut out movement of the picture on the screen, which were to be fundamental to the development of cinematography. However, the stop-start movement of the picture bands or discs did present mechanical problems. There was another solution which allowed the pictures to move continuously, but which still allowed the presentation of bright, sharp images in movement. The French artist and inventor Émile Reynaud may have been inspired to begin his experiments by articles on optical toys published in the magazine *La Nature* in March and April 1876. After making, and realising the drawbacks of, the Zoetrope, Reynaud hit on a clever idea. He constructed a shallow cylinder which could be rotated on its axis. In the centre of the cylinder he placed a drum covered with a number of pieces of mirror, one for each picture on a band set around the outside of the cylinder. The distance between the picture strip and the mirrors was the same as that from the mirrors to the axis of the cylinder. The result of this was that although the cylinder was rotating, the reflection of each picture seen in the facets of the mirror drum appeared to be stationary. As the facets of the mirror drum passed before the eye, they presented a series of stationary images which blended to give a clear, bright, undistorted moving picture. By stabilising the images optically, Reynaud had removed the need for awkward mechanical stop-start mechanisms and moving shutters. His pictures were seen continuously, with no dark intervals. Reynaud called his apparatus the Praxinoscope, and patented it on 21 December 1877. He began manufacturing the device in February 1878, at 58 rue de la Rodier, in Paris and the machine received an honourable mention in the Paris Exposition of 1878.

On 6 January 1879 he added a supplement to his patent covering an improvement – the Praxinoscope Theatre. In this model, the mirror drum and cylinder were set in a wooden box fitted with a panel cut out into a proscenium arch, as in a theatre. Only one figure at a time could be seen in the aperture, which was covered with a sheet of glass reflecting a series of interchangeable backgrounds and foregrounds which could be placed inside the lid. This

In Reynaud's Praxinoscope, 1878, a band of drawings placed around the circumference of a shallow cylinder was viewed in motion by reflection in a drum of mirrors in the centre

BELOW LEFT The Praxinoscope Theatre, 1879, used a transparent reflector to superimpose a moving image, seen in a mirror drum, on a variety of interchangeable backgrounds. BELOW An advertising card for a projection version of the Praxinoscope, 1880

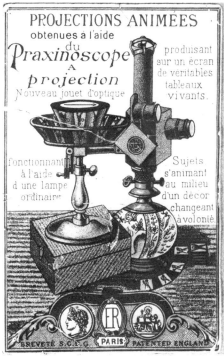

The Théâtre Optique

The *Pantomimes Lumineuses*, painted by Reynaud on long transparent bands and projected on a large screen, were first presented to the public at the Musée Grévin in Paris on 28 October 1892. The first three subjects were *Le Clown et ses Chiens* (300 frames, lasting six to eight minutes), *Pauvre Pierrot* (500 frames, lasting 12 to 15 minutes), and *Un Bon Bock* (700 frames, lasting 12 to 15 minutes). The projection apparatus was placed behind the translucent screen, which was set into a proscenium. Special music was composed for the shows by Gaston Paulin, and the scores were marked with 'synchronisation' instructions so that the musicians could follow the action closely. The shows were popular with the public, but Reynaud had problems with the picture bands, which became damaged with the heat from the lamp and from repeated projection. He worked at the painting of new bands between presenting the shows, but found it difficult to cope. On 26

Reynaud's Théâtre Optique in operation

April 1893, his contract with the Musée Grévin was renewed, but only on a monthly basis. The show was closed from 1 March 1894 until 1 January 1895, when Reynaud reopened with new subjects, *Un Rêve au Coin de Feu* and *Autour d'une Cabine*.

Soon, the Théâtre Optique was faced with competition from the new photographic moving pictures. Reynaud devised a cinecamera to speed up the production of new bands. The Photoscenograph was used to make sequences of photographs which he could use as the basis of his painted bands. The clowns Footit and Chocolat performed a sketch, *William Tell*, for the camera in April 1896 and Reynaud had a finished painted picture band ready for projection by the end of August. A second subject, the actor Galipaux miming *Le Premier Cigare*, was shot in November 1896, and the new picture band was prepared for showing by 30 June 1897. The constant public demand for something new and the growing popularity of the cinematograph, with its constantly changing programme, finally led the management to terminate the agreement with Reynaud and the last show took place on 28 February 1900. Before his death in January 1918, in a fit of depression, Reynaud smashed the surviving Théâtre Optique mechanism and threw all but two of his seven picture bands into the River Seine.

Picture band painted by Reynaud and (bottom) Photoscenograph band

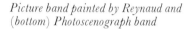

had a peephole through which the show was seen. Each subject, which was printed in colour on a black background, was thus seen superimposed upon a suitable scene – the juggler in a circus ring, a girl skipping in a garden and a swimmer in water simulated by a slip of mirror.

The Praxinoscope was very popular, especially in the Theatre form, and Reynaud followed up an idea covered by his first patent – the Projection Praxinoscope. A band of transparent pictures on glass joined together by pieces of black fabric was placed around the edge of a disc bearing as before a mirror drum in its centre. An oil lamp lit the transparencies as the drum rotated, and the successive reflections in the mirror drum were projected by a lens onto the screen. The same lamp supplied light for the projection of a lantern slide of a suitable decor, so that the moving pictures were seen in an appropriate setting, as in the Praxinoscope Theatre. All three models of the Praxinoscope were demonstrated to the Société Française de Photographie in 1880.

Had Reynaud's achievements ended with the production of these delightful toys, he would have earned his place in the history of the moving picture – but he did not stop there. On 1 December 1888 Reynaud patented his Théâtre Optique – a large scale adaptation of the Praxinoscope. It used a long band of pictures, painted on a flexible strip, or on inflexible material joined together by flexible material, and perforated between the pictures. The picture band was wound on rollers around the machine, in the centre of which was a large mirror drum carried on a horizontally mounted wheel with teeth which engaged in the perforations in the picture band, locating each picture accurately in relation to a facet of the mirror drum and allowing the wheel to turn as the band was wound from one spool to another. A lamp illuminated each picture as it passed before it, and the reflection of the successive pictures in the mirror drum was projected by a lens onto a translucent screen, while a second magic lantern projected a decor slide onto the same screen. The action was no longer limited to a cyclical movement lasting only a second or two but could last as long as the capacity of the reel, or the patience of the artist, would allow. It took Reynaud several years to work out the practical details of his apparatus, and to prepare the picture bands, each frame of which had to be carefully painted. On 11 October 1892 he signed an agreement with the management of the Musée Grévin in Paris to present the *Pantomimes Lumineuses* (see panel left). As a result, Reynaud has the honour of being the first person publicly to present animated moving pictures on a screen by the use of long, transparent bands of images. However, his pictures, delightful though they were, lacked the realism which could only come with the successful analysis and reproduction of movement by means of photography.

Émile Reynaud (1844-1918), inventor of the Praxinoscope and Théâtre Optique

3

Photographing movement

Plateau's Phenakistoscope, and the devices that evolved from it, demonstrated that an illusion of continuous movement could be created from a sequence of separate still pictures. However, this illusion was often imperfect, since the figures were hand-drawn and derived from the imagination of the artist rather than from a direct analysis of movement from life. The first camera to be designed specifically to photograph action was made by Thomas Skaife, a London photographer. Skaife had designed and patented in 1856 a camera shutter which used a pair of sprung flaps. Using the shutter attached to a stereoscopic camera, he claimed two years later to have photographed a 'monster shell' fired from a cannon. In 1859 he marketed his Pistolgraph camera. A small brass-bodied camera, it was fitted with a lens of very wide aperture, designed by Thomas Dallmeyer, of f2.2 and even f1.1. Skaife's flap shutter was fitted, and the camera took small wet collodion plates, making negatives about one inch (25.4mm) square. The Pistolgraph, which could be held in the hand, enjoyed some small success but made no great impact on photographers, who for many years continued to use cameras of large format and long exposure times.

The first suggestion for sequence photography to be used for making moving pictures was made in a supplement to a patent filed in France by Jules Duboscq on 12 November 1852:

'The reflecting stereoscope permits the construction of apparatus which combined the essential properties of the stereoscope with the marvellous properties of the Fantascope or Phenakistiscope of M. Plateau. The stereoscope gives the impression of depth to objects. The Phenakistiscope gives that of movement. The Stereofantascope or bioscope gives at the same time, as its name indicates, the sensation of depth and of movement, or an impression of life.

To change the fantascope into a stereofantascope it requires 1. to take two stereoscopic pictures of each of 12 phases of movement, 2. to place these 12 pairs of pictures on a rotating disc.'

Unfortunately, Duboscq did not have any idea as to how his 12 pairs of phases of movement should be produced.

Duboscq corresponded with the French photographer Antoine Francois Jean Claudet, who had for many years lived in London and who had made a number of important contributions to the early development of photography. Claudet was also working on attempts to animate photographs. On 23 March 1853 he applied for a patent for improvements in stereoscopes, to produce 'pleasing and novel optical illusions by means of a peculiar construction and arrangement

The birth of photography

Photography depends upon two basic operations – the formation of an image on a flat surface by an optical device and a chemical method of sensitizing that surface to light so that the image can be captured permanently. The first requirement was met by the camera obscura, known since the 16th century and used by artists as an aid to sketching. Thomas Wedgwood was the first to make a light-sensitive material, when about 1800 he treated white leather and paper with silver salts. He made prints of leaves and transparent paintings, but his material was far too insensitive to record the faint image of the camera obscura. The first permanent image produced directly by light was made by Nicéphore Niépce, probably in 1827, on a bitumen-coated pewter plate exposed for eight hours.

The first practical photographic processes were announced in 1839. Louis J. M. Daguerre, who had earlier collaborated with Niépce, demonstrated the Daguerreotype process, in which a silver surface on a copper plate was sensitized with iodine vapour and was then exposed in a camera. Development with mercury vapour revealed an image which could be fixed and made permanent. William Henry Fox Talbot in the same year described his Photogenic Drawing process, on which he had worked since 1834. He used paper sensitized with silver salts, which after a long exposure in the camera produced a negative image that could be fixed and then printed onto sensitized paper to give a positive image. This negative-positive principle forms the basis of modern photography. Talbot's process was improved in 1840 with his discovery of a method of developing the invisible latent image formed by a brief exposure in the camera. Daguerre's process, although capable of beautiful results, was a dead end. It was Talbot's improved process which evolved to make cinematography possible.

Louis Daguerre (1787-1851)

Fox Talbot (1800-77)

of some of the parts, which are made moveable so as to impart to the picture the appearance of moving figures'. The apparatus was designed for viewing Daguerreotype plates and used mirrors to reverse the normally inverted image produced in this process. A sliding shutter fitted behind the double eyepiece alternately covered and uncovered each lens as it was slid to and fro. 'The pictures are made differently, so that the objects are not similarly placed (but differently viewed) in each . . . one view shows a person with his hat on, for instance, the other the same with his hat off. By the action of the slide it appears that the figure is taking off his hat.' Claudet suggested that by placing the photographs on the arms of two crosses, four pairs of pictures could be viewed in rapid succession, the crosses being driven by a spring. Claudet, of course, had produced a photographic version of the slipping slide idea already familiar in the magic lantern world, but his Daguerreotype photographs had a much greater realism.

Henry du Mont applied for a Belgian patent on 7 April 1859 for a variety of viewing devices, under the general name of Omniscopes. They were variations of the Phenakistoscope combined with the stereoscope. Du Mont suggested that by using photographs, the Omniscopes could be applied to 'natural sciences, engineering, industry, arts and crafts, military strategy'. In a later French patent of 2 May 1861 he proposed various ways in which sequences of photographs might be made. His British patent of 8 June 1861 described

> 'a prismatic drum, whose periphery is mounted with sensitive layers, [which] is caused to revolve so that the sensitive layers succeed each other in the focus of the obscure chamber'.

Alternatively, the plates could be set

> 'behind each other in a long box with vertical grooves, and moving in a contrary direction to a similar box situated under it, and intended to receive the layers impressed by the light. A ratchet wheel and ratchet movement enable the sensitive layers to fall into the lower box as they are impressed. The exposure of the sensitive layers to light at the proper instant is accomplished by means of a black moveable screen, the regulated motions of which are connected with the motions of the system bearing the sensitive layers. The series of images thus produced, viz., the series of motions of a dancer, of one or more soldiers, of a machine, &ca, &ca, may be utilized both for the pleasure of the eyes and for other purposes.'

Du Mont had described the first camera design for sequence photographs, but unfortunately the photographic processes of his day would not have permitted its successful use. The wet collodion process required that the plates be prepared immediately before exposure and thus could not have been used in a magazine camera of the type described. The only dryplate processes available at the time were very insensitive, and would not have permitted exposures brief enough to photograph action.

The French pioneer of colour photography Louis Ducos du Hauron also patented a sequence camera, on 1 March 1864. He suggested a camera with multiple lenses, uncovered in turn by a black cloth band with holes, acting as a shutter. He further suggested that the apparatus could be used to record

> 'the progress of a funeral procession, military reviews and manoeuvres, the vicissitudes of a battle, a public fete, a theatrical scene, the movements of one or more people, the play of expression and, if one wished, the grimaces of a human face, etc., a marine view, the movements of waves (a tidal bore), the movement of clouds in a stormy sky, particularly in mountainous country, the eruption of a volcano etc., etc.'

Despite all these optimistically listed possibilities, of course du Hauron, like du Mont, was unable to put them into practice.

Since for the time being sequence photography of action was not practical, some workers turned to the next best thing – a sequence of posed photographs of phases of some easily arranged movement. Peter Hubert Desvignes, in his patent of 27 February 1860, described among other devices a form of Zoetrope for stereoscopic pictures in which

> 'the views may represent, for instance, a steam engine, and each view must be taken when the engine is at different parts of its stroke. The views being placed in the said cylinder [of the Zoetrope] and the cylinder being caused to rotate, will show to the eye the steam engine as if in actual movement in all its parts.'

William Thomas Shaw followed with a patent on 22 May 1860 suggesting a very similar application, taking a sequence of stereoscopic pairs of photographs of posed action, for viewing in various modified forms of the Phenakistoscope. Shaw described his Stereotrope in a communication to the Royal Society on 10 January 1861. Coleman Sellers, an American, patented his Kinematoscope stereoscopic viewer on 5 February 1861. He placed stereoscopic pairs of posed photographs on six equally spaced paddles fitted on a rotating shaft. Like Desvignes, Sellers photographed posed machinery, at the Baldwin Locomotive Works in Philadelphia. Gaetano Bonelli and Henry Cook proposed in a provisional English patent on 19 August 1863 to use

> 'a series of representations by means of photography of men or animals with limbs in motion arranged round a disc, to which rapid rotary motion is communicated by suitable mechanism, so that by the different figures in the series being brought in rapid succession before the eye of the observer, the effect of figures in motion will be produced.'

The unusual feature of this device was that it was proposed that the photographs be reduced to micro-photographs to be viewed through a microscope fitted with a rotating perforated shutter through which the disc of tiny photographs would be viewed. Bonelli and Cook did not suggest any way in which the photographs might be taken, although it was implied that they would be posed sequences. Cook showed a similar device he called the Photobioscope to the Société Française de Photographie in 1867 but appeared to be no nearer solving the problem of how to take the original photographs.

Probably the first public demonstration of projected picture sequences was that carried out by the American Henry R. Heyl, who presented his Phasmatrope at the Philadelphia Academy of Music on 5 February 1870. Heyl had photographed on wet plates six posed views of two people waltzing. By printing each negative three times, Heyl produced 18 transparencies on glass which he fitted around a large disc, which could be rotated intermittently by a ratchet and pawl mechanism, while an oscillating shutter covered the pictures as the disc moved. The apparatus was fitted into a magic lantern for projection. Heyl also demonstrated his Phasmatrope at the Franklin Institute on 16 March 1870, but neither presentation appears to have evoked much interest. At about the same time, Sir Charles Wheatstone in England invented a form of stereoscopic viewer in which a band of posed stereoscopic photographs, of a soldier presenting arms, for example, was fitted round a drum which was rotated intermittently by an eccentric device. Since no shutter was fitted to cover the pictures during the phase of movement, the results were necessarily somewhat blurred.

The last of these speculative inventions to be considered was provisionally patented by an English barrister, Wordsworth Donisthorpe, on 9 November 1876:

> 'This invention has for its object to facilitate the taking of a succession of photographic pictures at equal intervals of time, in order to record the changes taking place in or the movements of the object being photographed, and also by means of a succession of pictures so taken of any moving object to give to the eye a representation of the object in continuous movement as it appeared when being photographed.'

Wheatstone's stereoscopic viewer, c. 1870, in which a sequence of posed stereoscopic photographs could be viewed in motion by the use of an intermittent mechanism

The outline of the invention describes a camera virtually identical with that suggested by du Mont, using a magazine of plates dropping from one compartment to another after exposure. Donisthorpe suggested that the pictures could be printed onto a long band of paper 'wound onto a cylinder, and be unwound from it at a uniform speed onto another cylinder, and so carried past the eye of the observer, any ordinary means being used for ensuring that each picture shall only be exposed momentarily to the observer'. As it stood, Donisthorpe's proposal was neither original nor practical, although the newly developed dry plates were, as we shall see, sensitive enough for the purpose. However, Donisthorpe foresaw that his Kinesigraph apparatus might have important applications. On 24 January 1878, he wrote to the magazine *Nature*, which had just reprinted an article on Thomas Alva Edison's newly-invented tinfoil phonograph sound reproducer from the *Scientific American*. He started by quoting from the article which had speculated on the possibility of projecting a stereoscopic portrait on a screen and accompanying it with a phonograph record of the subject's voice. He went on,

'Ingenious as this suggested combination is, I believe I am in a position to cap it. By combining the phonograph with the Kinesigraph I will undertake not only to produce a talking picture of Mr. Gladstone which, with motionless lips and un-changed expression shall positively recite his latest anti-Turkish speech in his own voice and tone. Not only this, but the life-size photograph shall itself move and gesticulate precisely as he did when making the speech, the words and gestures corresponding as in real life. Surely this is an advance on the conception of the *Scientific American*!

The mode in which I effect this is . . . instantaneous photographs of bodies or groups of bodies in motion are taken at equal intervals – say quarter or half seconds – the exposure of the plate occupying not more than one-eighth of a second. After fixing, the prints from these plates are taken one below another on a long strip or ribbon of paper. The strip is wound from one cylinder to another so as to cause the several photographs to pass the eye successively at the same intervals of time as those at which they were taken.

Each picture as it passes the eye is instantaneously lighted up by an electric spark. Thus, the picture is made to appear stationary while the people or things in it appear to move as in nature. I need not enter more into detail beyond saying if the intervals between the presentation of the successive pictures are found to be too short the gaps can be filled up by duplicates or triplicates of each succeeding print. This will not perceptibly alter the general effect.

I think it will be admitted that by this means a drama acted by daylight or magnesium light may be recorded and re-acted on the screen or sheet of a magic lantern, and with the assistance of the phonograph the dialogues may be repeated in the very voices of the actors.

When this is actually accomplished the photography of colours will alone be wanting to render the representation absolutely complete, and for this, we shall not, I trust, have long to wait.'

Of course, Donisthorpe had no chance of putting his idea into practice. Even if the photographic apparatus could have worked, at that time the phonograph was certainly not up to the task. In fact, the world had to wait almost exactly fifty years before the arrival of the first effective talking colour film!

As we have seen, all these ideas for sequences of pictures of moving objects foundered on the rock of the insensitivity of the wet collodion process, coupled with its inconvenience. In the *British Journal of Photography* for 8 September 1871 a London physician, Dr Richard Leach Maddox, published details of a new process he had devised. He produced a suspension of light-sensitive silver bromide in a warmed solution of gelatin, which he then coated on plates. When dry this 'emulsion' retained its properties for relatively long periods, obviating the need to expose the plate immediately it had been sensitized. As his process was described, it was more convenient than the wet collodion process, but was hardly more sensitive. Several important improvements were made in the production of the gelatin dry plate during the next few years, notably by Charles Bennett in 1878. Bennett had discovered that if the gelatin emulsion was heated for long periods before coating it, the sensitivity of the plates was greatly increased. Bennett's publication of details of his 'ripening' process in the *British Journal of Photography* in March 1878 was followed rapidly by the appearance of commercially manufactured dry plates of a sensitivity never before available. Instantaneous exposures of a fraction of a second were now easily possible and the direct photography of action was at last fully practical.

The first photographic analysis of movement by sequence photography was carried out by the English photograper Eadweard Muybridge (born Edward Muggeridge in 1830 in Kingston upon Thames). As a young man Muybridge left England for America, to work in the book trade. In 1860 he returned to England to train in photography, an interest he had acquired through contact with a New York Daguerreotypist, Silas Selleck. He returned to America in the mid 1860s and spent five years recording the Far West with his camera, taking over 2,000 photographs which he sold at first under his pseudonym 'Helios'. He had acquired a significant reputation as a photographer by the spring of 1872, when he was asked by Leland Stanford, former governor of California and president of the Central Pacific Railroad, to attempt to photograph a horse trotting at speed. The object of the experiment was to determine whether at any point in the trot the horse had all four legs off the ground at the same time. The often repeated story that this was the subject of a large wager has absolutely no evidence to support it and would have been quite out of character for Stanford. Whatever the motive was, Muybridge in May 1872 made several negatives of the horse 'Occident' at the race course at Sacramento, but without any great success. He made a second attempt in April 1873 which was more successful. Muybridge claimed that the wet plate negatives 'were sufficiently sharp to give a recognisable silhouette portrait of the driver and some of them exhibited the horse with all four of his feet clearly lifted, at the same time, above the surface of the ground'. The photographs were good enough to answer Stanford's question. A lithographed print of 'Occident' trotting, published in 1873, may well have been drawn from one of the photographs.

For the next few years, Muybridge's personal problems prevented further work in this direction. He was tried for killing his wife's lover, Major Henry Larkyns, but was acquitted on the grounds of justifiable homicide. Until the trouble blew over, Muybridge went on a trip to Central America. He continued to experiment in photography and by his return to Sacramento in 1877 he had an improved shutter working in 1/1000 of a second. With it he produced a more detailed picture of 'Occident' in July 1877, which caused some controversy when an engraved version of it was published in the

Eadweard Muybridge (1830-1904), who pioneered the analysis of motion by sequential photography

43

'Apparatus for Photographing Objects in Motion'

In 1878 Eadweard Muybridge constructed the first successful device for sequence photography, at Palo Alto, Leland Stanford's farm in California. A long shed was built alongside a track and was fitted with 12 Scovill plate cameras placed side by side and equipped with fast Dallmeyer lenses specially imported from England. On the other side of the whitened track a white background was erected and marked off with vertical lines 21 inches apart and numbered consecutively. The bottom of the background was marked with several horizontal lines. In front of each camera was fitted a double drop shutter – two plates, each with a horizontal slot, tensioned with stretched rubber bands or springs. When released by an electromagnetic catch one plate moved up while the other moved down; as the slots crossed in front of the lens, a very brief exposure, of as little as one thousandth of a second, was made. When a single horse was to be photographed, thin threads were stretched across the track and attached to spring electric contacts. As the horse struck and broke each thread, the contacts were closed, completing the circuit and releasing the electromagnetic catch on the shutter. When the horse was drawing a carriage or sulky, wires stretched just above the track closed electrical contacts when run over by a wheel. By these means, a succession of photographs of the moving animal could be made in the right sequence and in a short space of time.

Muybridge filed a patent for the arrangement on 27 June 1878. Press and other visitors were invited for a demonstration on 15 June 1878 and saw 12 photographs made in about half a second of the horse 'Abe Edgington'. Muybridge was still using wet plates, as news of the improved gelatin dry plates had as yet made little impact in America, so the results were little more than silhouettes. Nonetheless, the

ABOVE *Sequence photography equipment at Palo Alto, California*

BELOW *Part of a sequence exposed in 1878*

press, so different was it from the conventional representations of the horse in motion. However, the photograph won a medal at the Industrial Exhibition in San Francisco in 1877. So far, Muybridge had been taking single photographs, and it was a matter of chance which phase of the horse's movement was caught when the shutter was fired.

In 1878 Stanford sponsored a much more ambitious scheme. Muybridge had decided to adopt a method which had been suggested by the photographer Oscar G. Rejlander in the *British Journal of Photography Almanac* for 1873. Rejlander discussed the 'vexed question' of the exact positions of a horse's legs when it was galloping and suggested:

successive actions of the horse were recorded with great accuracy. A set of six series of reproductions of the horses 'Occident', 'Abe Edgington', 'Mahomet' and 'Sallie Gardner' were published and sold throughout the world in 1878. Work continued in 1879 and the installation was increased to 24 cameras. By using a clockwork driven electrical contact wheel to release the shutters in sequence, Muybridge ensured that all the photographs were taken at precise and controllable intervals, eliminating uncertainties that the threads had introduced. It also made it possible to photograph not only horses but other animals and birds, as well as athletes who came to Palo Alto from the San Francisco Olympic Club.

In 1884, at the University of Pennsylvania, Muybridge extended his installation, using up to four banks of cameras which by simultaneous electrical release could photograph action from several angles. Muybridge's pioneering sequence photography provided the stimulus to other inventors, from whose work cinematography was born.

RIGHT *Sequence taken at University of Pennsylvania, 1884*

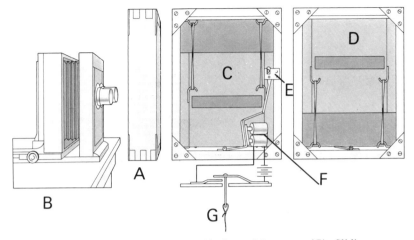

Muybridge's shutter unit (A) was placed in front of the camera (B). Sliding plates, one on each side (C, D), passed each other when a catch (E) was released by an electromagnet (F) when the switch (G) was closed

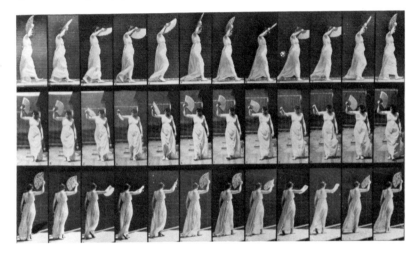

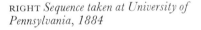

'Given a horse and rider, take a point near or on a sandy or dusty white road, 150 yards off . . . Then I would have a battery of cameras and "quick acting" lenses ready charged and loaded. The signal given, the rider starts some distance off the focussed point, and at the moment of passing it – bang! with a strong wrist and sleight of hand, the exposure and covering is done.'

Rather than have all the exposures at once, Muybridge arranged for them to be taken in sequence.

When Muybridge's photographs were printed in strips and placed in a Zoetrope, a remarkably realistic reproduction of the original movement was given. Accordingly, Muybridge designed a projector, based on the Phenakistoscope, first called the Zoogyroscope but later,

The Zoopraxiscope projector, 1879, was
designed by Muybridge to project glass
discs bearing sequences of pictures
painted from the photographic series.
Below is a Zoopraxiscope disc painted
with twelve images of a horse galloping.
The figures were deliberately elongated,
to compensate for the distortion
introduced by projection through a
rotating shutter.

in 1881, rechristened the Zoopraxiscope. The projector took large
glass discs round the edge of which were painted sequences of images
derived from the sequence photographs. Muybridge soon found that
he needed to distort the paintings by elongating them, to compensate
for the foreshortening effect introduced in all such devices. A counter
rotating shutter disc with the same number of slots as the disc had
pictures gave the necessary brief exposure to each picture as it
passed between the lamp and the projection lens. The machine was,
in fact, identical in principle to Uchatius' first model of many years
before but with the difference that Muybridge's pictures were very
life-like, having been derived from photographs. The projector was
finished in the autumn of 1879, and was first described in the *Alta
California* newspaper on 5 May 1880. Sets of original photographic
prints were bound up and sold in 1881, under the title *Attitudes of
Animals in Motion*, and in that year Muybridge left, with the Zoopraxiscope, for an important lecture tour in Europe. The French
physiologist, Professor Etienne-Jules Marey, whose own contribution
to the story we shall consider shortly, invited Muybridge to his
laboratory, where for the first time he worked with the new, very
sensitive, gelatin dry plates. Muybridge moved on to England in
1882, presenting his illustrated lecture with great success at, among
other places, the Royal Academy and the Royal Institution, where
his audience included the Prince and Princess of Wales, the Princesses
Louise, Victoria and Maud, the Duke of Edinburgh, Professors
Huxley, Tyndall and Owen, Mr Gladstone and the Poet Laureate!
This lecture was his first in England, held on 13 March 1882, and
was a tremendous success. *The Photographic News* said,

'Mr. Muybridge might well be proud of the reception accorded
him, for it would be difficult to add to the *éclat* of such a first
appearance, and throughout his lecture he was welcomed by a
warmth that was as hearty as it was spontaneous.'

On his return to America later in 1882 Muybridge fell out with Stanford over a book published in his absence, which gave him, he felt, inadequate credit. Until 1884 he toured America with his lecture; in that year he was given a grant of $40,000 by the University of Pennsylvania to carry on his work there. He built an elaborate arrangement using up to four banks of cameras which could photograph actions simultaneously from several angles. During 1884 and 1885 he produced over 100,000 photographs, of which 20,000 were reproduced in Muybridge's major publication *Animal Locomotion* (1887). By using gelatin dry plates, supplied by the St Louis Dry Plate Company, he was able to achieve a quality and detail in his photographs far in advance of the earlier results at Palo Alto. The subjects ranged in size from birds to elephants. Human figures, clothed and nude, were photographed in a very wide variety of activities. The publication, 11 volumes containing 781 photogravure plates, made a major impact not only on photographers, but also on artists who had to revise the traditional conventions of representing animals in movement.

In the years that followed, Muybridge travelled extensively, lecturing and projecting his pictures with the Zoopraxiscope. At the Photographic Convention in London in 1889 his lecture was followed by 'tremendous applause'. The chairman called it 'the most wonderful revelation of the age'. In 1894 Muybridge retired to his birthplace at Kingston on Thames, where he died in 1904. His was a considerable achievement. Not only did he carry out the first successful analysis of motion by photography and not only did he project the first motion pictures based on such analysis but his work was the direct stimulus to others who carried on from the start he had made to create cinematography as it is known today.

Étienne-Jules Marey, a native of Beaune, in France, was inspired by Muybridge's work. In the 1870s he was engaged on an investigation of animal locomotion. By using a variety of pneumatic and mechanical devices, he was able to make records of the sequence of hoofbeats of a horse trotting, galloping and so on. Turning to a study of the flight of birds, Marey had problems. The mechanical recording devices interfered with the free movement of the bird. Then, in *La Nature* of 28 December 1878 Marey read of Muybridge's photographs of the horse. Marey saw in this a possible solution to his problem. Through Gaston Tissandier, the editor of *La Nature*, Marey asked Muybridge to make pictures of birds in free flight. Muybridge photographed flying pigeons, but did not achieve an effective sequence of images, since his battery of cameras was not very suitable for recording small objects moving vertically. Muy-

ABOVE Étienne Jules Marey (1830-1904), the French pioneer of chronophotography whose research into photographic recording of movement led to his designing the first sequence camera using flexible film

LEFT A multiple image record of a fencer, exposed in Marey's fixed-plate camera

bridge brought his pictures with him on his visit to Màrey in August 1881. Marey was delighted to see that many of the individual images confirmed the results of his mechanical recordings, but he became even more anxious to make detailed sequences of pictures. He consequently began to experiment with an idea first suggested and used by the astronomer Pierre-Jules-César Janssen.

Janssen travelled to Japan to record and observe the transit of the planet Venus across the face of the sun, on 8 December 1874. Janssen described the problem of recording the phenomenon:

> 'It is well known that the observation of contact [the moment when the outline of the planet first encroaches on the sun's disc] must play a big part in the observation of the transit of Venus. . . . ordinary methods of photography cannot be of help in this, since one must know in advance the precise moment when the contact is about to take place in order to take a photograph of it. . . . I had the idea of taking, from the moment when the contact was about to happen, a series of photographs at very short and regular intervals in such a way that the photographic image of the moment of contact must of necessity be included in the series, giving at the same time the precise moment of the phenomonen.'

Janssen built an 'astronomical revolver', in which a circular Daguerreotype plate was rotated intermittently by clockwork through a modified form of Maltese Cross mechanism. A rotating shutter with 12 apertures exposed the plate each time it was at rest, giving 48 exposures in 72 seconds. The by then obsolete Daguerreotype process was preferred since the metal plate would have better dimensional stability than the film of collodion on the wet plate, which in any case would have been inconvenient to use in such a camera. The total absence of halation or flare on the metal plate was another of its advantages over a glass negative, while the insensitivity of the process was no problem when the subject was the sun itself. However, some records were also made on collodion plates. The apparatus worked well, and in a lecture to the Académie des Sciences in Paris in April 1876, Janssen suggested that his apparatus might be used for the study of animal movements, especially those of birds, if only materials sensitive enough to permit the very brief exposures needed became available. Within two years such materials were available, with the advent of the commercial gelatin dry plates.

Starting from Janssen's camera, Marey produced a photographic 'gun' which was working by February 1882. Marey described the camera:

> 'The barrel of the gun is a tube containing a photographic lens. Behind, and mounted solidly on the butt, is a large cylindrical "breechblock" in which is a train of clockwork . . . when the trigger is pressed, the train of clockwork is set in motion and communicates the necessary movement to all parts of the instrument. A central axis, turning 12 times a second, operates all the parts of the apparatus. There is first an opaque metal disc, perforated with a narrow window. This disc forms a shutter, and only lets through light from the lens twelve times a second, and each time only for 1/720 of a second. Behind this first disc, another turns freely on the same shaft, carrying 12 windows, behind which the circular or octagonal sensitised plate is fixed. This perforated disc turns intermittently, stopping twelve times a second, in line with the rays of light entering the instrument.'

Marey used his photographic gun to record the flight of birds,

The 'photographic gun' designed by Marey in 1882 to take sequences of photographs of birds in flight. BELOW A plate from Marey's 'photographic gun', with twelve pictures exposed in one second

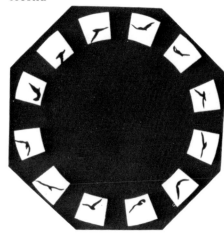

Marey's camera in which a rotating shutter made ten exposures in one second on a fixed photographic plate, giving superimposed multiple images of a moving subject

capturing in the picture sequences all the positions of the wings. The inertia of the relatively heavy glass plate prevented higher speeds than 12 pictures a second being achieved. Marey had been lobbying the public authorities to persuade them to establish a physiological station for the study of animal movements, and in August 1882 he received a grant from the government for such a project, while the Paris Municipal Council provided some land near the Porte d'Auteuil.

For work in the new station, Marey decided to use a different camera. He fitted a large camera with a rotating disc shutter $4\frac{1}{4}$ feet (1.3 metres) in diameter and perforated with very narrow slots. A single, fixed plate was exposed ten times a second, with an exposure time of 1/1000 of a second, when a handle was turned. The moving subject was photographed brilliantly lit against a totally black background, so that the camera recorded multiple images on the plate, more or less overlapping depending on the speed of movement of the subject. The camera was carried in a truck on rails so that it could be quickly set up at a distance appropriate to each subject. The chronophotographic fixed plate camera was used for motion studies by Marey from March 1883 until 1888, when, as we shall see, he made a major step forward.

The Prussian photographer Ottomar Anschütz was another to have been inspired by Muybridge's work. In 1883 he began a series of photographic studies of military manoeuvres and the like, using a camera fitted with a focal plane shutter of his invention which would work at speeds down to 1/1000 of a second. In the autumn of 1885 he set up a series of cameras on Muybridge's pattern, using electromagnetic shutter releases, with which he made studies of horses, other animals and men, taking 24 pictures in about three quarters of a second. In 1887 he invented a device for the public presentation of his sequence pictures. The negatives were printed as

Anschütz's Electrical Tachyscope, 1887. Sequence photographs taken in a series of cameras were printed as transparencies and fitted around the edge of a wheel rotated in front of a Geissler tube. This produced a very brief flash of light as each picture passed in front of it. Through persistence of vision, the audience saw an apparently continuously illuminated moving picture

9 × 12cm transparencies and were arranged around the circumference of a large steel disc, which could carry up to 24 pictures. The disc was turned in front of a spiral Geissler tube (a glass tube containing a gas which produced a brilliant light when a very high voltage was momentarily applied to it – rather as in a modern electronic flashgun). As each picture passed before the face of the tube an electrical contact was made, and a high voltage pulse applied to the tube caused it to flash, the duration – about 1/1000 of a second – being so short that the moving picture was 'frozen'. The pictures followed each other at intervals of about 1/30 of a second and presented the illusion of a continuously lit, moving photograph. The whole apparatus was hidden behind a partition, with only a small aperture for the picture to be seen through.

The first show of the Electro-Tachyscope was given in Berlin from 19 – 21 March 1887, at the Kulturministerium. The subjects on display included horses, marching soldiers and gymnasts. The Electro-Tachyscope was shown in London in December 1892 under the name of 'An Electrical Wonder' operated, said the *British Journal of Photography* 'by dropping the omnipotent penny into the inevitable slot'. The *Amateur Photographer* thought 'So exquisitely are these produced as transparencies, and so life-like the impression . . . that we think this new wonder will become a very good thing'. Not everyone was so impressed, though. In London's Strand one lady was overheard to say to another 'It's a show of pictures of moving figures. It's awfully stupid.' A series of 100 of the machines were made by Siemens and Halske, and were widely shown throughout Europe and America. The *St Louis Photographer*, reporting on the Electro-Tachyscope set up in Chaplin and Gore's Restaurant in Chicago, said,

'Dropping a dime in a slot, an observer waits for a few moments, when with a wirring [sic] noise the machinery starts. A personal inspection is necessary to enable one to appreciate fully the realistic manner in which a horseman is represented riding along a boulevard. Every movement of the man and animal may be clearly seen – the movements of the rider's body, hands, arms, legs and feet, the motion of the bridle, every step of the horse and even the dust stirred up by his hoofs, and what is most astonishing of all, every movement of the muscles in the horse's flank.'

In November 1894 Anschütz devised for his pictures a projector in which 24 transparencies were arranged on two discs of 12 each. The discs were rotated alternately and intermittently by a form of Maltese Cross mechanism, and were projected by two lenses. A rotating shutter allowed each picture to blend rapidly into the next with no dark interval. The first public demonstration was given in Berlin on 25 November 1894, on a screen which measured about $19\frac{1}{2} \times 26\frac{1}{4}$ feet (6 × 8 metres). From 22 February 1895 they were on regular show to audiences of 300 in a building on the Leipzigstrasse. Admission charges were from 1 mark to 1 mark 50 pfennigs. Anschütz's pictures reached a wider public with the publication of the Tachyscope viewer for the home. It used the principle of the Zoetrope, and the photographs were mechanically reproduced on strips of card, with narrow slots punched between the pictures. The bands were placed around the circumference of a shallow cylinder, which could be rotated on a central spindle. The figures were seen in lifelike movement when viewed through the slots. The Tachyscope, on sale in 1891, cost 7s. 6d. for a set of ten strips in a box containing the wooden stand.

George Eastman

George Eastman, a young American bank employee, became interested in photography in 1877. Dissatisfied with the cumbersome apparatus and messy chemicals of the current wet collodion process, he turned to the newly invented gelatin dry plate. He mastered the process so well that in 1880 he was able to begin the commercial manufacture of dry plates. Eastman's plates rapidly acquired a good reputation, but Eastman looked for ways of making photography simpler, in order that more people should be able to take it up. In 1885, with William Walker, he invented and marketed a roll-holder which could be attached to the camera in place of the conventional plate holder. It carried a roll of sensitized paper sufficient for 48 exposures. The roll-holder proved popular, and Eastman worked on a new camera design in which the roll-holder was built in. The new camera was introduced in 1888; it was a simple box camera sold ready-loaded with a paper roll sufficient for 100 exposures. To

George Eastman (1854-1932)

Eastman-Walker rollholder, 1885

First Kodak camera, 1888

identify his new camera, Eastman created the trade name 'Kodak'. The Kodak camera, supported by a developing and printing service, brought photography to the general public for the first time. In 1889 Eastman introduced a thin, flexible, transparent celluloid roll film for the Kodak camera. This provided the movie experimenters with the material they had been waiting for.

Albert Londe, a French medical researcher, designed in 1883 an apparatus which condensed the multiple camera arrangement of Muybridge into a single unit, fitted with nine lenses arranged in a circle. A series of electromagnets energised in sequence by a metronome device released the shutters in quick succession, exposing nine pictures on a 12×18cm plate. The camera was intended for use in the study of the movements of patients in epileptic fits at La Salpétrière hospital, in Paris. In 1892 Londe produced an improved version with 12 lenses in three rows of four, exposing a 20×30cm plate. The apparatus was used only for medical studies of muscle movement, and it could make a sequence of 12 pictures in anything from 1/10 of a second to several seconds.

All these chronophotographic sequence cameras used glass plates. Glass is not an ideal medium for making rapid sequences of photographs. Its weight is such that to stop and start a plate sufficiently large for a useful series of pictures presents almost insurmountable problems. Until the mid 1880s, however, the photographer had no choice. In 1885 George Eastman, an American manufacturer of photographic plates, revived an earlier idea which had never previously had much success. With William H. Walker, Eastman designed a rollholder – a device which replaced the conventional plate holder on a camera, and which took a roll of sensitized paper, enough for a large number of exposures. The negative material, called 'American Film' by Eastman, consisted of a gelatin emulsion coated on paper with a thin layer of soluble gelatin between them. After exposure and processing, the thin gelatin film with the image could be stripped from the paper and transferred to glass, sheets of insoluble gelatin, or simply kept as it was between the pages of a book.

The new stripping film and the rollholder began to revolutionise photography. In 1888 Eastman introduced his Kodak camera, a simple box form model with an integral rollholder holding enough American Film for 100 exposures $2\frac{1}{2}$in (6.3cm) in diameter. The influence of this camera on still photography was considerable, but the long bands of flexible material that it used provided the long awaited substitute for glass plates in sequence photography.

Marey had been frustrated by the limitations in the numbers of pictures he could take with his early cameras. With the appearance of the new roll films he designed a new camera. On 8 October 1888 at the Académie des Sciences he proposed the use of a long roll of paper film of the type used in the newly introduced Kodak camera, $2\frac{3}{4}$in (7cm) wide and about 22 feet (6.7 m) long. At a later session, on 29 October 1888, he showed a roll of exposed paper film he had used in his new camera, with a series of pictures made at the rate of 20 in a second. His new flexible film camera used a large disc shutter like that on the fixed plate camera; in a chamber at the back the roll of paper was passed from one spool to another, passing on the way through the exposing aperture (or gate, in the jargon of cinematography) and round a driving roller which pulled it through the camera at constant speed. In the first model, the film was intermittently arrested at the gate by an electromagnetically operated clamp, while the rotating shutter made the exposure. While the film was held in the gate, the driving roller kept on turning, and would have torn the film but for a light spring which bore on the film. The increasing tension bent the spring inwards until the clamping was released, when it sprang back to its former position, pulling a length of film through the gate, when the cycle began again. This camera ran quite well, taking up to 40 pictures per second, but the spacing

The mechanism of Marey's film camera (1890). A roll of film (M) was drawn through the exposing aperture (F) by a continuously turning roller (L). A rotating star wheel (C) intermittently clamped the film while a rotating shutter made the exposure

Marey's film camera, designed in 1888 and improved in 1890, was the first to embody the essential elements of a cine camera – flexible film moved intermittently and exposed while stationary, with accurate spacing of successive exposures

of the photographs was not always even. This was no real problem to Marey whose first concern was to analyse the content of individual frames. On the 3 November 1890 he told the Académie des Sciences of an improved camera in which he had replaced the electromagnetic clamp with a mechanical one. A cylindrical clamp was periodically pressed against the film by each of six protruding points on a rotating star wheel. This new mechanism gave much more evenly spaced exposures.

In the autumn of 1889 Eastman had introduced a thin, tough, flexible transparent celluloid roll film to replace the paper rolls in his cameras and rollholders. It was available in a range of widths, and in long lengths. It was an almost ideal material for recording long sequences of pictures. Marey used this new film in his cameras, as well as shorter lengths of sensitized celluloid sold by the French manufacturer Balagny. The length of Marey's films varied between about $14\frac{1}{2}$ feet (4.4 metres) and four feet (1.25 metre) and the width was $3\frac{1}{2}$in (9cm), the size of film used in Eastman's No 2 Kodak camera. The combination of tougher material and more reliable mechanism allowed Marey to achieve picture frequencies of up to 100 pictures per second. By altering the starwheel arrangement and changing the masking in the gate, Marey was able to adapt the format of his pictures to suit the subject. Details of a horse's hooves trotting were filmed as long narrow images, permitting many exposures on the film; a horse jumping a fence, or a seascape, would be recorded on fewer, but larger frames. He was able to adapt his cameras to take close-up pictures of insects and other small creatures, and even to couple them to microscopes.

Marey's principal aim was to analyse the movements of animals, but from time to time he made attempts to synthesise movement from his picture sequences. Although they could be viewed successfully in the Zoetrope, Marey had little success in projecting his bands of pictures. The unperforated bands of film made the successive pictures difficult to register on the screen. However, although Marey's camera was very simple in design, it functioned well and embodied the basic elements of a cinecamera – use of a flexible transparent film moved intermittently through the camera, exposed while stationary and moved on while covered by a rotating shutter. Only the addition of perforations in the film to ensure accurate registration of successive frames was wanting for it to be a true cinecamera of the modern type. Marey had shown the way; it was now up to the inventors, interested more in commercial exploitation than scientific study, to carry on.

ABOVE Part of a sequence record of a seascape exposed by Marey on stripping film in his film camera

BELOW Part of a sequence study of the hooves of a trotting horse, recorded by Marey on celluloid film. Note the timing clock measuring the interval between frames. The film was exposed at the rate of about 80 frames in one second

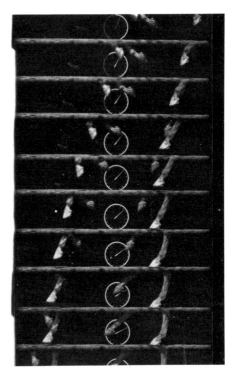

4

Enter the inventors

By the middle of the 1880s everything was ready for the appearance of cinematography. The wide publicity given to the work of Muybridge and Marey, the great interest of the public in the latest developments in science and technology and the availability of the new, faster gelatin-based photographic materials all contributed to the inspiration of the inventor. The most significant factor of all was the introduction of a flexible paper roll film by George Eastman in 1885, which provided a useful experimental material for the production of sequences of pictures.

The first experimenter to explore its possibilities was the Frenchman Louis-Aimé-Augustin Le Prince. Born in Metz in 1842, in 1860 he moved to Leeds in England at the invitation of his brother-in-law to be, and worked in the Whitley family's brass founding business. After returning to France to serve as a volunteer in the Franco-Prussian War, he went back to Leeds and with his wife opened a school of applied art in Park Square. In 1881 he moved to America where he became manager of a chain of Panoramas in New York, Washington and Chicago. He is known to have commissioned the production of lantern slides showing military scenes in 1884, to be used in the preparation of large paintings for the Panorama, and it may have been this experience, coupled with the publicity given to Muybridge at the time, which led him to investigate the photography of movement. He designed a form of camera carrying a number of lenses, fitted with electromagnetic shutters, which exposed sequences of pictures on rolls of paper negative film. In an American patent, applied for in November 1886, granted on 10 January 1888, he claimed

> 'The successive production by means of a photographic camera of a number of images of the same object or objects in motion and reproducing the same in the order of taking by means of a "projector" or "deliverer", thereby producing on the eye of the spectator a similar impression to that which would have been produced by the original object or objects in motion . . . In an apparatus for producing "animated" pictures the continuous alternate operation of the film and its corresponding shutter or series of shutters . . . As a means of producing "animated" pictures of a photographic receiver provided with one or more lenses and one or more shutters, in combination with one or more intermittently operated film drums.' (See panel opposite)

Le Prince's work, which was quite promising, came to an abrupt end on 16 September, 1890, when, after being seen boarding a train for Paris at Dijon, he disappeared, never to be seen again.

Louis Le Prince

Le Prince was the first inventor to explore the possibilities of Eastman's paper roll film, introduced in 1885, as a means of recording sequences of images. He was granted an American patent on 10 January 1888 but those parts of the claim referring to single lens camera designs were removed by the American Patent Office on the somewhat unjust grounds that they had been anticipated by Du Mont's English patent of 1861 for a sequence plate camera. The American patent as issued covered a form of camera and projector fitted with 16 lenses exposing two roll films.

The lenses were arranged in two groups of eight. The roll of paper running behind one set was clamped in the exposing aperture, while the

Le Prince (1842-90?)

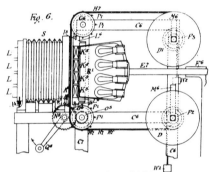
English patent drawing, 1888

eight lenses exposed in sequence through electromagnetic shutters. After this, the film was released and moved on, while the second film was clamped and exposed in turn. Sets of eight successive exposures were thus carried alternately on the two films. Le Prince proposed that the not always evenly spaced exposures be printed onto sheets of sensitized transparent material – glass, mica, horn or whatever – cut up and mounted on flexible bands with perforated edges which could be wound through a projector of similar construction to the camera.

Le Prince's English patent, applied for on 10 January 1888, described in addition the single lens version of his apparatus:

'When the receiver is provided with only one lens it is so constructed that the sensitive film is intermittently operated at the

Single lens camera design

rear of the said lens, which it provided with a properly timed intermittently operated shutter; and correspondingly in the deliverer, when only one lens is provided, the band or ribbon of transparencies is automatically so operated as to bring the pictures intermittently and in the proper order of succession opposite the said lens . . . Sensitive film for the negatives may be an endless sheet of insoluble gelatine coated with bromide emulsion or any convenient ready-made quick acting paper such as Eastman's paper film.'

This was a perfectly good statement of the necessary principles involved

in the construction of a cine camera and projector, although Le Prince's single lens camera design had several deficiences. The paper negative film was moved on in the camera by an intermittent rotation of the take-up spool, the film being clamped and held flat in the exposing aperture while the exposure was made. This led to a progressive increase in the separation between exposures as the diameter of the reel increased. This would not have been of serious consequence if the uncut film was projected on an identical machine, or if the individual frames were cut up and remounted, as in the multiple lens version. Short lengths of film made in 1888 and still surviving show that the camera worked at a picture frequency quite adequate for analysis and synthesis of motion, but show rather uneven location of the frames, some of which overlap.

Film shot in Leeds, 1888

William Friese Greene (1855-1921), the English professional photographer and early experimenter with moving pictures. A cartoon by 'Peter' from *The Bioscope*, 9 April 1919

The next inventor to enter the field was an English professional photographer, William Friese Greene, whose tombstone proclaims him to have been the inventor of 'commercial kinematography'. This claim has been often repeated, and formed the basis of the feature film *The Magic Box*, made for the Festival of Britain in 1951. Therefore, his contribution must be considered in some detail. Friese Greene seems to have been introduced to the business of animated photography by John Arthur Roebuck Rudge, a talented mechanic of Bath, who had begun experiments with magic lantern devices for moving picture projection in the early 1870s. On 12 November 1884 Rudge applied for a provisional patent for 'Improvements in the method of showing dissolving views and all kinds of slides, and producing life-like effects with the optical or magic lantern'. This lantern was based upon Beale's Choreutoscope. Rudge arranged seven lantern slides on a rotating ring placed around a cylindrical lamphouse. A form of Maltese Cross movement was used, with notches in the slide-carrying ring being engaged with a tooth on a rotating disc, and so being moved on one slide at a time as the handle was turned. While the slides were changing, a pair of shutter blades, acting like a pair of scissors, moved to cover the lens. The series of seven posed photographs shown thus in quick succession were combined by persistence of vision to give a moving picture.

Friese Greene met Rudge in 1880, and as a young up and coming photographer it seems likely that Rudge asked him to help in providing sets of photographs for his lantern. In the later 1880s Friese Greene demonstrated Rudge's lanterns on several occasions. On 26 January, 1886, at the Photographic Society in London he

'exhibited and explained a piece of apparatus for use in the optical lantern, designed by Mr Roger [sic] of Bath. In front of four transparencies, four lenses are placed, each one having its optical axis converging to a common centre, and the light coming through the condenser is transmitted, by opaque divisions, in four channels, so that each lens receives its own light . . . in front of the lenses a revolving diaphragm is attached, which permits only one lens at a time to act, and, by turning this diaphragm, one image after another is thrown upon the screen. In portraits from life, by changing the position of the eyes or other parts of the face in the original negatives, a living motion is given to the image on the screen.'

This machine was Rudge's Phantascope lantern, which Friese Greene demonstrated again in 1887 to the Photographic Society as an invention 'he had designed' with no mention of Rudge's part. He showed a new version on 27 January 1889 to the Photographic Society, in the form of

'an appliance for exhibiting a more life-like effect upon the screen . . . The apparatus consisted of a pair of lanterns furnished with a series of portraits of the same person with varying expressions. These portraits were mounted in frames linked together in a sort of endless chain and the pair of chains were actuated by clockwork driven by a heavy weight. On setting the apparatus in motion the portrait in one of the lanterns was covered by a dissolver, and whilst this portrait was hidden, the slide was changed by a movement of the chain, so as to bring another portrait into place. The other lantern objective was then covered, and the portrait behind it changed in the same way. It thus became possible by using a series of gradually changing images to represent the movements of a person when bursting into a laugh, when winking, etc. . . . In order to get a perfect representation of motion, Mr Greene considered that it would be necessary to take the photographs at the rate of five in one second.'

Rudge was provoked by reports of this demonstration to draw attention to the fact that he had invented the apparatus, which he had sold to Friese Greene. Despite this, the double projector was exhibited at the Crystal Palace in March 1889 by Friese Greene as 'an automatic biunial lantern . . . of his own invention'.

In order to produce sets of slides for the Rudge lantern, in 1889 Friese Greene, with a civil engineer, Mortimer Evans, designed a sequence camera which they patented on 21 June 1889. It has been claimed that Friese Greene worked on such a camera as early as 1886, but such a claim is not substantiated by contemporary sources. Indeed, there is no evidence that Friese Greene worked on the preparation of continuous sequences of photographs, as opposed to posed series, until after the publication of reports of Marey's film camera in late 1888, and of Le Prince's patent in the same year. The patent described

John Arthur Roebuck Rudge (1837-1903), the inventor of a number of lantern devices for creating movement on the screen

'improved apparatus for taking photographs in rapid series . . . Our invention has for its object the formation of Photographic Pictures, and relates chiefly to the production of such pictures as are necessary to illustrate and register the movements of animals, insects or moving objects either taken singly or in masses as may be desired.

For this purpose we construct an apparatus by which with a single camera and lens a rapid series of such pictures may be taken and by which a series of fresh photographic sensitive films or portions of such photographic film may be substituted for those which have been exposed to the action of light with sufficient rapidity for the desired end.'

The reference to 'films' in the patent has led some to assume that the patent was the first to refer to transparent celluloid film – but no mention of this was made in it. The paper negative materials

Rudge's Phantascope lantern, 1884, by which seven lantern slides could be projected in quick succession by means of a form of Maltese Cross mechanism. Scissor-like shutter blades covered the lens during movement of the slides

Part of a length of film exposed in
Friese Greene and Evans' 'machine'
camera, probably in 1890. Notice the
big difference between the frames, due
to the very low picture frequency

commercially available at this time were referred to as films, as we
have seen – Le Prince so described them in his earlier patent. Indeed,
the complete specification of Friese Greene and Evans' patent, filed
on 13 March 1890, refers specifically to 'a roll of any convenient
length of sensitized paper or the like'. The camera was described as
being for 'photographic representations of quarter-plate size' – that
is $4\frac{1}{4} \times 3\frac{1}{4}$in ($10.8 \times 8.3$cm). The sensitized material was driven intermittently by a driving roller worked by a spring and escapement
tooth of rather unreliable design. The driving roller had serrated
ends, to give a positive grip on the paper, which was not perforated,
however, as has been claimed. The driving winch-handle was geared
to take two exposures with one turn, limiting the exposure rate to
four or five pictures a second only. From the low picture frequency,
the large image size, and the fact that the flip-flop shutter design
allowed for adjustment of exposure time, it is obvious that the camera
was intended to produce short picture sequences to be cut up,
printed as separate lantern slides and shown in the Rudge lantern.
Indeed, it is apparent from subsequent demonstrations of the camera,
and Friese Greene's own statements, that this was the case. There is
no record of any successful projection of such picture sequences in
public and certainly no indication that Friese Greene made any
attempt at this time to project picture sequences on transparent
flexible film.

The claims, based on this patent, that Friese Greene invented
'commercial kinematography' cannot be substantiated. Both Marey
and Le Prince anticipated him in the use of an intermittently moved
flexible film in the camera. The design of the camera and the few
fragments of surviving film show it to be capable of operation only
at very slow speeds, certainly nothing like the 16 pictures per second
frequency required for successful synthesis of motion. The claim that
Friese Greene manufactured and coated his own celluloid film in long
strips in his basement darkroom is simply incredible. Such a task
was at the time beyond the skill of many commercial manufacturers.
The earliest mention by Friese Greene of the use of celluloid film
came over two months after Eastman's transparent film had been
introduced to the English market. He made no authenticated use of
perforated film until after the introduction of the 35mm film of
Thomas Edison, which we shall consider shortly. He did not con-
ceive of the use of a projector using long strips of transparent positive
film in his early experiments, nor did he even achieve successful
projection with the Rudge-type lantern. The demonstration at the
Chester Photographic Convention in 1890, which is often claimed
to have been the first public presentation of projected moving
pictures, was a failure: the *British Journal of Photography* reported,
'The apparatus or lantern by which these were to have been thrown
upon the screen having suffered some derangement in the course of
its transit to Chester, the audience were deprived of the opportunity
of witnessing the full effects intended to be produced'.

Soon after Friese Greene and Evans filed their patent, Wordsworth
Donisthorpe (whose Kinesigraph camera was mentioned in the last
chapter) and W. C. Crofts filed a patent for a new model, on 15
August 1889. The patent referred to 'a sensitive film carried by a
roll of paper or other material'. The paper film, of the size and type
used in the first Kodak camera introduced the year before, was
wound continuously from one reel to another at constant speed. The
whole of this film transporting mechanism was mounted so as to be
free to slide up and down behind the lens and was operated by an

eccentric drive from the flywheel shaft. As the mechanism moved upwards, its speed matched that of the film on it, which was moving downwards, so that the film was effectively stationary relative to the lens, during which time the exposure was made. As the mechanism moved down again, the shutter covered the film, and by the time that the mechanism began to move upwards again, enough film had been wound through the exposing aperture to bring an unexposed portion into it. The projector was built to a similar pattern. Although the design was unconventional, it seems to have worked quite well.

The Kodak Museum in London possesses nine frames of celluloid film printed from a negative strip exposed in Trafalgar Square in 1890. The evenly spaced pictures are circular, $2\frac{1}{2}$in (6.4cm) in diameter, like those of the first Kodak camera. The movement recorded suggest that they were taken at a speed of 8 to 10 frames per second. Donisthorpe tried to get financial backing to develop the Kinesigraph. He

> 'submitted the matter to two "experts", selected by Sir George Newnes, to pronounce on its merits. One (I afterwards learnt) was an artist, a painter who was as ignorant of the physical sciences as Noah's grandmother; and the other was, I believe a magic-lantern maker.
>
> I need hardly tell you that both these "experts" reported adversely. They agreed that the idea was wild, visionary and ridiculous, and that the only result of attempting to photograph motion would be an indescribable blur.
>
> What could Sir George Newnes do in the face of such "expert" testimony?'

It is unfortunate that Donisthorpe could not develop his device further at the time, since of the several experimenters in the field, he was perhaps the nearest to success.

The next attempt at animated photography was patented by Frederick H. Varley, a London engineer and an associate of Friese Greene's. The patent, filed on 26 March 1890, described a twin-lens camera for stereoscopic photographs in rapid series. The film was moved on intermittently by a cam-operated rocking roller, which bore on the film, pulling through the exposing aperture a length of film equal to the height of one picture. Each turn of the operating handle made one pair of exposures, so that the camera

Part of a film exposed by Wordsworth Donisthorpe in Trafalgar Square, 1890, in his Kinesigraph camera

A stereoscopic film camera designed and patented by Frederick Varley in 1890. A virtually identical design was patented by Friese Greene in 1893. This camera could operate at only two or three frames a second

59

Part of a film exposed by Friese Greene in Varley's camera in 1890. Since the successive pictures were taken at quite long intervals, there is considerable difference between the frames

RIGHT A drawing from Varley's patent of 1890 for a sequence stereo camera
FAR RIGHT A similar drawing from Friese Greene's later patent of 1893

could not have taken more than two or three pictures a second. The stereoscopic pairs were about $3\frac{1}{4}$in (8.3cm) square, the normal stereoscopic picture size. The patent mentioned the provision of a removable back 'so as to permit the camera being used for . . . projecting on a screen strips of translucent positives (obtained from the strips of negatives obtained by the aforesaid operation of the camera) sufficiently near each other in time, to convey the idea of life and motion'.

Varley was the first to suggest the projection of transparent film strips derived from negative film exposed in the same mechanism but unfortunately the picture frequency possible in the camera was far too low for successful motion synthesis. Friese Greene used and demonstrated Varley's camera in 1890 but once again there is no record of a successful projection demonstration. The lack of any method, such as perforated film, to register each picture accurately with the preceding one would have made the machine impractical. Three years later, on 29 November 1893, Friese Greene patented a virtually identical apparatus under the title 'Improvements in apparatus for exhibiting Panoramic, Dissolving, or changing views, and in the manufacture of Slides for use therewith'. The grant of a patent for a device bearing an astonishing resemblance to that of Varley of three years before is explained by the fact that at that time the granting of a British patent was no guarantee of originality, since no systematic search for novelty was made by the patent authorities. None of the efforts of these inventors – Le Prince, Friese Greene, Evans, Varley, Donisthorpe and Crofts, mostly working at the same time, in the same country and all apparently completely unaware of each other's work – came to any commercially applicable conclusion. The first public exploitation of cinematography took place in America.

The great inventor and industrialist, Thomas Alva Edison, became interested in the possibility of producing an optical equivalent to the sound recording and reproducing phonograph that he had invented in 1877. The stimulus seems to have been, once again, the work of Muybridge, who lectured at West Orange, home of Edison's laboratory, on 25 February 1888. Muybridge visited Edison two days later and discussed with him the possibility of coupling the Zoopraxiscope projector with the phonograph. What followed from this meeting was for many years inaccurately reported. The false

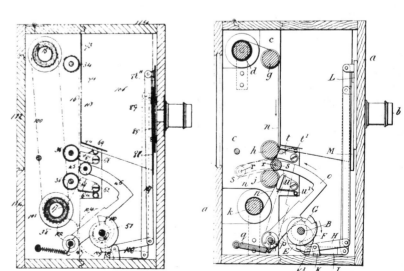

picture arose from Edison's own biased accounts, deliberate falsification of facts, dates, and even equipment during legal proceedings in the 1890s and 1900s, and above all the inaccurate, if loyal, accounts by Edison's chief collaborator in the work, William Kennedy Laurie Dickson, who, for reasons of his own, placed the key developments two years earlier than they had actually occurred. Dickson, a young Scot, had joined the Edison Company in 1883 (not 1881, as he often stated) and was soon in a position of responsibility in Edison's research organisation. Among other duties, he was the official photographer to the organisation, and it was logical that Edison should give him the task of working out his ideas for sequence photography.

The first step that Edison took was to file a caveat with the Patent Office. In American patent law, a caveat enabled an inventor to warn others of an impending patent, thus barring applications from other inventors for a similar invention for one year. If another such application were filed, the original inventor then had three months' grace to file his full patent specification. The first caveat, on 8 October 1888, referred to a camera using an intermittently rotated sensitized cylinder, on which a spiral arrangement of tiny pictures might be produced 25 per second, with a total running time of 28 minutes. This optical equivalent of the cylinder phonograph was mechanically unsound but it set the direction of Dickson's experimental work for the next three years. A limited amount of work was done during the winter of 1888-89, when Dickson experimented with micro-photography to establish the best way to make minute photographic images but he made no progress with sequence photography. A second caveat on 3 February 1889 repeated the cylinder idea, discussing methods of overcoming the problems of photographing on a curved surface. By this time Edison had created a name for the viewing device – which did not yet exist – the Kinetoscope. Again, only a small amount of work was done developing the cylinder idea during 1889; on 20 May Edison wrote a third caveat, this time suggesting the use of electric sparks to take and view the images. Interestingly enough, this was the idea suggested by Donisthorpe in his proposed combination of Kinesigraph and phonograph back in 1878. This caveat Edison filed on 5 August, 1889.

Up to this time, Dickson had had great problems in producing sensitive surfaces on cylinders. In November 1888 John Carbutt, a leading American photographic plate maker, announced that he was manufacturing sensitized sheets of celluloid, supplied to him by the American Celluloid Manufacturing Company. He offered them as a lightweight substitute for glass plates; they were the first commercially successful application of celluloid as a base for a photographic material. Dickson acquired some sheets of the Carbutt film in June 1889 and exposed some wrapped around the cylinder of a larger model camera but he achieved no real success before Edison's trip to Paris in August 1889. In Paris, Edison met Marey and saw his rollfilm sequence camera. On his return from Europe in October 1889 Edison, it was claimed, saw a projected moving picture synchronized with a phonograph, but this cannot possibly have been the case. Edison may have seen the first really successful results obtained with a cylinder machine. Armed with his knowledge of Marey's work, in November Edison drafted a fourth caveat which for the first time mentioned the use. of a long band of film passing from one reel to another, with toothed sprocket wheels engaging in

William Kennedy Laurie Dickson (1860-1935), the British employee of Thomas Edison, who was chiefly responsible for the development of the Kinetograph and the Kinetoscope

rows of perforations on each side of the film, with an escapement mechanism to provide the necessary intermittent movement. To view the pictures, he proposed the use of an electric spark briefly to light each frame, or light from a lamp flashing through a narrow slot in a rotating shutter.

Dickson at first used short strips of the relatively thick Carbutt film in a prototype camera but a more suitable material was now to hand. In June 1889, George Eastman had announced the introduction of a celluloid roll film, suitable for his Kodak camera, $2\frac{3}{4}$in (7cm) wide and about 24 feet (7.3m) long. 'It is as thin as a blister and as clear as glass' said the editor of *Wilson's Photographic Magazine*. The new material went on sale in July. On 2 September 1889 Dickson wrote to Eastman acknowledging receipt of a roll of the new film: 'it looks splendid – I never succeeded in getting this substance in such straight long pieces'. Whether this film was to be used in the sequence picture experiments is not clear although a footnote to the letter, requesting samples of the most sensitive film available suggests that it might have been. Another letter, sent a week or two later, requested six rolls cut $\frac{3}{4}$in (1.9cm) wide and 54 feet (16.5m) long, or even longer if available. 'I have made all my astronomical experiments on the samples', Dickson said. Such narrow celluloid film would have had little use for astronomical photography, and it is most likely that the film was intended for the motion picture experiments. Dickson noted on the margin of the letter, 'Have you a good method for slowly developing the strips?' This may well have related to the problem of making positive prints from the exposed negatives, for which the relatively fast negative film was less suitable.

During much of 1890, Dickson was preoccupied with other work on an ore-milling machine and work only began again on the Kinetoscope project in the autumn, when the successful, but final, experiments with a cylinder machine were carried out. The fact that in March 1891 only a single roll of $3\frac{1}{2}$in (8.9cm) wide film was purchased suggests that little work was being carried out at that time. Matters must then have moved quickly, for on 24 August 1891 Edison filed specifications for patents covering a Kinetograph camera and a Kinetoscope viewer, using perforated bands of film. Dickson had already made a successful camera using a horizontally running perforated film, as outlined in the fourth caveat. A Kinetoscope viewer using a strip film was shown to the delegates of the National Federation of Women's Clubs, who visited the Edison Laboratory on 20 May 1891. The *Sun* reported,

> 'The surprised and pleased clubwomen saw a small pine box standing on the floor. There were some wheels and belts in the box . . . In the top of the box was a hole perhaps an inch in diameter. As they looked through this hole they saw the picture of a man. It bowed and smiled and waved its hands and took off its hat with the most perfect naturalness and grace. Every motion was perfect. No wonder Edison chuckled with the effect he produced with his Kinetograph.'

A later report in the same paper gave more details, referring to 'rolls of gelatine film' with photographs 'about half-an-inch square'. The machine was the first prototype of the Kinetoscope.

In July 1891 Dickson visited the Eastman factory in Rochester, New York, and ordered four rolls of film one inch (2.54cm) wide and 50 feet (15.2m) long to carry on the experimental work, and by the end of the year had made such progress that in June 1892 Edison decided on the commercial introduction of the Kinetoscope. A new

Kinetograph camera, with a vertical film feed was designed, taking a wider film strip $1\frac{3}{8}$in, or about 35mm, wide. This was exactly half the width of the film Eastman produced for his original Kodak camera, probably produced by slitting such film down the centre and joining the two ends to give a length of almost 50 feet. The film was perforated with four roughly rectangular perforations on each side of the $1 \times \frac{3}{4}$in (2.5×1.9cm) frame. Thus the film had approximately the same dimensions and arrangement of perforations as is still in use. The film was moved intermittently through the camera by means of a toothed sprocket wheel, which engaged with the perforations, giving reliable traction and precise registration of each frame. An escapement consisting of a toothed disc bearing upon a slotted disc at right angles to it gave the necessary stop-go movement to the sprocket wheel, while a rotating disc shutter made the exposures. The whole was driven by an electric motor.

Edison's contribution to the development of the motion picture was a most significant one. It is true that most of the development work was carried out by Dickson and that the apparatus used no fundamentally new principles. Nonetheless, it *was* Edison who brought photographic motion pictures, in the form used today, to the public. The Edison Kinetograph camera was the first to employ perforated celluloid film for accurate registration of the images and effective transport through the camera and to use a size and disposition of film still in use today. The appearance of the Kinetoscope in America and Europe in 1894, like Muybridge's earlier demonstrations, acted as a powerful stimulus to the development of motion picture apparatus by others, who took the process to the final stage of theatrical projection. Possibly because of its close association with the phonograph in its early stages of development, the moving picture was seen by Edison as being best exploited in a peepshow form. The phonograph parlours, in which the public paid to hear the talking machine through ear tubes, were highly successful, and this undoubtedly conditioned the thinking of Edison and Dickson. The mechanism of the Kinetograph camera could have been adapted for projection but this was not done. Nonetheless, after the appearance of the Kinetoscope in America and Europe in 1894 (see pages 64-5), other inventors turned to the investigation of the problems of projecting moving pictures onto a screen.

In America there has been considerable argument over who first projected films. Jean Aimé LeRoy claimed that in 1893 he had acquired a short length of Donisthorpe's film taken in Trafalgar Square in 1890, and had projected it using a home-made projector in which the film was moved intermittently by being gripped periodically by a pair of partially cut-away rollers. His claim to have projected two Edison Kinetoscope films to an audience of about 25 theatrical agents on 5 February 1894 is certainly not substantiated. The two films were supposed to have been *Washing the Baby* and *The Execution of Mary, Queen of Scots*, but the latter film was not produced until 28 August 1895. The existence of theatre playbills advertising 'LeRoy's Marvellous Cinematographe' in the early months of 1895 does however suggest that he may have had a successful working machine by that time.

Woodville Latham and his sons Otway and Gray, inspired by the Kinetograph in May 1894, proposed to present complete film records of prize-fights. The Edison Black Maria studio was modified for the purpose in May, and on 14 June 1894 Mike Leonard fought Jack Cushing for six one-minute rounds, each round being filmed by an

Edison's Kinetoscope

The Kinetoscope, designed by Edison's assistant, W. K. L. Dickson, was based on a patent filed on 24 August 1891. An upright wooden box contained a bank of spools over which almost 50 feet (15.2m) of perforated 35mm wide film ran in an endless loop. The continuously moving film passed over an electric lamp and under a magnifying lens set in the top of the box. Between the lamp and the film passed a rotating disc

some demonstrations it was coupled with a reproducing phonograph.

To produce films for the Kinetoscopes, Dickson designed a studio which was completed at the end of 1892. It was built from a pine timber frame-work covered with tarpaper so that it would be as light as possible. It could be rotated on a turntable so as to give the best light throughout the day through the glass roof. Edison's employees christened

ABOVE *T. A. Edison (1847-1931)*

LEFT *The 'Black Maria' studio*

BELOW *Inside the 'Black Maria'*

shutter perforated with a narrow slit. As each frame passed under the lens, it was lit by a flash of light passing through the slit, a flash so brief that it 'froze' the movement of the film. Thus a series of apparently stationary images, about 40 per second, were presented to the eye in rapid succession. Persistence of vision did the rest. The film was driven by a large sprocket wheel operated by an electric motor, set in motion by inserting a coin and gave a 'show' lasting about 20 seconds. Experimental production of the machines began in the summer of 1892 and full manufacture began in 1893. One of the new models was demonstrated at the Brooklyn Institute on 9 May 1893, the subject shown being a blacksmith at work. Another Kinetoscope was installed in the Edison exhibit at the Chicago World's Fair (the World's Columbian Exposition) during the summer of 1893. It appears that for

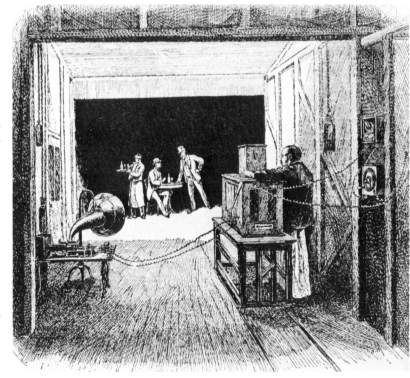

Edison's Kinetoscope

Carmencita, filmed in March 1894

Sandow, a wrestling match, a barber's shop, Highland dancing and a trapeze act. In August 1894 the Werner brothers, Michel and Alexis, installed Kinetoscopes in premises on the Boulevard Poissonière in Paris. The public in London first saw the Kinetoscope on 18 October 1894 at 112 Oxford Street. By the end of the year, Kinetoscope parlours were open all over North America and Europe. Altogether over 1,000 machines were sold, before their popularity began to wane.

The new entertainment soon ran into trouble. Senator Bradley, seeing the Kinetoscope in July 1894, was shocked:

'The view was that of Carmencita in her famous butterfly dance and the Senator watched the graceful gyrations of the lovely Spanish dancer with interest that was ill-concealed. But near the end . . . the Spanish beauty gives the least little bit of a kick, which raises her silken draperies so that her well-turned ankles peep out and there is a background of white lace.

That kick settled it. The Senator left the peephole with a stern look on his face . . . The Mayor was also greatly shocked and agreed . . . that the picture was not fitted for the entertainment of the average summer boarder, and the exhibitor was told he would have to send for some new views or shut up shop.'

So reported the *Newark Evening News.*

it 'the Black Maria'. As film production got under way in earnest, celebrity performers were enticed to appear before the Kinetograph camera. Eugene Sandow, the strong man, came to the studio on 6 March 1894 and a week later the famous Spanish dancer Carmencita danced in the Black Maria. By the beginning of April 1894 a batch of ten Kinetoscopes was sent to the premises of Holland Brothers at 1155 Broadway, New York City, where the first Kinetoscope parlour opened to the public on 14 April 1894. The ten machines all showed different subjects, including the film of

A Kinetoscope parlour

'The Butterfly Dance'

A picture sequence exposed by
C. Francis Jenkins in his Phantascope
camera, (from *The Photographic Times*,
6 July 1894)

enlarged Kinetograph camera taking 150-foot (45.7m) rolls (Cushing was knocked out in the sixth round). From around late July, the film was exhibited in enlarged Kinetoscopes in a parlour on Nassau Street, Manhattan. Each round was shown in a separate machine, requiring the insertion of six ten-cent pieces if the whole fight was to be seen. The film showing the knock-out wore out first!

Later in 1894, the Lathams became interested in the possibility of projecting the films. In April 1895, Dickson resigned from the Edison organisation, and came to work with Latham, who was already employing Dickson's old colleague, Eugene Lauste, of whom we shall hear much more. They produced a projection version of the Kineto-scope, using exactly the same principle of a moving film briefly illuminated on each frame. While not very efficient, the Panoptikon projector was shown privately to the New York press on 21 April 1895. Renamed the Eidoloscope, the projection show opened to the public at 153 Broadway in May 1895. *The Photographic Times* reported there was 'considerable room for improvement, and many draw-backs have yet to be overcome . . . but even in its present state the results are interesting and often startling'. The Latham Eidoloscope remained on show for a couple of years, but the inevitably dim picture and the low quality of its definition meant that it made little impression.

The first projection of films in America based upon the inter-mittent projection of the film strip was the joint work of C. Francis Jenkins and Thomas Armat. In later years much controversy developed between the two as to who did what, and when. Jenkins' first documented work resulted in a patent filed on 12 January 1894, for the Phantascope – a camera using a continuously moving film, in front of which rotated a disc bearing a ring of lenses, whose speed of rotation matched that of the downward movement of the film. Since the images produced on the film were thus stationary relative to the sensitive surface, they were recorded as quite sharp and clear. Jenkins used celluloid films obtained from Eastman and Blair; his subjects were 'dressed in solid colour, preferably black and white . . . before a dead white or black surface, respectively'. The camera measured only $5 \times 5 \times 8$in ($12.7 \times 12.7 \times 20.3$cm). On 6 July 1894 *The Photographic Times* reported on Jenkins' camera, and reproduced part of a film sequence of a man shot-putting. Jenkins proposed both to present the films in Kinetoscope-type viewers, and to project them, and even to couple his machine to the phonograph.

In the autumn of 1894 Jenkins met Thomas Armat, another worker stimulated by sight of the Kinetoscope. After working together for a time, they signed an agreement on 25 March 1895, in which Jenkins undertook to drop a patent application for a projector using a 'beater' intermittent movement. This device, which had been patented by the Frenchman Georges Demeny in 1893, used an eccentrically mounted roller which bore on the film once per turn, drawing fresh film through the exposing aperture. The agreement cleared the way for a joint patent for an intermittent movement based upon the Maltese Cross principle. This new Phantascope proved impractical and in the late summer of 1895 they turned to the beater movement again, incorporating it in three projectors demonstrated at the Cotton States Exposition at Atlanta, Georgia in October 1895. At this time, Armat's contribution seems to have been largely financial and entrepreneurial, with the mechanical ideas worked out by Jenkins. The new Phantascope moved the film intermittently but no shutter was fitted, the movement being so rapid

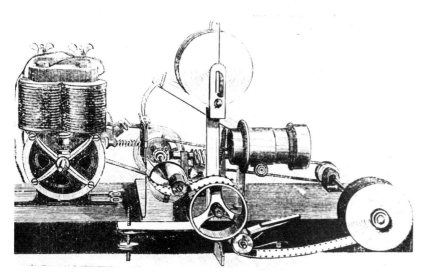

The improved Phantascope projector of Armat and Jenkins, shown at Atlanta, Georgia in October 1895. It used a 'beater' movement

from one frame to the next that it was not thought necessary.

After the Atlanta show, Jenkins and Armat separated; Armat redesigned the machine, adding a second, continuously rotating sprocket wheel above the gate to give a more even feeding of the film. The new design was filed in a patent application on 19 February 1896 under the new name Vitascope. Armat had already been in touch with Edison's agents for the Kinetoscope, Raff and Gammon, about a supply of films. Through them a demonstration was arranged of films projected by the Vitascope for Edison in February 1896. Edison dropped his so far unsuccessful attempts to develop a projector and reached an agreement with Armat for the supply of Vitascope projectors to be promoted under Edison's name. On 23 April 1896, Armat supervised the presentation of the first public show of the Vitascope, at Koster and Bial's Music Hall in New York. The 12 subjects, all Kinetoscope films, included a barber's shop, a boxing match, umbrella dance, a serpentine dance, a scene from *The Milk White Flag*, *A Rough Sea at Dover* and *The German Emperor Reviewing his Troops*. The last two subjects were supplied by an Englishman, R. W. Paul, and had been shot by Birt Acres, both of whom will be discussed in the next chapter. The show was a great success, and the Vitascope was shown subsequently in theatres all over America. Its reception in Europe was less enthusiastic. The *British Journal of Photography* reporting the news of the New York show in its issue of 1 May 1896 said,

> 'The "Vitascope" appears to partake of the nature of the screen kinetoscope of Lumière, Paul or Acres. The great genius of Menlo Park [Edison] seems to have developed quite a passion for following in the footsteps of other inventors, a sign, maybe, of greatness and genius as it is understood across the Atlantic.'

For by this time Europe was already familiar with the new medium of the projected motion picture.

5

Living pictures on the screen

In France, the first attempts at commercial exploitation of animated pictures were made by the ex-collaborator of Dr Marey, Georges Demeny. Demeny had been Marey's chief assistant at the Physiological Station from 1882 and he played a significant role in the development of the chronophotographic cameras. In 1891 he began a study of the movements of the face and lips during speech. He discovered, for example, that to record the phrase 'Je vous aime' required 18 images in one second. He made transparencies from the sequence exposures, and arranged them around a metal disc, with a slotted shutter disc rotating before it – yet another version of the Phenakistoscope. When operated, the rotating discs reproduced the facial movements of the speaker. He called his device the Phonoscope and patented it on 3 March 1892. With it he projected pictures at the first Paris International Exhibition of Photography in 1892, and the demonstrations excited a good deal of interest. Demeny saw a glorious future for his machine and formed a company to exploit it commercially.

Demeny could not reach agreement with Marey over the use of the chronophotographic cameras to make the negatives and resigned from the Physiological Station. He patented his own camera design in France on 10 October 1893. His first camera used a band of film moved on intermittently by an eccentrically mounted take-up spool, but this gave poor registration of the successive frames, although this was of little consequence when they were to be cut up and mounted on the Phonoscope discs. In his English patent of 19 December 1893, he included an important improvement. The unperforated film was wound from reel to reel through the gate of the camera, through which it was moved periodically by a beater movement – an eccentrically mounted roller, which in every turn bore on the film, pulling it through the gate. We have seen how later Jenkins and Armat adopted this principle in their apparatus and for the next 20 years it remained one of the principal intermittent movements for cine projectors. The new camera design was able to produce more accurately spaced exposures on the film but Demeny still proposed to view the results in the disc projector. It was only in 1896 that Demeny applied his beater principle to a commercially successful film camera and projector, as we shall see.

The two brothers Auguste and Louis Lumière were the first to achieve a satisfactory system for taking *and* projecting moving pictures made on a celluloid strip. Their father, Antoine, had founded in Lyons a business for the manufacture of photographic materials and the two talented brothers turned the struggling firm into a highly successful concern, the leading supplier of photographic plates in France – and even in Europe. In the summer of 1894 they were shown a piece of Edison Kinetoscope film, which had just reached Paris. Because of the high prices charged by Edison's agents, the local exhibitor was interested in the possibility of producing films in France. Auguste first applied himself to the problem of designing a camera but with little success, until Louis suggested a mechanism like that used in a sewing machine to advance the cloth step by step. A successful machine based on this principle was patented in France on 13 February 1895, in the name of both brothers. The machine was a combined camera and projector and the perforated film was moved intermittently by a claw mechanism – a pair of pins which, inserted into perforations in the film then moved down, carrying the film with them. At the bottom of the stroke, the pins were withdrawn and moved up past the now stationary film to be inserted in the next set of holes. The up and down movement was produced by a circular cam rotating in an almost oval hole in the pin frame and the in and out movement was executed by a pair of wedges on a rotating arm, one pushing the pins in, and the other withdrawing them. In an improved design, described in a supplement to the patent dated 30 March 1895, a triangular cam rotating in a roughly rectangular hole and a stepped groove on a rotating disc were used to provide the two movements. This new arrangement formed the basis not only of the Lumières' instrument but of a large number of later camera mechanisms, some still in use today. The Lumière claw mechanism was smooth and reliable in operation, and reasonably quiet.

The Lumières called the apparatus the Cinématographe, but the name was not original to them. The Frenchman Léon-Guillaume Bouly had used it for two designs for sequence cameras patented in France on 12 February 1892 and 27 December 1893. The second version, Bouly claimed, could be used for projection but there is no record of any successful achievement of this. At least two examples of his apparatus survive, suggesting a number may have been produced. As we have seen, LeRoy used the name 'The Marvellous Cinématographe' for his apparatus shown in America in the early months of 1895. (Curiously enough, the claimed early projection of Donisthorpe pictures by LeRoy is said to have been made with a machine using two cutaway rollers to give an intermittent grip – the principal feature of Bouly's apparatus. Could it be that LeRoy had acquired a Bouly Cinématographe in 1893 or 1894? At least one is now in America, in the collection of the International Museum of Photography at George Eastman House, Rochester, New York.) The first public presentation of the Cinématographe was given at the Société d'encouragement a l'industrie Nationale in Paris on 22 March 1895. The film showed workers leaving the Lumière factory. The Society's records reported that 'this animated picture, showing everyone in full movement coming out into the street, produced a gripping effect, and a repetition of the projection was demanded by all of the amazed audience. This scene, which lasted only a minute, comprised of no less than 800 successive pictures. There was everything, a dog coming and going, bicycles, horses, carriages at full trot, etc.'

The Cinématographe was shown again on 17 April 1895, at the Sorbonne, to the acclamation of an audience of distinguished academics. After this auspicious start, the Lumières began to produce new subjects. By the time of their next presentation, on 10 June 1895, at the Congrès des Sociétés Françaises de Photographie, at

The Lumière Cinématographe show

The first public presentation of the Lumière Cinématographe was given in Paris on Saturday 28 December 1895. The Lumières rented a basement room at the Grand Cafe, 14 Boulevard des Capuchines. The owner refused an offer of 20% of the receipts and charged a flat rate of 30 francs a day. The room was simply furnished, with about 100 seats, and the entrance fee was one franc. The 30-minute show included twelve film subjects. It was an immediate success and soon long queues formed on the boulevard. The first day's takings were 33 francs; after three weeks they were taking 2,000 francs a day.

The impact of these first projected films was considerable, even on such an experienced lanternist as G. R. Baker, a columnist on projection matters for the *British Journal of Photography*. On 6 March 1896 he wrote an account of his visit to the Marlborough Hall at the Polytechnic in Regent Street, London, to see Lumière's agent, Trewey, present the Cinématographe:

'Imagine yourself sitting in a nice-sized hall, and a small screen, five or six feet square, or rather oblong,

Auguste and Louis Lumière

with a dark border, hanging in front of you, well above your head . . . after a little introduction a picture appears on the screen, at the same time as the electric lights are turned out in the hall. What is it ? . . . It is a steamship pier, and there is a gangway in the mid distance. A little whirr is heard in the gallery above our heads, and the picture on the screen is all animation. Some one is walking up the gangway carrying a

The Lumière Cinématographe, 1895

camera, and he is followed in quick succession by a hundred or so of others. Some turn to the left at the end of the gangway, and others to the right; every third or fourth person raises his hat, as if he recognised some one that the audience cannot see; but when two or three run across the intervening space, one concludes they wish to be quickly out of the field of view of the camera, and that the salutations are for M. Lumière, who is photographing this wonderful scene. It was stated that the gentlemen coming from the boat were those attending the Photographic Convention at Lyons (I think). Certainly the marvellous detail, even to the puffs of smoke from the cigarette spoke volumes for the perfection of the apparatus employed.

The subjects are considerably varied, the first being a domestic scene, *The Family Tea Table*, in fact with father and mother and little baby [Auguste Lumière and family] seated at the table; the child is in turn fed, and the lady sips her tea or coffee, and every

The Lumières' first film, of workers leaving their factory

The Cinématographe set up for projection

Queen Victoria's Jubilee, 1897

movement is gone through with all the exactness of life. *The Railway Station* again forms another scene. The station is apparently empty when the train is seen approaching, and gradually gets nearer and larger until the engine passes where we are apparently standing, and the train stops, the guard comes along, passengers get out and in, and all is *real*. *The Forge* again gives an opportunity of showing that the apparatus can faithfully reproduce delicate objects, for, when the hot iron is plunged into the barrel of water, the steam rises in a most natural manner.

The scene outside a café of three gentlemen playing cards, and the waiter bringing in refreshments, drawing the corks, pouring out the contents of the bottle, and each of the three toasting the other during an interval in the game, was rather "mouth-watering", and the hilarity of the garçon at the results of the game seemed almost bound to produce laughter among the audience. The photographic reproduction of Monsieur Trewey's wonderful girations of a strip of long calico whipped round

and round must be seen to be realised, for it baffles description.

The same may be said of the *Street in Paris*, and finally the pièce de resistance, viz., *Sea Bathing in the Mediterranean*, for here we have the breaking waves on a shingly shore, a diving or jumping board, and the bathers in succession going down this board, jumping into the sea, battling with the breakers, climbing the rocks, and getting once more on the diving board, all so faithfully to life that one "longed to be there" ... My advice to all lanternists is this, take the first opportunity ... to see the "living photographs" I have described, and country readers should time themselves to be in Regent Street (Oxford Street end) five or ten minutes before any of the hours between two and ten p.m.'

LEFT *Professor Marey leading Photographic Congress delegates at Lyons, 1895*   RIGHT *'Feeding the Baby', 1895*

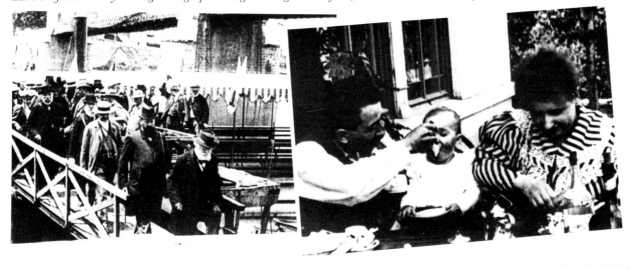

Lyons, they had seven more subjects: *The Place de la Bourse at Lyons*, *A lesson in vaulting*, *Baby and the fish bowl*, *Feeding a baby*, *The gardener watered*, *A blacksmith* and *Firemen extinguishing a fire*, as well as the original scene of the lunchtime exodus from the works. The films were received with great enthusiasm, and on 11 June the delegates were filmed by Antoine Lumière as they disembarked from a boat at Neuville-sur-Saône after an excursion. The film was shown to them the next day during the Congress, together with a film record of Messieurs Jannsen and Lagrange talking on the terrace of the Hotel du Lyon d'Or. More demonstrations followed, at the offices of the *Revue Générale des Sciences* on 11 July, at a meeting of the Association Belge de Photographie in Brussels on 10 November and again at the Sorbonne on 16 November. In the autumn of 1895 Antoine Lumière began to look for suitable premises in Paris to bring the Cinématographe to the public.

The first Lumière films had been made on rolls of celluloid imported from the American Celluloid company but they had difficulty in coating them with emulsion, so at the end of 1895 the Lumières entered into an agreement with Planchon, a maker of celluloid film in France, to combine their resources. The Lumière film, 35mm wide with one circular perforation to each side of the frame, was from this time manufactured at Lyons. At the same time, they ordered the production of 200 Cinématographes from an engineer, Jules Carpentier.

As they were produced, Lumière agents took them all over Europe and to America, where the first show was given at Koster and Bial's Music Hall on 34th Street, New York, and subsequently at theatres in many other cities. The first presentation in London was given by the Lumières' friend, the conjurer and shadow-graph artist Felicien Trewey, who brought the Cinématographe to the Marlborough Hall, in Regent Street. The first show was given in the afternoon of Thursday 20 February 1896. Eight films were shown, and they received a favourable press. Each show of the regular programme was made up of a selection from about 25 films. Within a few days, the management of the Empire Theatre of Varieties in Leicester Square began negotiations for the Cinématographe show, and it was included in their programme from 9 March 1896. A few days after, the shows at the Marlborough Hall ceased, and the Cinématographe ran continuously in Leicester Square for over a year with great success. The *Amateur Photographer* said,

> 'To see the carriages rolling up to the Empire matinées one would suppose that Society had only just discovered Leicester Square. The "boom" is tremendous, and apparently as catching as measles, for, besides the afternoon shows, Society is flocking so unconcernedly to see the new thing that there is never a stall to be secured in the evening.'

However, the Cinématographe show was not the first to be given in England, where since the end of 1894 developments parallel to those in France had taken place. Two men were involved, the London instrument maker Robert W. Paul and the photographer Birt Acres. After working well for a time, the partnership split up, and a rancorous relationship developed, each man claiming that the other had made only minor contributions. Both have presented their own views of what happened during the critical year – 1895. In the absence of documented evidence, one must deduce from their

Birt Acres (1854-1918), who gave the first successful presentation of projected films in England, in January 1896

ABOVE RIGHT Drawing of the mechanism of the Paul-Acres camera, 1895. Mechanically, it was essentially the same as the earlier film camera of Marey

BELOW Birt Acres (top left) films the 1895 Derby with the Paul-Acres camera

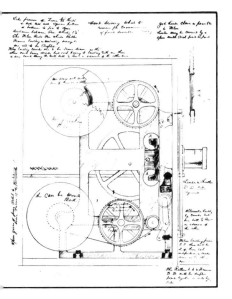

ABOVE A frame from the first film exposed by Birt Acres, outside his home, Clovelly Cottage, in March 1895

subsequent records who contributed what to the early development. Paul was an instrument maker and electrical engineer with a business in Hatton Garden, London. After the opening of the first Kinetoscope parlour in Oxford Street, in the autumn of 1894, Paul was approached by two Greek entrepreneurs, Georgiades and Trajedes, who had acquired six Kinetoscopes and installed them in a shop in Old Broad Street. Needing more machines, they asked Paul to make them. Paul soon established that the Kinetoscope had not been patented in England and there was no legal barrier to making copies of it. By the end of the year he had made six but found that Edison's agents supplied films only to purchasers of the original machine. At about this time he was brought into contact with Birt Acres, a photographer, who was working for a photographic manufacturing company.

Some years later, Paul stated that Acres visited him on 4 February 1895 and showed him some ideas as to how a camera might be made. Paul said that he rejected or modified most of them but developed one idea into a working model by 5 or 6 February. By 16 March the camera was finished and Acres found and fitted a lens for it. On the other hand, Acres claimed that Paul had no idea how to make a suitable mechanism and had to be shown by working drawings and constant supervision. Since Paul was a skilled engineer and Acres was an amateur, this seems a trifle unlikely. Whatever the truth of the matter, the camera was not an original design. The Paul-Acres camera was virtually identical in principle to Marey's chronophotographic film camera of 1890, details of which had been widely published. The film was periodically clamped in the gate during the exposure, while the film was taken up against the action of a sprung roller. As the clamp was released, the roller sprang back to its former position, drawing the film through the gate. The only difference between the cameras of Paul-Acres and Marey was in the use of perforated film and this, we have seen, was the invention of Edison and Dickson. The camera worked well enough to make test films and on 29 March 1895 Paul wrote to Edison, enclosing a sample of the first film, shot by Acres outside his home, Clovelly Cottage in Barnet, Hertfordshire, and offering to supply film subjects for the Kinetoscope.

On the same day, Paul and Acres made a ten-year agreement, with Acres to be responsible for producing films for the Paul-made Kinetoscopes. On the 30 March, Acres filmed the Oxford and Cambridge boat race, and on 29 May he recorded the Derby at Epsom. On 27 May 1895 he patented the Kinetic camera, which embodied the principles incorporated in the Paul-Acres machine. Perhaps because of this unilateral action, relations between the two became strained. When Acres returned from Germany, where he had filmed the opening of the Kiel Canal in June, Paul and he split up. Acres withdrew from the agreement on 12 July, having paid for the camera and work related to its development. Some 13 subjects were shot by Acres during his short association with Paul; two of them, as we have seen, were among the films presented at the first Vitascope show in America, in April 1896.

After July 1895 the two men went their own ways. Paul does not appear to have made more films during 1895, although he had designed a new camera with a more efficient mechanism driven by a Maltese Cross intermittent. Acres turned his attention to the construction of a projector, obviously necessary to him now that the outlet for his films, the Paul Kinetoscopes, was denied him. The

Paul's Theatrograph projector, 1896

The mechanism of Paul's improved cine camera, late 1896

claim that he showed a film demonstration to the Royal Photographic Society is undocumented; his first recorded presentation of projected films was to that Society on 14 January 1896. With his Kinetic Lantern, Acres projected a number of films he had made between March and June of the previous year. Although the films were shot at 40 pictures per second, to suit the Kinetoscope, he projected them at about 15 pictures per second. Of the films shown, it was *Rough Seas at Dover* which brought the most acclaim, as it was to do in the later New York showing. The *Amateur Photographer* said,

> 'simply wonderful in its realistic effect . . . Very rarely indeed has such enthusiastic applause as greeted Mr Acres . . . been heard at the Royal.'

The *Photographic News*, reporting another showing at the Photographic Club, called it 'Mr Acres' masterpiece'. These were the very first successful shows of projected motion pictures to take place in England. At the end of the month Acres went into business with his own company, The Northern Photographic Company. 'Kinetoscopy is to occupy his attention', said a report. The new company offered to supply sensitive film, to develop and print exposed films, and to supply finished film productions.

The first public showing of the Kinetic Lantern, renamed the Kineopticon, was given at 2 Piccadilly Mansions, Piccadilly Circus on 21 March 1896, almost a month after the first Lumière show in London. Most of the programme consisted of the 1895 films, but some new subjects were shown including the arrest of a pickpocket and a visit to the Zoo. The admission charge was sixpence and the shows ran from 2pm to 6pm and 7.30pm to 10pm. After a short time, a fire destroyed the show and Acres gave up this form of exploitation in favour of lecture and demonstration tours around the country. The high spot of his year was a Royal Command Performance on 21 July 1896 at Marlborough House, before the Royal Family. During 1896, Acres made many more film subjects for the Kineopticon, but apart from his own demonstrations and those of a few other operators, little commercial use was made of it.

As with Acres, so Paul seems to have done little with the animated picture business in the second half of 1895. By the early weeks of 1896 he was working on a projector design using a seven-armed Maltese Cross mechanism driving a sprocket wheel intermittently, described in the *English Mechanic* on 21 February 1896. It had been shown at the Finsbury Technical College the evening before and on 28 February was presented at the Royal Institution before an audience of 320 people. The films shown were mostly Edison Kinetoscope originals, but at least three of the films shot by Acres in 1895 were included. The first model of the projector gave trouble with picture unsteadiness, and on 2 March 1896 Paul patented a new design in which a second intermittent sprocket wheel was placed above the gate, both turned by a double seven-armed Maltese Cross mechanism. Soon, he improved the projector further by adding continuously moving sprockets above and below the intermittent ones. He produced and sold over 100 of these improved models, which sold at £80 each. A similar mechanism was incorporated in a new camera, which he seems to have brought into operation in the autumn of 1896. It was a well-designed, efficient machine.

After the first demonstrations in February, Paul was engaged to present his Theatrograph regularly at a number of theatres in London. They included the Egyptian Hall (from 19 March), Olympia (from 21 March), and the Alhambra Theatre of Varieties, Leicester Square (from 25 March). The last hall was just across the square from the Empire, where the Lumière Cinématographe was doing great business. For the shows at the Alhambra only, the apparatus was renamed the Animatograph.

Paul had begun to film new subjects for the Theatrograph early in 1896. A comic piece, *The Soldier's Courtship*, was shot on the roof of the Alhambra Theatre in April. The big success of the year was Paul's film of the Derby, won by the Prince of Wales' horse 'Persimmon'. Paul developed and printed the negative overnight and had it on the screen the next day before huge audiences at the Alhambra and Canterbury Theatres. Paul commissioned a major film-making programme in the summer of 1896 and a series of films made in Spain by Paul's cameraman Henry W. Short included a very popular subject *A Sea Cave near Lisbon*. Paul's film business was very profitable. In the first year of operation, from March 1896 to March 1897 'in spite of initial expenses and difficulties of manufacture, which have now been overcome, it has yielded a net profit of 12,838£ 15s. 4d. on a capital of about 1,000£, or 1,200£ per cent'.

Paul played a major part in the founding of the British film industry through his readiness to supply projectors, films and all other necessary apparatus, at a time when many other inventors jealously guarded their apparatus for sole exploitation. Among early purchasers of Paul Theatrograph projectors was David Devant of the Egyptian Hall 'Cave of Illusion and Mystery'. Carl Herz the showman took his Theatrograph projector with him to South Africa, and later to Australia, giving the first ship-board film shows on the way. The photographers W. & D. Downey bought a machine from Paul and gave a performance before Queen Victoria and other members of the Royal Family at Windsor Castle on 23 November 1896. Mr George Belmont, of Sadler's Wells Theatre, famous for his alliterative advertisements, announced his presentations of 'Paul's Perfect Palpitating Promethean Photos' in December 1896. Paul went on to become a leading producer of films, specialising in trick effects, the use of many of which he pioneered. His manufacture and widespread sale of reliable equipment and his film-making earned him the deserved title of 'Father of the British Film Industry'.

What then of the rival claims of Acres and Paul? There seems little doubt that the first move came from Paul, seeking someone to make films for his version of the Kinetoscope. The first working camera was based on an idea of Acres, practically developed by Paul. Acres deserves the honour of being the first Englishman to take, and later to project, successful motion pictures. Acres was no showman and was perhaps temperamentally disinclined to exploit commercially his Kinetic Lantern. Paul, a talented and skilled engineer made and sold reliable projection apparatus to the newly developing film trade. So, the honours are even, perhaps.

The other European country where early motion picture development took place was Germany, where from 1879 a showman, Carl Skladanowsky, presented dissolving view lantern shows, helped by his sons Emil and Max. It is claimed that Max built and used a sequence camera in 1892 using a continuously running film exposed through a very narrow slot in a rotating shutter. The spacing of the pictures was very uneven, the film being that produced for the No. 2 Kodak camera by Eastman. The film was $3\frac{1}{2}$in (8.9cm) wide, and

Poster advertising 'Living Photos' by Paul, for an Animatograph show

The Soldier's Courtship, a popular film, shot by Paul on the roof of the Alhambra Theatre, London in April 1896

Skladanowsky cut it in half to make two narrower strips.. Once exposed, the negative films were cut up and reassembled to remove the unequal spacings and alternate frames were separated and joined up to make two strips of eight frames each. These were printed on 24×30cm sheets of sensitized celluloid, four eight-frame strips to a sheet. The sheets of positives were cut up into four strips and joined end to end using three small eyelets, while the edges were perforated and fitted with larger eyelets. The strips were made up into loops; in one example, ten strips of pictures were joined up. The Bioscop projector was patented in November 1895; it took two bands of positives with alternating frames, moved in turn by a worm-drive 'drunken screw' intermittent mechanism driving a sprocket wheel engaging with the eyelets in the film edge. A rotating 'dissolving view' shutter allowed a frame from each film to be shown in turn, with a gradual transition between them and no dark interval. On the day the patent was filed, Max and Emil gave their first public show at the Berlin Wintergarten, presenting a fifteen-minute programme of eight films, including a boxing kangaroo, a juggler, peasant and Russian dances and a wrestling match between Sandow and Greiner. They toured Europe in 1896 using a new Bioscop projector and a programme of films made with a much improved camera, with an intermittent mechanism.

By the end of 1896 the moving picture had become an established form of entertainment. Eager showmen carried their apparatus all over the world in search of new audiences and new subjects for the camera. New designs appeared almost weekly; in England alone 42 new patents for moving picture equipment were applied for in 1896, and even more the following year. On 4 December, the *British Journal of Photography* burst into verse:

'Such a bustle and a hurry
O'er the "living picture" craze,
Rivals rushing full of worry
In these advertising days.
Each the first and each the only
Each the others wildly chaff
All of them proclaiming boldly
Their's the first A-Kind-O-Graph.
But it is a wonder really
How the constant flood of life
O'er the screen keeps moving freely
Full of action – stir and strife.
There the waves are wildly breaking
There the swimmer stems the tide.
The cyclist his record making,
With countless varied scenes beside.
'Tis far from perfect in its movements,
'Tis very hard upon the eyes;
The jolty wobble no improvements,
Smooth running films a surprise.
Still successful beyond reason,
Spite of all its erring ways,
Holding first place in the season
Is the "Living Picture" craze.'

With the proliferation of new designs came an equal proliferation of jawbreaking names. The Vitamotograph, the Chronophotographoscope, the Kinesetograph and many others soon disappeared into oblivion; the name Cinématographe, coined by Bouly and popularised by the Lumières, remained to serve as the name for the new medium.

There have been an enormous number of developments in movie cameras and projectors in the eighty years since cinematography was born but the fundamental principles have remained the same. Cinematography is based upon the intermittent movement of a strip of perforated transparent film, exposed while stationary, and moved on between exposures while covered by a shutter. All but a very few specialised devices have followed this pattern ever since the beginning. However, before we consider the introduction of sound, colour and so on, we can look at a few of the more interesting and influential developments in the process of cinematography.

While a substantial number of even the earliest workers employed the 35mm film width created by Dickson for the Kinetoscope, some went for wider films. In 1896, Léon Gaumont's company, Le Comptoir General de Photographie, persuaded Georges Demeny to redesign his camera based on the 1893 patent, so that it could use perforated film and be adaptable for projection. The result was the Demeny-Gaumont Chronophotographe camera, marketed in the autumn of 1896. It used perforated film 60mm wide, transported by the beater movement Demeny had invented. The same mechanism could be used for both taking and projecting films. The *British Journal of Photography* reported on a show given to the Photographic Club in London on 9 December 1896. Of the films, it said, 'They struck us as being the best, photographically and mechanically, that we have seen'. The films were printed on Eastman celluloid film and since the area of each frame was four times that of the standard 35mm

60mm wide film for the Demeny-Gaumont Chronophotographe, 1896

The Demeny-Gaumont Chronophotographe, 1896. An outfit for the projection of 60mm wide film. The mechanism also doubled as a camera

77

picture the pictures on the screen were much more detailed. The programme included a film shot on the roof of the Chatelet Theatre in Paris in November 1896, designed to be part of a spectacular show, *La Biche au Bois*, in which it was presented with the simultaneous projection of still pictures and combined with live action – the first multi-media theatrical performance.

Another important early wide-film process was the American Biograph. On 21 November 1894 Herman Casler filed a patent for the Mutoscope, an animated picture device in which a series of sequential images printed on thin cards were attached radially to a cylinder. As the cylinder rotated, the cards came up against a stop which held each one momentarily stationary, before it flipped over to reveal the next. The idea of a flip or flicker book was not new. The Linnet Kineograph, patented in March 1868, used the same idea in the form of a book of cards flipped over by the thumb. Variations of this idea appeared regularly in the years that followed.

In December 1894 Casler began the design of a camera to produce the picture sequences for his Mutoscope viewer. He was almost certainly guided in this by W. K. L. Dickson, at that time still working for Edison. It was probably for that reason that the camera patent filed on 26 February 1896 was in the name of Casler alone. A working camera was built and made to make a test film in June 1895, and the same mechanism, modified, was used to show a film in a workshop in Canastota, New York in November. The original purpose of the camera, to produce the flip-book reels, was temporarily put aside in favour of a projection arrangement. On 27 December 1895 the American Mutoscope Company was formed, with Casler, Dickson, Henry N. Marvin and Elias Koopman as sole stockholders. Dickson designed a studio built on the roof of 841 Broadway, New York. Like Edison's Black Maria, the studio was mounted on a turntable to catch the best light and the camera was in a cabin running on rails for easy movement to and from the stage. Film production of a wide variety of subjects began in June 1896. On the

The studio designed by W. K. L. Dickson for the production of Biograph films, in 1896. Like the 'Black Maria' before it, it was mounted on a turntable to keep the best light on the set

The electrically driven Biograph camera filming an express train

same day as the camera patent was filed, a projector design was also entered and the Biograph projector gave its first show in a week's run at the Alvin Theatre in Pittsburg, starting on the 14 September 1896. After runs in several other theatres, the Biograph made its main debut at Hammerstein's Olympia theatre in New York on 12 October 1896. After a two week run it moved to Koster and Bial's theatre on 26 October, and thence it went to Keith's theatre on Union Square on 18 January 1897, where it ran almost without a break until 15 July 1905.

The Biograph camera and projector used similar intermittent mechanisms. The camera film, about $2\frac{3}{4}$in (68mm) wide was transported intermittently by a pair of 'mutilated' rollers, with part of their circumference cut away, so that once per turn they ceased to grip the film. The principle had been used by Bouly in his Cinématographe camera some years before. In the camera a pair of registering perforations was punched between the successive frames, to act as a registration device, compensating for a tendency to uneven spacing. The projection film was the same width, but unperforated. The film was run at about 40 frames per second, and was driven by a large, $2\frac{1}{2}$ horse-power electric motor at first, although later models were hand-turned. The very large picture size, 2.7×2.1in (68×54mm) was over $7\frac{1}{2}$ times the area of the picture on the Edison film, and produced images of exceptional photographic quality. The unperforated projection film did give trouble, however, with framing and registration of the pictures on the screen. The English engineer and inventor, Arthur Newman, noted, 'Sometimes the screen was showing only half a picture. The adjustment of the regulating screw required extreme ability on the part of the operator'. Nonetheless, the Biograph enjoyed considerable popularity throughout the world. It opened at the Palace Theatre in London in April 1897, and the next month Dickson left the United States to run the European operation, travelling widely to make Biograph subjects, including a film of Pope Leo XII in 1898, and recording scenes during the Boer War in South Africa in 1899. Well over a thousand titles were produced for the Biograph before its slow decline in popularity in the early 1900s.

The flip-book application, the original motive behind the Biograph camera, was not launched until early in 1897. The Mutoscope was reported in the 7 February issue of the *New York Herald*, and was

A Biograph film of Pope Leo XII, photographed by W. K. L. Dickson in the Vatican in 1898

A fairground bioscope show, c. 1900. Travelling showmen in England were quick to take up the new medium, and brought it to most communities in the country in the first few years of the century

Prestwich's cinecamera, 1898, with external, detachable 400-foot (118-metre) film magazines

described in detail in the *Scientific American* for 17 April. The subjects on the early Mutoscope reels were shot for the Biograph and were made by enlarging the Biograph negatives onto cards about 6 × 4in (152 × 102mm). The Mutoscope coin-in-the-slot viewers became a regular feature of amusement parlours and arcades, fairgrounds and seaside piers, surviving in some places almost to the present day. Many were still in use in England until decimalisation of the coinage in 1971 (see panel right). The flip-book principle was used in several other early moving picture devices. In 1896 Henry W. Short, Robert Paul's cameraman, filed a provisional patent for a flip-book device he called the Filoscope. The Anglo-French Filoscope Syndicate Ltd was formed in September 1897 to exploit the invention, which used a lever device to facilitate the flipping over of the pages which were printed with photomechanical reproductions of film frames, mostly from productions by Short's employer. The Lumière Kinora viewer, introduced in 1897, worked in much the same way as the Mutoscope, with a vertically placed reel of pictures. Both commercial coin-feed and small domestic versions were produced but the Kinora did not come into wide use until some years later, in a form for amateur use, as we shall see in chapter nine. An idea mooted by Casler in a British patent of 1897 suggested mounting the picture cards on a flexible belt wound on rollers, the more supple mounting giving a better flip-over effect. The principle was embodied in the Theoscope viewer, on sale in 1901.

The basic design of early movie cameras was essentially similar. They usually had a capacity of only about 50 feet (about 15 metres) of film and this small quantity was usually loaded directly into the camera in a darkroom, or could be pre-loaded into a small light-tight wooden box which could be placed in the camera in daylight. One of the first cameras to be fitted with detachable external film

'What the Butler Saw'

Casler's Mutoscope, using a reel of prints working on the flip-book principle, was introduced early in 1897. The coin-operated viewers were a feature of amusement arcades and the like almost until the present day. The early subjects were edifying or entertaining, but soon less wholesome topics were available. The English moralist and Member of Parliament, Samuel Smith, wrote to *The Times* in April 1899

H. W. Short's Filoscope printed from R. W. Paul's film subjects

about a report he had received of a visit to an amusement arcade in Southport, Lancashire, to have, as the correspondent put it, 'three or four pennyworths'. He was 'literally astounded that the Southport authorities permitted such viciously suggestive pictures to be publicly exhibited . . . as the pictures are all moving, it makes them all the more dangerous in their influence. Whilst we were in

the exhibition, three or four girls were going round.' Mr Smith stated, 'It is hardly possible to exaggerate the corruption of the young that comes from exhibiting, under a strong light, nude female figures represented as living and moving, going in and out of baths, sitting as artist's models, &c. Similar exhibitions took place at Rhyl in the men's lavatory, but . . . they have been stopped.' Things were no better in 1900, when one of the good Mr Smith's informants reported on Mutoscopic views at the Earl's Court Exhibition. 'One machine . . . contained a series of pictures of girls in short frocks engaged in kicking at a hat which was held above their heads, there being at each attempt a liberal display of underclothing.' Mr Smith observed 'Scoundrels take an empty shop . . . and fit up their machines with such pictures putting suggestive headings in the windows, and a crowd of children are enticed within, and gradually brutalised by the disgusting sights they witness. In a primitive state of society these men would be lynched, but here they are allowed to do as they like.' Alas for Mr Smith's efforts, the Mutoscope continued to be used to display doubtful subjects.

Mutoscope 'flip-book' viewer, 1897

Inspector Sewell, of D Division of the Metropolitan Police, giving evidence in a case of displaying obscene materials in April 1907, reported on machines which 'when a penny was placed in the slot, exposed to view objectionable pictures. On one of the machines was written "What Tommy Saw through the Keyhole", on another "Spooning in the Park", a third bore the legend "Matilda's Courtship", and a fourth had written on it "What the Butler Saw".' The latter title was the name by which the Mutoscope machines have become better known over the years.

Seaside-pier Mutoscopes, 1912, and one of the exciting subjects!

magazines was that designed by J. A. Prestwich in 1898. The wooden film magazines could take up to 400 feet (120 metres), and when the film was exposed, one magazine could be quickly changed for another. Since a number of scenes could be exposed on a longer length of film, a footage indicator was necessary, and the Prestwich camera was one of the first to be so equipped. The 400-foot magazine soon became established as a standard size. The English camera manufacturers of the early years of this century, including Darling, Williamson, Prestwich, the Warwick Trading Company, Charles Urban and Moy, favoured a pattern in which the magazines were carried inside the camera, one above the other. This English pattern camera remained in widespread use until the late 1920s. An alternative arrangement placed the magazines side by side inside the camera, giving the camera a long rather than tall shape.

The best known and most widely used camera of this type was the Debrie Parvo, patented by Joseph Debrie on 19 September 1908 and built by his son André. The film was fed from the magazine through the gate to a take-up magazine through two skewed loops. The Parvo remained in use for the next 40 or more years, remaining basically the same, although undergoing minor changes of design including the change from a wooden to a metal body in 1922 and the development of a model T version for sound films in 1930. The English Newman and Sinclair Reflex cinecamera of 1911 also used side by side magazines. The wooden body of the early model was replaced later by a distinctive aluminium case with a lozenge pattern milled on its surface. The twin magazines were replaced by a single magazine with a built-in sprocket wheel. Many of these highly efficient cameras are still in use. The Akeley camera, designed in 1918, also had its film chamber carried inside the camera, which had a very distinctive drum shaped body. It was designed by Carl Louis Gregory Akeley, explorer, sculptor, taxidermist and curator of the American Museum of Natural History. The film was carried in a single combined magazine; a cylindrical shutter ran around the inside of the cylindrical body. The telescopic finder had a most

TOP A typical English upright-pattern professional cinecamera, made to a design by Moy and Bastie, 1909

ABOVE Inside the Moy and Bastie camera the two 400-foot (118-metre) film magazines were placed one above the other

Carl Akeley's unusual cinecamera, designed in 1918, was popular with newsreel cameramen. Robert Flaherty shot *Nanook of the North* (below right) mostly with an Akeley

BELOW André Debrie built the Parvo camera from a design patented by his father Joseph in 1908. It remained one of the most popular professional cinecameras for the next forty years.

BELOW LEFT The film magazines were placed side by side in the Debrie Parvo camera, the film being fed to the gate through skewed loops

ingenious optical system which kept its eyepiece in the usual level position regardless of the tilt of the camera, a great boon for a cameraman following rapid action, the special aim of the design. A reviewer said, 'The Akeley is unique in its field, and for that reason it has met with approval of certain cinematographers who specialise in the recording of sports, wild life, military events, races and so on'. Robert Flaherty shot most of his famous documentary film *Nanook of the North* (1922) with the Akeley.

The alternative was to fit the magazines externally; the early Prestwich had a magazine on top and one behind. The Pathé Professional studio camera, introduced in 1905, had its two square magazines in line on the top of the camera. This had the advantage that it left the back of the camera clear for indicators and controls and enabled the photographer to get close to his viewfinder. Unlike most other cameras of its day, the Pathé had its handle on the back and not on the side. This model was extremely popular with film makers the world over and was the choice of D. W. Griffiths' cameraman, Billy Bitzer. It was used to film many of the Chaplin and Sennett comedies. An American version of the Pathé, made with a metal instead of a wooden body, was the Wilart, introduced in 1919.

The Bell & Howell Studio camera appeared in 1912 and was

The Pathé Professional studio camera, introduced in 1905, was popular for many years with European and American cameramen. Billy Bitzer used it to film *Birth of a Nation* for D. W. Griffiths

The Bell & Howell Studio camera, launched in 1912, remained one of the leading professional cinecameras almost to the present day

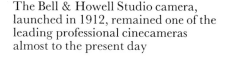

described as representing 'the last word in motion picture cameras being provided with almost no end of attachments that expedite filming and make possible the numerous unusual effects that characterise America's leading film producers'. The camera was of all metal construction and carried a one-piece double magazine in line on the top of the camera, the figure of eight shape giving the characteristic 'Mickey Mouse's ears' look to the camera. It was fitted with a rotating turret which allowed up to four lenses to be fitted. The Bell & Howell cameras have remained in almost constant use ever since their introduction, with only minor changes of design.

Although some of the very earliest cameras, the Kinetograph and Biograph for example, were driven by electric motors, the vast majority of cameras made up to the general adoption of sound in the late 1920s were turned by hand. Most cameras were provided with a handle which exposed eight frames per turn, so that it was operated at two turns per second for the 'normal' running speed of 16 frames per second. This speed was an average speed only; there was no standard speed as such. Cameramen would 'undercrank' to speed action up on the screen and 'overcrank' to slow it down. After the novelty of the moving picture wore off, audiences became conscious of the flicker on the screen when the projectors ran at 16 frames per second, especially when the projector was fitted with the widely used Maltese Cross type of intermittent. Exhibitors began to increase the projection speed to reduce the effect and by 1921 it was reported that nearly all studio production in Hollywood was being shot at around 20 frames per second. By 1923, speeds of up to 23 frames per second were not at all unusual. This increase in taking speeds was coincident with the increasing adoption of electric drives for cinecameras. In 1927 it was proposed that all film should be taken at 16 frames per second and projected at about 21, but within a few years the general adoption of sound led to 24 pictures per second being adopted as the professional standard.

One of the first cameras to have an integral electric drive was the English Moy Gyro camera of 1912. A small electric motor inside the casing drove the film and a detachable, flat electric motor could be

Early film studios

The limited sensitivity of the films used in early cine cameras required very strong lighting. Most early films were shot out of doors with open sets, especially in America. Film studios were constructed on the pattern of still photographic studios, albeit on a larger scale. Glass roofs and walls admitted as much daylight as possible. Artificial light could be used to supplement daylight. The first studio, Edison's 'Black Maria', had electric arc lighting;

available in the 1920s, high intensity incandescent lamps largely replaced the earlier light sources, although arc lamps were still used when very bright lighting was needed, especially for colour films.

In early film studios, it was not unusual for several productions to be shot side by side on adjacent sets in the same studio. Since there was no sound recording this presented no problems, other than, perhaps, confusion between the

Mary Pickford, star of silent films

different directors' instructions. At first, the studio cameras were fixed on their tripods and the actors had to perform within the field of view of the lens. In scenes with lively action, they were not always successful! Soon, panning and tilting of the camera allowed action to be followed. Cameramen had to acquire the special skill of turning the camera crank at constant speed with one hand while turning the panning handle at another speed with the other. The technique of mounting the studio cameras on a wheeled dolly so that it could be moved about while filming did not come into general use until after the First World War, although it had been used from time to time in earlier productions.

Day-lit professional silent film studio

A studio stage c. 1916

this very high intensity light source remained in use into modern times. Another very efficient form of lighting used in early film studios was the mercury vapour lamp. This had a very high output of the blue and ultraviolet illumination to which the early film stock was especially sensitive. The 'cold' light from such lamps distorted the total values of certain colours (as can be seen when such lamps are used for street lighting) and strange compensating make-up was needed. When panchromatic films, equally sensitive to all colours, became generally

The Cinex Electro-Automatique camera, 1926, was electrically driven. Its small size made it very suitable for newsreel filming in difficult conditions

RIGHT The Moy Gyro camera of 1912 was one of the first cinecameras to have an integral electric motor.

The Debrie Sept camera, 1922, took small chargers of film sufficient for 17 seconds of filming, driven by a clockwork motor. It was used for pirating newsreel material in the 1920s

fitted on the front of the camera to act as a gyroscopic stabiliser when the camera was held in the hand. It was designed primarily for newsreel work but the need to carry very heavy wet-cell batteries around with the camera restricted its use. Later, improvements in light-weight electric motor and battery design led to their adoption for movie cameras. The Newman and Sinclair Kine Camera model 3, of 1922, had a detachable electric motor, driven from a battery box, fitted to the front. It was used on the Royal Geographical Society's expedition to Everest in 1922. A. Bourdereau's Cinex Electro-Automatique camera of 1926 was driven from an external 12-volt motor on a baseboard fitted with a pair of handgrips and a trigger switch. This, and its light weight and small size, made it a useful camera for newsreel work under difficult conditions, although it had only a 200-foot (60-metre) capacity. The larger studio cameras, such as the Bell & Howell and the Mitchell, introduced in 1920, could be (and usually were) driven by electric motors. After the coming of sound at the end of the 1920s, constant speed drive, impossible by hand turning, became obligatory and virtually all professional cameras were motor driven.

An alternative to electric drive was the clockwork motor. The problem here was that the power needed to drive a 35mm film camera for a useful time was beyond the capacity of a readily portable spring motor at first. A few small cameras of the 1920s did use clockwork drive. The Debrie Sept camera, a seven-function machine which combined still and movie camera, printer, enlarger and projector, took small chargers holding only 17 feet (5 metres) of 35mm film, enough for only 17 seconds' filming. It was used for some professional applications where its very small size was an advantage.

The chase sequence in Douglas Fairbanks' film *Robin Hood* was shot with a Sept and it was used often by newsreel photographers during the 1920s to 'pirate' events exclusive to another company. The Sept could be carried past rival operators, concealed in an overcoat pocket. Among the first full-scale professional cameras to use clockwork drive were the Bell and Howell Eyemo camera of 1923 and the Newman and Sinclair Autokine camera of 1927. For the latter, Arthur Newman designed a very reliable double spring motor which would run a full 200 feet (60 metres) on one wind. It was used by Robert Flaherty to film *Man of Aran* in 1933.

One of the strangest but yet widely used cameras to be self-powered was designed by the Polish inventor Kasimir Proszynski. In 1911 he established a company, Aeroscope Ltd, to promote a cinecamera driven by compressed air. The Aeroscope camera contained a small air motor in the form of a miniature beam engine, driven by compressed air from a bank of cylinders held within the body of the camera and charged with a foot or hand pump. One full charge would run several magazines and a heavy flywheel helped to stabilise the camera gyroscopically when it was hand-held. The first cameras were ready by the end of May, 1911; one of their earliest uses was to film the Coronation procession of King George V on 22 June. The natural history photographer Cherry Kearton used and promoted the camera, which because of its very silent operation and great portability was very suitable for wild life photography. The camera was made by the Warwick Trading Company for some years. A new model was marketed in 1921 by Eracam Ltd, in which the cylinders were recharged on the 'Sparklet' principle from precharged containers.

The earliest film stock, as we have seen, was made from the celluloid film designed for still cameras. Much of the early material was supplied by Eastman and by Blair, who were the first producers of celluloid roll film. The Eastman film, on a thinner base, was preferred by many for making the negatives and the thicker Blair film was more suitable for the positive prints which had to withstand many projections. By April 1896 the demand for film had grown to

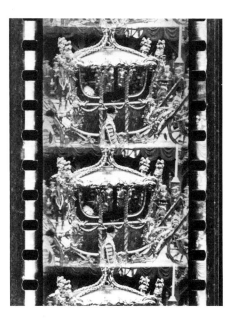

Film of the Coronation Procession of King George V, taken with an Aeroscope camera on 22 June 1911

Kasimir Proszynski's Aeroscope camera introduced in 1911, was driven by compressed air from cylinders charged by a hand- or foot-pump

A rotary film perforator sold by
Wrench of London in the first years of
this century

such a level that the Eastman company introduced special films made
for both negative and positive work. Generally, the film manufacturers supplied the film in 35mm widths, unperforated, since there
were so many variations in apparatus that it was desirable for the
user to perforate the film to suit his particular requirements. The
first film perforators were rotary, the film being wound between two
drums, one with protruding studs, the other with matching recesses.
Unless the drums were of large diameter and very precisely made,
this method gave rather uneven perforation. Soon, reciprocating
perforators were introduced in which accurate punches made six or
eight holes at a time, each set being registered by the holes made on
the previous stroke. After the initial proliferation of film shapes and
sizes, the original Edison gauge of 35mm film, with four rectangular
perforations on each side of the frame, became the most widely used
and was finally adopted by an international conference of film
makers in Paris in February 1909 as the professional standard.

The film base was celluloid – cellulose nitrate – which is a highly
inflammable material, liable to ignite and burn fiercely if subjected to
only moderate heat. If the film stopped for only a moment in the
projector, the heat from the lamp would ignite it immediately. Film
fires were quite common in the early years and a major tragedy in
1897 almost killed the infant film business before it had really
started. At a charity bazaar in Paris, on 14 May, a cinematograph
show was in progress, with a projector lit by an ether saturator. The
operator paused to refill the still warm saturator with ether and
through a misunderstanding an assistant brought a naked light close
to the machine. The ether ignited and sent a huge jet of flame from
the projector which set fire not only to the film but to the adjacent
stand as well. Within ten minutes the whole bazaar was burnt out.
The single exit was blocked and more than 120 people died. Although
this tragedy was not directly attributable to the inflammable film, it
led to stringent safety regulations being imposed on cinematograph
shows in many countries.

Clearly, a film which would not burn so readily was required. In
the 1900s several companies produced slow-burning films. Cellit

film, invented by Eichengrünn in 1908, was on the market for a few years; Lumière made safety film in 1908 and Eastman in 1909. These materials were based on cellulose acetate but did not come into general professional use, since they were inferior to nitrate film in their wearing properties and dimensional stability, although they were widely used for amateur systems where these problems were not so significant. The development of cellulose triacetate film, without these disadvantages, led to nitrate film being discontinued in the cinema. The Eastman Kodak Company introduced safety film in 1948 and by the end of 1949 had ceased to manufacture inflammable film; most major manufacturers followed suit soon after.

The first movie films were shot on materials coated with 'ordinary' emulsion, sensitive to blue and violet colours, slightly sensitive to green and not at all to yellow and red. By the First World War, orthochromatic film stocks were in common use, with sensitivity to green as well as blue. The lack of red sensitivity required that the film be exposed in strong daylight, or if, indoors, by the light from high intensity arc lamps or mercury vapour lamps. The latter seriously distorted the monochrome rendering of colour values in the scenes, making red lips very black, for example, and strangely coloured make-up had to be used to produce an acceptable result on the film.

The first panchromatic movie films, sensitive to all colours, were produced for the experiments in colour cinematography before the First World War. Such films were made by bathing the ordinary film in special dyes which extended its colour sensitivity but this method gave uneven results. From 1913, the Eastman Kodak Company made available a panchromatic cine film, developed for the Gaumont Chronochrome colour process. Produced at first on an experimental basis, small quantities were used for conventional filming, notably by the Hollywood cameraman Charles Rosher in 1919. The first production to be shot entirely on panchromatic film was *The Headless Horseman* by Ned Van Buren in 1922. Robert Flaherty used panchromatic stock in filming *Moana* in 1923-24, achieving a subtlety of tone range which made a great impression at the time. At first more expensive, in 1926 the cost of panchromatic film was reduced to the same as the conventional film and it was widely adopted. It had arrived at just the right time. As the studios turned over to sound production, they had to stop using the noisy carbon arc lamps in favour of noise-less incandescent lamps, whose high red light output had made them unsuitable for use with the non-colour-sensitive films. So now the studios were in a position to exploit the new 'talking pictures', the development of which we shall consider in the next chapter.

6
Sight and sound

During the first few years of the moving picture, it was a sufficient novelty in itself to attract audiences and nothing more was required than to project the short film subjects, lasting only a minute or two. Often, especially in England, the films were shown as part of a music hall performance, and they were then usually accompanied by the pit orchestra. This could sometimes produce less than adequate results. Henry Hopwood in his book *Living Pictures* described the presentation of Paul's film of the tragic sinking of HMS *Albion* at her launching in 1897 'the horrors of which were repeated before an audience at a London music-hall to the strains of "Rocked in the cradle of the deep".' The travelling showman in the fairground would present his show to a background of music from the fair organs.

Soon, the moving picture settled down as a regular form of entertainment and converted or purpose-built establishments were set up as cinemas. Films became longer and the 'actualités' of the early years gave way to more elaborate dramatic and narrative films. In the absence of dialogue and other sound, music was widely used to create and enhance the emotional, dramatic or comic mood of the film. We have seen already that Reynaud's Théâtre Optique used specially composed music to accompany the presentations and it was not unusual for elaborate magic lantern shows to have a piano accompaniment. Writing in 1915, R. B. Foster said,

> 'it is now rarely that a Cinematograph exhibition is given without a musical accompaniment of some sort. A suitable and appropriate selection of pianoforte music greatly improves an exhibition, and, on the other hand, an inappropriate selection, or a bad rendering of a good selection, is worse than no music at all. An ordinary piano is all that is used in many places, but a piano, organ, orchestra or orchestra substitute, such as the Cinephonium, however excellent the instrument may be, have limitations; and while these can be adopted to give music harmonizing to a large extent with most pictures, there are many sounds and noises, musical and otherwise, which require special devices for imitation . . . Invention and ingenuity have not failed to supply means for imitating these . . .'

Sound effects had been used for many years before the coming of the cinema, to accompany dissolving view shows, especially those at the Royal Polytechnic Institution in London. Some effects could be improvised by the operator, but sound making machines were soon supplied to the trade. In 1910, A. H. Moorhouse devised the Allefex machine which produced fifty individual sounds. F. A. Talbot described it as 'the most comprehensive and ingenious machine

A Victorian magic lantern show, accompanied by piano music and an elocutionist

ever made for the mimicry of sound', and he described some of its effects:

'The shot of a gun is imitated by striking a drum on the top of the machine, on which a chain mat has been placed . . . At the bottom of the machine is a large bellows worked by the foot. Their manipulation in conjunction with one or other of the handles will produce the sound of exhaust steam issuing from a locomotive, the rumbling of a train rushing through a tunnel, and so on. Running water, rain, hail and the sound of rolling waves are obtained by turning a handle, which rotates a ribbed wooden cylinder against a board set at an angle from the top of which hang a number of chains . . . The puffing of an engine is made by revolving a cylinder with projections against a steel brush; the crash of china,

The Allfex sound effects machine for cinemas, 1910

I AM IT!!

SUBLIME EFFECTS.
UNIQUE EFFECTS.
REALISTIC EFFECTS.
PERFECTION EFFECTS.

£29 15 0

What was the Order
and who gave it ? . .

The comments of a well known Property Master
of 25 years' experience :

"The greatest marvel of the age, simply astonishing:
seen others, but, undoubtedly the 'Allefex' is a masterpiece of ingenuity. Deliver the first machine May 25th."
Good Enough, Strand, London.

EACH NUMBER TELLS ITS OWN TALE AND BRINGS THE MONEY IN.

pots and pans, &c., is due to the revolution of a shaft on which are mounted a series of tappets striking against hammers which in turn come into contact with a number of steel plates. The crackling of a machine gun is caused by turning a shaft having tappets which strike and lift up wooden laths, subsequently releasing them to strike smartly against the framework of the machine. The same device serves for imitating the crash attending the upsetting of chairs, tables, and so on. Pendant tubes serve to produce the effects of church bells, fire alarm, ship's bell, and similar noises; the sound of trotting horses is caused by revolving a shaft carrying three tappets which lift up inverted cups . . . a trot can be converted into a gallop and *vice versa* . . . Thunder is made by shaking a sheet of steel hanging on one side of the machine; the press of a bulb gives the bark of a dog; the bellows and another attachment operate the warbling bird; while the cry of the baby is emitted by the dexterous manipulation of plug-hole and bellows.'

So with his pit orchestra and his Allefex machine the go-ahead cinema proprietor could embellish the screen performance. The cost to the exhibitor of a small orchestra or even a pianist was an additional financial burden in an industry which was always precarious. If the sound could be produced mechanically as part of the film presentation the worries of the exhibitor would be over, it was hoped, and the film-maker could rely on his production being accompanied by the music and sounds that he felt were appropriate. Above all, dialogue would make obsolete the constant stream of titles necessary to give the audience the nuances of the plot in a dramatic film. So, from the beginning of cinematography, the hunt was on for a practical method of combining sound with moving pictures.

We have seen how Wordsworth Donisthorpe predicted the sound film very soon after the introduction of Edison's Phonograph in 1877. This machine was the first practical device for the recording and reproduction of sound, although in its earliest form it was extremely primitive. A brass cylinder was mounted on a threaded rod fitted in threaded bearings. When the rod was rotated by a handle, the cylinder moved horizontally as well as rotating. The cylinder was incised with a spiral groove matching the threaded rod in its pitch. It was covered with tinfoil, and a stylus, set in the centre of a diaphragm, bore on the foil. As the cylinder was rotated by hand, the user spoke into a mouthpiece, causing the diaphragm to vibrate, and as a consequence the stylus produced indentations in the foil along a spiral track as the cylinder moved along. To reproduce the recording, the cylinder was wound back to the start, and a reproducer, similar to the recorder, was rested on the drum. When the handle was turned, a faint, distorted but recognisable reproduction of the original speech was heard. Tradition has it that Edison's first successful recording was of him reciting 'Mary had a little lamb' – the verse which to this day sound recordists are wont to recite when setting up their equipment. Edison's invention was described in the *Scientific American* in December 1877, and it was a reprint of the article in *Nature* that prompted Donisthorpe's prediction.

Alexander Graham Bell, with his cousin, Chichester Bell, and Charles Sumner Tainter, devised an improved recorder which they named the Graphophone which they demonstrated in 1885. The mechanism was basically similar to that of the Phonograph, but they used a wax-covered cardboard cylinder to receive the recording. The recording head moved along the cylinder, instead of the cylinder itself moving. The wax-coated cylinders could be interchanged easily, unlike the Edison foil recordings. Faced with the competition, Edison improved his machine and in June 1888 introduced the 'perfected' Phonograph, which used a wax cylinder. Both the Graphophone and the Phonograph were intended primarily for use with ear tubes, rather than a horn, although one could be fitted if required. The new Phonograph was driven by an electric motor, while the Graphophone was treadle operated. Both were intended for use as business machines and in a form suitable for dictation they were both put on the market. There was little demand for either at the time but entrepreneurs brought the new sound reproducers before the public as an entertainment. In the early 1890s coin-released devices were used to set Phonographs in motion, to be listened to by one person at a time through ear tubes. Sometimes as many as 17 people could listen at once through a multiple tube system. The great success of the Phonograph parlours led Edison to introduce his moving pictures to the public in the same way, as we have seen.

From the beginning, Edison had seen the moving picture as an adjunct to the Phonograph. His first caveat said 'I am experimenting upon an instrument which does for the eye what the phonograph does for the ear'. Despite repeated claims of successful combination of the two devices in the years that followed, no one really achieved it until the end of 1894, when some progress was made. Attempts to record the sound and picture in synchronism had proved totally unsuccessful but the Edison Kinetophone used non-synchronised music to accompany the pictures. The new machine was described in *The Orange Chronicle* on 16 March 1895. Externally, the Kineto-phone was like the Kinetoscope except that a set of rubber ear tubes, like a stethoscope, was fitted to the top, connected to a cylinder phonograph inside and coupled with the film mechanism. The first model was shipped to a Kinetoscope parlour in San Francisco in April 1895. Only 45 Kinetophones were produced; a few reached London. *The Photographic News* reported on 13 September 1895,

> 'It was long ago suggested that the kinetoscope could be wedded to the phonograph, and, if we remember rightly, a promise was held out that entire operas would be produced in this way. The first attempt which we have met with in this direction forms a side show at the Indian exhibition and it is a dismal failure. Possibly the particular instrument we sampled may have been a faulty specimen. The phonograph part was certainly badly adjusted, the sounds being crude and very disagreeable. The poetry of motion should be wedded to good music or to none at all.'

Edison's tinfoil phonograph, invented in 1877

A cylinder player from an Edison Kinetophone – a combined Kinetoscope and Phonograph, 1895

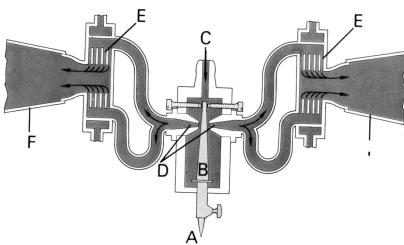

The principle of mechanical amplification. The stylus (A), vibrated by the record groove, caused the tapered needle (B) to more or less close the apertures (D) through which compressed air from the inlet (C) was passing. The small movements of the stylus were converted thus into large changes of air pressure. The baffles (E) reduced random noise from the compressed air and the amplified sound emerged from the horns (F). The Auxetophone in the engraving above was based on this principle

The inadequacies of the phonograph, especially its limited volume and the cylindrical form of the records, made it unsuitable for application to synchronised sound and picture work. On 16 May 1888 Émile Berliner demonstrated his Gramophone at the Franklin Institute in Philadelphia. He used a zinc disc covered with a thin layer of beeswax. A recording sound-box was moved across the disc as it rotated, cutting a spiral groove in the wax, the vibration of the stylus producing side to side variations in the groove. The recorded disc was etched with chromic acid which attacked only the exposed metal, producing a groove in the metal which followed faithfully the movements of the recording stylus. The disc could be played many times without damage. The first gramophone was sold as a toy in Germany in 1889 but in 1893 the US Gramophone Company sold 7-inch discs pressed in a hard rubber from a metal master disc, a technique which opened up the possibility of the mass production of cheap records. Each phonograph cylinder, on the other hand, had to be individually recorded, either directly, or by copying from another cylinder. After the introduction of a spring motor-driven model in 1896 (the original models were hand-turned) the Gramophone became a major competitor to the Phonograph and by 1900 disc records were in common use.

While the Gramophone produced adequate volume for home use, its output was rather limited for use in a hall or large auditorium. The use of very large horns did give a greater volume; some models were fitted with three, or even four horns. One model, the Victor Triplephone, played to an audience of 20,000 people at the Crystal Palace in London in 1904. An important advance, foreseen by Edison in his original phonograph patent, was developed by Sir Charles Parsons in 1902. His apparatus used the vibrations of the stylus as it followed the grooves of the record to control the passage of compressed air into a large horn. The original very small movements of the stylus were thus translated into considerable variations in air pressure, with a great increase in the volume of the reproduced sound. Parsons' Auxetophone was shown to the Royal Society in 1904, and was sold by the Gramophone Company for £100 in 1906. Its sound output was adequate for successful use out of doors as well as in large halls. Similar methods of mechanical amplification were used in Gaumont's Elgephone of 1906, based on an invention in 1902 by G. Laudet, and in Pathé's Orphone, introduced in 1907. So, by the early years of this century, sound reproducing devices were sufficiently advanced to make them potentially applicable to a combination with the cinematograph.

The first successful demonstration of synchronised sound and picture appears to have been given by Léon Gaumont at the Paris Exposition of 1900. He showed a 'Portrait Parlant' of himself speaking, using a mechanical coupling between the camera and a cylinder phonograph to record the sound and picture and a similar coupling between the phonograph and a Gaumont Chrono projector to reproduce them. The presentation was not very successful because of speed variations in the phonograph transmitted to it from the projector mechanism. Gaumont constructed a new model which he demonstrated to the Société Française de Photographie in November 1902. The projector was driven by an electric motor, the speed of which was controlled by an electrical contact wheel driven by the gramophone. If the sound record changed speed, the projector speed was changed automatically to maintain synchronism.

Gaumont showed three films, one of himself demonstrating his 'Block-Notes' still camera, and two showing dancing to a musical accompaniment. The latter two films were shot to the replaying of an existing record, since the inadequate sensitivity of the recording machines of the day required that the source of sound be placed very close to the horn, permitting close-up filming only, if the horn was not to appear in the picture. Gaumont's Phono-Scenes were shown at the Musée Grevin and elsewhere in 1903, but the presentations were limited by the inadequate volume from the unassisted gramophone.

In 1906 Gaumont built the Elgéphone compressed air amplifying gramophone, which produced enough volume to fill a large hall. He also introduced an improved coupling between the projector and the Elgéphone, using electric motors in each, electrically coupled so as to run in synchronism, with provision for manual adjustment of the projector speed if synchronism were lost for any reason. The new Chronophone was first shown at the Académie des Sciences on 27 December 1910, when a synchronised talking film of Professor d'Arsonval lecturing at the Académie was shown. This film was recorded by a synchronised camera and gramophone. To make films away from the studio, Gaumont first recorded the sound, and on location the performers mimed to a play-back of the record. The first public shows were given in 1912 at the Gaumont-Théâtre on the Boulevard Poissonière in Paris, and then at the huge 5,000-seat Hippodrome, in which the twin-horn Elgéphone performed very well. The 'Filmes Parlantes' included recitations, scenes from opera and ballet and comic and dramatic sketches, 'recorded and projected with a perfect relationship between sound and movement' said a contemporary writer. When the Chronophone was demonstrated in London at the Royal Institution in May 1912, the *Kinematograph Weekly* wrote of the 'startling realism' of the films of a den of lions roaring and a cock crowing.

In Germany, Oskar Messter patented several synchronisation methods in 1903, the most significant of which involved the electrical interconnection of two electric motors, which Gaumont used later. Messter demonstrated his 'Kosmograph' system on 30 August 1903 at the Apollo Theatre in Berlin. In 1904 he presented sound films at the St Louis World Exposition, showing subjects specially shot in English versions, such as 'The Whistling Bowery Boy'. His Biophon Theatre presented five or six sound films each day, for a 25-cent admission fee. About 500 people a day visited the show during the run of the Exposition. Messter used the Auxetophone amplifying gramophone. A later, improved system devised by Messter used a synchroniser which was mechanically coupled to the projector but electrically coupled to the gramophone, eliminating the effects of varying gramophone motor speed that had been obtrusive in the earlier system. By 1913, the improved Biophon sound system had been installed in 500 theatres in Germany.

The Frenchman Georges Mendel designed a synchroniser which used a similar principle to Messter's improved model. The shutter shaft of the projector was connected by a flexible cable to the synchroniser, where through a worm gearing it slowly turned a drum. The gramophone was fitted with a contact breaker in circuit with a battery and an electromagnet in the synchroniser. As the gramophone motor turned, the contact breaker developed a series of electrical impulses which caused the electromagnet to turn a pointer mounted concentrically with the drum. The film was set up in the projector with a marked frame in the gate, and the needle of the gramophone was placed on a synchronising mark at the edge of the disc. The gramophone-operated pointer was aligned with a mark on the projector-turned drum, and both machines were started together. The operator adjusted the speed of the projector so as to keep the drum turning at the same speed as the pointer, to maintain synchronism. If they parted company, the operator adjusted the projector speed to bring them into line again. The Mendel synchroniser was used by the English Walturdaw company for their Cinematophone system in 1911. Walturdaw 'Singing Pictures' were made by performers miming to existing gramophone records, including a number of Gilbert and Sullivan songs, which brought the company into legal conflict with the D'Oyly Carte opera company, whose permission they had not sought or obtained! The Cinematophone outfit, including projector and Auxetophone, cost £120.

The British Cinephone sound system was based on a patent by William Jeapes and Will Barker and was exploited by the Warwick Trading Company from 1908. First, a film was shot of performers miming to a record. Included in the bottom corner of each scene

The essential elements of the Walturdaw Cinematophone system. An acoustic gramophone (left), which in use was electrically connected to a Mendel synchroniser (centre) which in turn was mechanically coupled to a projector mechanism (right)

was a dial with a pointer driven round by the gramophone motor. In the theatre, a similar gramophone connected to an illuminated dial was set up close to the screen. When the film started, the operator had to match the rotation of the pointer on the screen with that of the gramophone, by adjusting the speed of the projector. This was not easy on the operator. F. A. Talbot wrote in 1912,

'Synchrony between picture and talking machine is dependent upon the operator, and until the latter has become accustomed to the combinations, the results are disconcerting. It is no simple matter to keep the hands of the two dials rotating harmoniously. When the film lags behind the talking machine, a pronounced speeding up is requisite to bring the two hands into synchrony. The increased work thrown upon the operator is also far from being a negligible quantity. He has to watch the two dials intently, and cannot centre his mind upon the projector, as he should be free to do. More than once I have seen a film snap under the strain imposed in the effort to catch up with the talking machine, or the light has demanded attention, and the result has been far from pleasing.'

None the less, some 483 theatres were equipped with Cinephone apparatus, which had the great advantage that it could be used with any projection apparatus, and with any sound reproducer, requiring only a small modification.

Cecil Hepworth's Vivaphone method introduced in 1911 used a synchroniser with a pointer, fitted in the projection box. The synchroniser had a vertical pointer, the position of which was set by two electromagnets, one on each side. One was fed with impulses from a contact breaker on the gramophone spindle, the other with pulses from a contact breaker fitted to the projector driving shaft. Behind the pointer was a narrow slot, with a light behind it, covered by the pointer when it was central. On either side of the pointer was fixed a small glass, red on one side, green on the other, so that if it moved from vertical, one or other of the glasses came in front of the light. When the machines ran in synchronism, no light showed, but if one got ahead of the other, a red or green signal was given and the operator adjusted the projector appropriately, so as to return the pointer to the central position. The method was simple and reliable and worked well in practice. As with most other systems, the Vivaphone films were made by miming to pre-recorded discs. The very popular song 'Meet Me Tonight in Dreamland' was made into a Vivaphone film in January 1912; the *Kinematograph Weekly* said 'the synchronism is perfect . . . an item on no account to be missed'. The Vivaphone system could be fitted to any make of projector for five guineas. It was shown with some success in America in 1913.

Thomas Edison's dream of creating a combined sound and picture reproducing device took him a quarter of a century to realise. His Kinetophone was shown first in March 1913. A long-playing phonograph was set up behind the screen and was connected by a long endless belt running overhead on idler pulleys to the projection box, where it passed through a synchroniser which applied a brake to the projector in proportion to the variation in synchronism. The phonograph used a mechanical power amplifier to create the necessary volume to fill the theatre. Compared to the relative sophistication of the electrically synchronised, automatic methods in use in Europe, the Kinetophone was astonishingly crude, coming from the man known as the 'Electrical Wizard'. The Kinetophone ran at Keith's Colonial theatre in New York for about four months and was later shown in other places in America and Europe. It was first shown in England on 10 July 1913, before the King and Queen at Knowsley Hall. Despite the mechanical crudity of the system, it seems to have worked well enough. The *Kinematograph Weekly* spoke of the 'nearest approach to perfection that singing pictures have yet attained', describing the one-and-a-half-hour show before their Majesties. The films included comedies, dramas, opera, nursery rhymes and a performance by the Edison Minstrels. By January 1914 the Kinetophone was installed at the West End cinema in London, and the *Kinematograph Weekly* enthused '[it] makes the moving picture a living and breathing substance and, consequently, adds intrinsically to the value of our art'.

The fundamental problem with all these early sound systems was that the direct recording of sound and picture at the same time was made very difficult by the need to have a large recording horn very close to the subject. In addition, the acoustic gramophone was severely limited in the tonal range of its reproduced sound. Talbot said in 1912,

'What is the future of the phono-cinematograph? In the first place, until the peculiar nasal sound is eliminated from the talking machine it will not prove popular. It is well-nigh impossible, unless a speaker or singer has peculiar characteristics, to identify voices on this instrument. Furthermore expression in tone is practically non-existent.'

Electrical recording, using a less obtrusive microphone to pick up the sound, feeding an electromagnetic cutter on the recording gramophone was tried by the Pathé company, among others, in 1909, but the results were unsuccessful. In the absence of any method of amplifying the weak signals from the microphone, not enough power was available to drive the cutting head on a gramophone. The development of electrical recording had to wait for the invention of the electronic amplifying valve.

The valve was based upon a phenomenon noticed by Edison during experiments with incandescent electric lamps in the 1880s. He noticed that although his early carbon filament lamps tended to blacken all over inside the glass, there was a thin, clear line left, in the plane of the filament, and in line with the leg of the filament connected to the positive pole of the battery or dynamo. By placing a plate inside the bulb, he was able to show that a current would flow from the positive side of the filament to the plate across the intervening gap. The 'Edison effect' was studied by a number of scientists and in 1904 J. A. Fleming made a valve in which the filament was passed through the centre of a tubular electrode. He found that the valve was a one-way device, a current flowing only from the filament to the electrode, called the anode, and not the other way. It could be used as a rectifier, or detector, for radio waves. Lee de Forest experimented with the Fleming valve, and on 20 October 1906 at the American Institute of Electrical Engineering in New York he read a paper on 'The Audion, a new receiver for wireless telegraphy', in which he discussed an improved version of Fleming's diode valve. In 1907 he added a third electrode to the valve, a grid placed between the filament and the anode. By connecting a battery between the filament and the anode a current would flow. By varying the electrical charge on the grid, the current flowing to the anode could be varied. He saw this as an improved detector for radio waves and at the time failed to see that with the right connections the 'triode' valve could be made to amplify a signal applied to the grid. Almost simultaneously, in the summer of 1912, E. H. Armstrong and de Forest discovered that if a small proportion of the signal passing through the valve was fed back to the grid from the anode, a considerable increase in the current flowing through the valve occurred. A single triode valve could amplify a signal five times, while with three valves connected one after the other an amplification of 120 times was possible. The feed-back circuit and the triode valve led to a rapid development in electronics, given an impetus by various military applications during the First World War. The amplifying valve solved the problem of providing enough power to drive electromagnetic cutting heads on the gramophone, and allowed the development of amplifiers capable of filling a hall with sound from loudspeakers. Everything was set for the rapid development of the sound film. One method, which we shall consider shortly, involved systems for recording sound on film. The other method was a modernisation of the separate sound on disc methods which had been so widely used before the First World War.

The first of the sound film systems to make a real impact on the public, although by no means the first to be demonstrated, was the Vitaphone system. The Western Electric Company in America had been involved in investigations of sound recording methods before the First World War and had pioneered systems of electrical recording and reproduction of sound, developing in the early 1920s a much improved magnetic cutting head for disc recording. Experiments were begun in the synchronisation of sound with pictures and demonstrations were given at Yale University in 1922 and 1924. In order to make a satisfactory sound system for the feature length films which had now replaced the short films of the earlier years, the playing time of the discs had to be increased. The sound engineers decided on a 16-inch (40.6cm) diameter disc, recorded at $33\frac{1}{3}$ revolutions a minute, playing from the centre outwards. The camera and disc recorder were driven by selsyn (*self-syn*chronous) electric motors which ensured precise synchronisation, and starting marks had to be made on both the disc and the film. The effective exploitation of the Western Electric system had to wait for the development of an

Don Juan, 1926, was the first film to be presented with a synchronised musical score by the Vitaphone system

The Coming of the Talkies

In 1925 Samuel L. Warner, of Warner Brothers, saw a demonstration of the Western Electric sound film system using synchronised discs and became enthusiastic about its possibilities. Extensive tests were made in the winter of 1925-6 in the Warner Vitagraph studios in Brooklyn, New York. The Vitaphone Corporation was formed in April 1926 and took over the Manhattan Opera House in New York. A number of short musical items were filmed, and a specially composed musical score was recorded for the film *Don Juan* by the New York Philharmonic Orchestra. *Don Juan*, starring John Barrymore, was presented at the Warner Theatre in New York on 5 August 1926. The programme began with a synchronised film of Will H. Hays introducing the Vitaphone system and this was followed by the overture to *Tannhäuser*, played by the New York Philharmonic Orchestra. Other musical items, including excerpts from *Rigoletto* and *Pagliacci* and instrumental performances by Efrem Zimbalist, Harold Bauer and Mischa Elman followed. *Don Juan* was a great success, although the sound track carried only the musical score, no dialogue. Warner Brothers began

ABOVE *Advertisement for* The Jazz Singer
LEFT *Ross sound projector, 1929*
BELOW *16-inch Vitaphone disc*

Jolson in The Jazz Singer

production of a new sound film, *The Jazz Singer*, in the spring of 1927. George Jessel was to play the lead, but he got into a dispute with the studio over extra pay for singing as well as acting and the part was offered to Al Jolson. The sound track was to consist of a synchronised musical score and

songs only, but Jolson adlibbed some words of dialogue. After singing the song *Dirty Hands, Dirty Faces*, Jolson said as the customers applauded, 'Wait a minute, wait a minute, you ain't heard nothing yet', a favourite catch phrase of his. The film was premiered on 6 October 1927 and was an immediate success, especially with Jolson speaking. The occasion was also a sad one for Sam Warner, who had worked so hard and taken such a risk with the new Vitaphone System had died from pneumonia the day before.

While Vitaphone was by no means the first sound system to be demonstrated it was *The Jazz Singer* which caught the public's imagination. The next year Warner Brothers produced the first all-talking synchronised sound film, *The Lights of New York*, released on 15 July 1928. Although the Vitaphone sound films started a great public enthusiasm for talking pictures, the system lasted only a short time. By 1930, the cost of shipping the heavy 16-inch records and their frequent breakage added to the complicated handling problems for the projectionist and led Warner Brothers to discontinue the sound-on-disc method in favour of sound-on-film.

efficient loudspeaker, provided by Dr Wente's moving coil design, introduced in 1923 and much improved in 1926. For projection, the film was threaded in the projector with a frame marked START in the gate and the pick-up needle was placed in the centre groove of the disc, opposite an arrow. The projector and the turntable were driven by the same motor and started together when the switch was thrown. The two remained in exact synchronism throughout the reel.

Samuel L. Warner, of Warner Brothers, was one of the first major film-makers to see the potential of the Western Electric system and he backed his hunch with extensive resources (see panel left). In 1928, Warner Brothers produced the first all-talking synchronised sound film, *The Lights of New York*, released on 15 July. Although the Vitaphone sound film, and particularly its use in *The Jazz Singer*, started a great public enthusiasm for talking pictures, the system itself lasted only a short time. By 1930, the cost of shipping the heavy 16-inch records, and their frequent breakage with consequent replacement costs, together with the complicated handling problems for the projectionist, led Warner Brothers to discontinue the sound on disc system in favour of sound on film.

If the sound record was carried on the same strip of film as the pictures, all problems of synchronisation would be solved. Some early workers tried to combine the mechanical recording of the gramophone with the film. From 1913 F. von Madelar patented a series of inventions for mechanically recording sound on film. In one, a rotary cutter, vibrated by a connection with the diaphragm of a recording horn, bore on the edge of the film, cutting a wavy line which was to be followed in the projector by a flat-ended sapphire attached to a gramophone sound box. In another, a vibrating red-hot platinum wire was to be used instead of the rotary cutter. Although a company was formed to exploit the patents, nothing came of it at the time. The idea was revived in 1929 when von Madelar used a diamond stylus on a magnetic cutting head to record the sound in the form of a groove on the base side of a 16mm film. The projector was fitted with a pick-up which played the recording as it passed over a drum. The sound track groove, which was duplicated on each side of the frame, was easily visible on the screen – one of the several disadvantages of the process!

The future of the sound film lay in the development of methods of optical recording, in which the variations of sound were converted into a varying photographic image recorded on the film with the pictures. From the middle of the last century, a number of scientists and inventors investigated ways of recording sound waves as visible traces. Some used moving photographic plates on which thin beams of light were reflected from vibrating mirrors. The result was a wavy line on the developed plate, which represented the variations of the sound which had vibrated the mirror. Many experiments of this type were carried on in the last decades of the last century. By 1900 the principles of the recording of sound as a photographic image, in which the sounds were reproduced either as a track of varying area, or as one of varying density, had been discussed theoretically, and demonstrated, notably by Bell, Bell and Tainter (as early as 1886).

As well as a method of recording sound as an optical image, a method had to be found of 'reading' the sound. A material was required that would respond to the variation in a light beam passed through the sound record, so that electrical impulses could be generated and heard in, say, a telephone receiver. In a lecture to the English Society of Telegraph Engineers in February 1873, Willoughby

Von Madelar's 16mm sound system, 1929, used two modulated grooves scribed in the film base about one-eighth of the way in from each side of the picture. A pick-up 'read' the groove in the projector. BELOW A scanning electron micrograph of the groove on the Von Madelar film

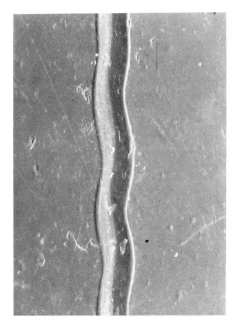

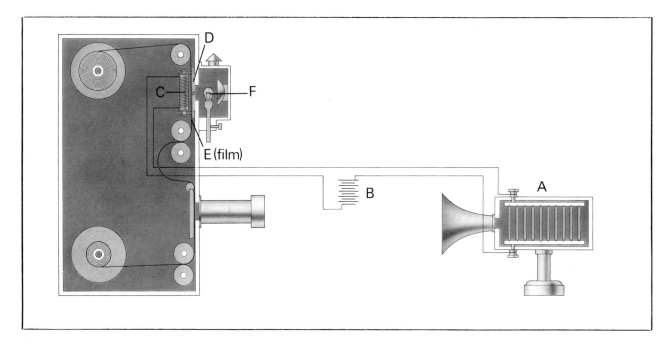

Smith described the discovery that the metal selenium had an electrical resistance which varied when light fell on it. This discovery was to be of great significance for the sound film. A photo-electric cell, made of a thin layer of selenium coated on an insulating material and with an electrical contact on each side, when placed in a circuit with a battery and a telephone receiver, would vary in resistance in proportion to the light falling on it; in the same proportion, current flowing through the circuit would vary. Light passing through a photographic sound record onto a photo-cell would thus produce variations which could be heard in a receiver as a reproduction of the original sound. Professor Ernst Rühmer in 1901 published details of the Photographon, in which he used 35mm cine film exposed through a narrow slit to a light source varying in brightness in proportion to the variations of a sound source. He produced a variable density sound track occupying the whole width of the film, which ran at the very high speed of ten feet (3 metres) per second. He was able to reproduce the recorded sound by passing a narrow beam of light through the film onto a selenium cell. As a scientist, Rühmer was concerned primarily with the analysis of sound, but he did say, 'For practical uses the application of the Photographon in combination with the Kineomatograph whereby on one and the same film both motion and speech may be recorded should be kept in mind'. Although there had been a number of earlier suggestions and patents for similar devices, Rühmer appears to have been the first to make a working optical sound recorder.

Eugene A. Lauste, a Frenchman, worked in the Edison Laboratory during the early years of the development of the Kinetoscope. Some time after leaving Edison, Lauste worked with the Lathams and Dickson, playing a leading part in the development of the Panoptikon and Eidoloscope projectors. Then he joined the American Mutoscope company, where he worked once again with his old colleague, Dickson. After moving to England at the beginning of the century, Lauste began experiments in sound recording. His first work was done in 1904, with apparatus he later described as little more than a toy. It was a box containing a roll of film onto which a beam of light was directed through a slit close to the film, via a mirror

BELOW Lauste recording a sound film with his improved camera of 1910. RIGHT The sound was recorded as a wide variable area sound track on the same film as the picture

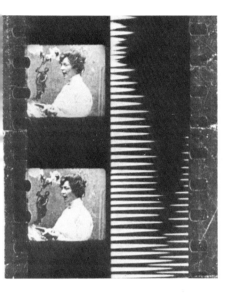

mounted on a vibrating diaphragm. It worked well enough to demonstrate the principle required and after further research, on 11 August 1906 Lauste, together with his two financial backers, R. T. Haines and J. St Vincent Potts, applied for a patent for 'A New and Improved Method of and Means for Simultaneously Recording and Reproducing Movements and Sounds'. In a cinecamera, the film was at one point carried round a roller behind two grids. One was fixed, and the other next to it was vibrated by an electromagnet connected to a microphone. A beam of light from a lamp passing through the two grids onto the film was more or less obstructed by the vibrating element, in proportion to the sounds received. A variable density sound track was produced, occupying about one-third of the width of the film between the perforations, and the pictures, rather smaller than usual, filled the rest of the width of the film. The processed and printed film was run in a projector in which a lamp was provided, in the same relative position as the recording unit in the camera, and a narrow beam from the lamp passed through the film onto a selenium cell, connected in series with a battery and a telephone receiver. As the light passing through the film varied, so did the current passing through the cell and receiver and the original sounds, or a recognizable version of them, were heard, at the same time as the appropriate action was seen on the screen.

Lauste visited Rühmer in Berlin in 1908, and bought from him a Photographone and improved selenium cells. The mechanical grate light valve was not very efficient, since its inertia was too great for it to respond to the very rapid vibrations needed to record a full range of sounds. Lauste worked constantly to improve the system. In 1910 he tried using a string galvanometer, in which a small mirror was fixed on a silicon bronze wire stretched between the poles of two electromagnets. When a varying current was passed through the latter, the varying magnetic field caused the wire and the mirror to vibrate. A beam of light reflected from the mirror fell on a narrow slit close to the film as it passed through the camera, and the vibration of the light beam produced a sound track of varying area on the film. The new string galvanometer was much more sensitive than the light grate, although it was also more prone to picking up vibrations from the camera. The new variable area sound tracks now occupied half the usable width of the film, with the pictures on the other half.

Between 1910 and 1913 Lauste made many experimental sound film records, some shot in America in 1913, when on a visit in search of financial backing. His work ended with the coming of the First World War, without any commercial development of his pioneering system. In the absence of any method of amplifying the signals generated by his sound projector there was no way of showing the films to a large audience. Nevertheless, the principles Lauste used were fundamentally those used for the successful sound on film process introduced a decade later, and still in use today.

The solution to the problem of the inadequate sound reproduction came, as we have seen, with the development of the triode valve, which was greatly improved during the First World War with new techniques for improving the vacuum inside the valve. The selenium cell used for the early experiments had drawbacks. In particular, it did not respond with the speed necessary to reproduce the higher frequencies of sound. A new form of photo-cell was developed in 1917 by the American Theodore W. Case. His Thalofide cell used a layer of thallium oxy-sulphide coated on a glass plate and enclosed in a glass bulb filled with inert gas, or evacuated to a vacuum. The

Lee de Forest's Phonofilm system used a variable density sound track recorded on the film. This example was made by British Talking Pictures in 1929

new cell was very sensitive, especially to infra-red radiation, and for this reason was used by the United States Navy in a communications system during the First World War. The Thalofide cell did not have the lag of the selenium cell and was much more responsive.

Lee de Forest turned his attention to methods of sound recording and in 1919 filed a patent for a 'glow-lamp' – a nitrogen gas-filled tube which glowed when a high-frequency current from a modified radio telephone transmitter was applied to it. The light output from the tube, which de Forest called the 'Photion', varied as the signals from a microphone were applied to the transmitter. The film was exposed to the light from the lamp through a very narrow slot about one-and-a-half thousandths of an inch (.04mm) wide placed very close to the film as it passed through the sound camera, producing a variable density sound track. The sound was replayed using a Thalofide cell connected to an amplifier. Several demonstration films were made and shown in the spring of 1921, although the system was still rather crude.

In 1922 Case devised the AEO-light, a glow-lamp filled with hydrogen, and which required about 350 volts of direct current to make it glow. Amplified alternating signals from the microphone could be made to vary the brightness of the lamp. New equipment using the AEO-light was much more successful and de Forest demonstrated the Phonofilm system to the press on 13 March 1923, and in the week of 15 April 1923 Phonofilms were shown to the public at the Rivoli Theatre, New York. In 1924 a Bell & Howell camera was modified for sound work, with an AEO-light fitted in the back of the camera, close to a fine slit six ten-thousandths of an inch (.02mm) wide, ruled in a silver coating on a quartz plate, behind which the film ran. The Case laboratories continued to make improvements until the working arrangement with de Forest ended in the autumn of 1925. The Phonofilm system was used to make a few demonstration short films and by 1925 about 34 theatres in eastern America had sound installations. In the spring of 1924 President Calvin Coolidge made a speech recorded by the Phonofilm camera; this film and others showing dancers and singers were shown to the Royal Photographic Society in London on 17 February 1925, together with a filmed address by Lee de Forest. The demonstrator, C. F. Ewell, 'had to admit that this fell short of perfection'. The sound quality still left much to be desired, with a limited range of tone and volume. 'So unmistakably a "canned" product', as one writer put it.

After the split with de Forest in 1925, Theodore Case developed new and improved apparatus, particularly in the form of a sound reproducing head which could be fitted to existing projectors. Case chose to fit the sound head under the projector mechanism, so that the sound track was offset from the picture by 20 frames, and fixed on a picture frequency of 24 frames per second, the extra speed being necessary to give adequate sound quality. Both became the standard for sound on film systems. In 1926, the Case apparatus was demonstrated to the Fox Film Corporation, who on 23 July 1926 purchased the rights from Case. Fox christened the system Movietone. Western Electric amplifiers and speakers were used for the sound reproduction systems. The first test recordings of Movietone were made on 25 October 1926, including films of Sir Harry Lauder, and several short sound films were shown as part of the introductory programme at the premiere of *What Price Glory?* on 21 January 1927. Various news subjects were recorded, including a speech by Mussolini on 6 May

Sound-on-film

Although Emil Lauste had demonstrated sound-on-film recording methods before the First World War, practical applications were not made until the 1920s. A number of individuals and organisations worked on sound film systems in the early 1920s, in Europe and America. In America two principal commercial sound systems were developed. One evolved from the work of Lee de Forest and Theodore Case. The Phonofilm variable density method created by de Forest and Case was demonstrated in 1923 and was in small scale commercial use by 1925. Case then independently developed an improved system which was taken up by the Fox Film Corporation, who launched it under the name Movietone in 1927. The first regular sound newsreels, Movietone News, began in October 1927 and feature film production began the following year. The equipment for Movietone was made by the Western Electric Company, whose rivals, General Electric Company, Westinghouse and RCA, collaborated in the introduction of

an alternative sound system based on an invention by Charles A. Hoxie. The Photophone method used a variable area sound track; the first feature film to use it was released in June 1928. Incompatible features of the two systems were removed by agreements in 1928, paving the way to the general adoption of sound by the American film industry.

Movietone News the first regular sound newsreel, began in 1927

1927 and the reception of Charles Lindberg in Washington on 12 June. The first of the regular weekly Movietone News programmes was shown at the Roxy Theatre, New York on 28 October 1927. Within a year there were two issues each week of this pioneering sound newsreel and by December 1928 it had been increased to three.

In 1928 Fox went into large scale sound film production; the first all-talking feature film to be made on location, *In Old Arizona*, was released in December 1928, with a premiere at the Criterion Theatre, Los Angeles. It was a great success. Harold B. Franklin said in 1929, 'the scenes and human voice and all the accompanying sounds were reproduced with a clearness and naturalness that attracted wide attention. The Movietone process caught and reproduced with fidelity not only the voices of the actors, but actually the natural sounds of the outdoors: the whispering of the wind, the song of the birds.' In March 1929 Fox announced that henceforth they would discontinue all silent film production – the first major studio to take the plunge into sound production exclusively.

The General Electric Company entered the sound film business with sound recording equipment developed by Charles A. Hoxie in 1921. He devised a vibrating mirror type optical recorder, which he called the Pallophotophone. It recorded a variable area track down the centre of a 35mm film strip. Hoxie recorded speeches by President Coolidge and other politicians which were broadcast over the radio. In 1925 GEC developed a variable area sound recorder based on Hoxie's machine; their Kinegraphone system was used in 1927 for applying a sound track to *Wings*, which had been shot as a silent film by Paramount. The Kinegraphone was used to add a sound track of

The Wall sound-on-film recording camera, used extensively for newsreel work in the 1930s and 1940s

ABOVE RIGHT A Bell & Howell camera used in the aerial sequences in *Wings*, 1927

sound effects. The sound version of *Wings* was toured as a road show, since few theatres were equipped for sound at the time. RCA, acting as a marketing organisation for the products of GEC and Westing-house took over the commercial exploitation of the sound on film process and formed RCA-Photophone Inc. A bolt-on sound head to convert silent projectors for sound was designed, the arrangement following Case's design. This apparatus was available from the autumn of 1927, for direct sale to theatres. A service of post-recording of musical scores for silent films was available to any company who would supply a silent print for the preparation of the score. The first feature film shot in Photophone was *The Perfect Crime*, released on 17 June 1928.

The sudden proliferation of sound film processes in the late 1920s created some complication, since not all were made to the same standards. The question of interchangeability arose in July 1928 when the Western Electric Company agreed that the Cecil B. de Mille production in Photophone of *The King of Kings* could be shown on their equipment at the Rivoli Theatre in New York. The Photophone variable area sound track was 25% wider than the variable density track used on the Western Electric equipment, and had to be reduced to make it compatible. On 30 December 1928 it was announced that the various companies had agreed on standardisation, so that there would be no bar to the showing of any kind of sound film on any make of projector. Standardisation was certainly needed. In December 1929 there were 234 different types of theatre sound system, including a number only for sound on discs. The popularity of talking pictures led all the major studios to commit themselves to sound productions. By February 1930 it was reported that only 5% of Hollywood production was silent and in September of that year it was estimated that about one-third of the world's cinemas were already converted, including 47% of cinemas in the United Kingdom. In 1930, Warner Brothers finally discarded the Vitaphone sound on disc method and changed to sound on film, using a light-valve recorder designed by Dr E. C. Wente and developed by Bell Telephone Laboratories for Western Electric in 1922. It gave a variable density sound track.

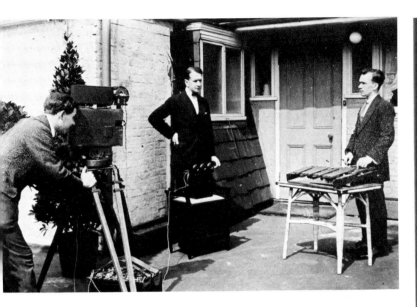

Sound film developments in the 1920s were not confined to America. In 1919, the English inventor H. Grindell Matthews devised a sound on film system not unlike that of Lauste. With the help of the engineer Arthur Kingston, and B. J. Lynes, who developed the electronics, a functioning sound recording camera was made in 1921. It used a galvanometer movement to produce a variable area sound track beside the picture on the film. Several demonstration films were made and in September 1921 Arthur Kingston filmed an interview with Sir Ernest Shackleton just before he left on his last voyage. The results were promising, but the money ran out and the project ceased in April 1922.

In Germany, the Triergon company was formed in 1918 by Josef Engl, Joseph Massolle and Hans Vogt, to develop sound reproduction and recording equipment. They devised a glow-lamp recording camera and a photo-cell for reproduction, using a 42mm wide film, the extra 7mm being outside the perforations on one side carrying the sound track. The Triergon sound films were demonstrated on 17 September 1922 at the Alhambra in Berlin, showing musical numbers and sketches. Other demonstrations followed in the next few years. The Tonbild-Syndikat AG, known as Tobis, was formed in 1928 to exploit the process. In that year the Siemens and Halske, Polyphon and AEG companies formed a joint company called Klangfilm GmbH to exploit sound films; after attempts to release

ABOVE LEFT Arthur Kingston operating the sound camera invented by H. Grindell-Matthews, CENTRE, in 1921. ABOVE Film from the Grindell-Matthews sound camera

Sound recording head for the Grindell-Matthews variable area sound system. Light from the lamp (far right) was projected by a lens (centre) onto a mirror galvanometer (left) the mirror of which was vibrated by the signal from a microphone. Light reflected from the mirror played on a slit in the sound head (right of centre) behind which the film ran

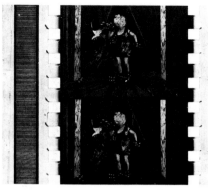

The German Tri-Ergon sound film system, 1922, placed the sound track on the outside of the perforations on a 42mm wide film

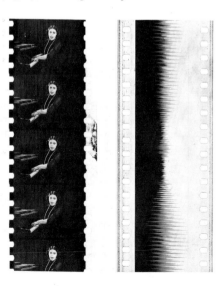

Petersen and Poulsen's sound system (1924-1928) used separate picture films (left), running at 20 fps and sound films (right), running at 32 fps

American-made sound films in Berlin, they were prevented by an injunction from Tobis on the grounds that such presentations infringed the Tobis patents. As a result Klangfilm and Tobis signed an agreement to cooperate in March 1929. Tobis-Klangfilm during the next few years became involved in litigation with various American sound film companies and their agents, until on 22 July 1930, at a conference in Paris, agreements were reached over the exploitation of sound films between the European and American producers.

In Denmark E. Petersen and V. Poulsen worked on methods of recording sound tracks on film strips separate from those carrying the pictures. In 1923 they used a variable area track occupying the whole area between the perforations; the sound film ran at 32 fps, and the pictures at 16 fps. From 1924 to 1928, the picture frequency was increased to 20 fps. In 1925 British Acoustic Films Ltd was formed to exploit the Petersen-Poulsen sound system in England and made a number of short demonstration films. In Germany, Deutsche Tonfilm AG acquired the German rights to the Danish system, which was used for a sound film *Tonfilm Kabarett* shown in the Capitol Theatre in Berlin in November 1926. Gaumont bought the French rights and in 1928 produced the first French sound on film production, *Eau de Nil*, in the G.P.P. system. It was shown at the Cameo Theatre in Paris on 18 October 1928. A variety of problems were inherent in the separate sound film method and it was never commercially successful, especially against the competition from the single-film methods from America. Petersen and Poulsen developed a single film system in 1928.

The general changeover to sound films occurred in Europe a year or two after the move in America, but it happened just as quickly when it came. The *Bioscope* in February 1930 listed 16 different sound systems available to the British exhibitor. Almost all were for sound on disc as well as sound on film. The average cost for an installation of medium size was well over £1,000. Although sound recording methods improved considerably during the next few years, with significant reductions in background noise and improved fidelity and frequency response, there was no significant change in the principles underlying the optical sound film. An optical sound recorder, electrically synchronised with the camera, made the sound record through one or more microphones. A clapper board marked the beginning of each shot, marking the sound track and the picture with a reference mark so that the separate records could later be matched in synchronism. To eliminate the noise from the camera, at first it was placed inside a soundproof booth in the studio. This was at first no restriction, since the insensitive microphones had to be hidden in the set and thus each shot was static. Later, with improved and more directional microphones, the camera was liberated from its booth, being covered by a 'blimp' – a soundproof box or jacket which surrounded the camera, but left it free to move.

An alternative method of recording sound, which later was to bring about significant changes in sound film production, was to use a magnetic material, in which the variations in the sound were recorded as variations in the degree of magnetism on a band. The first practical magnetic recorder was built by Valdemar Poulsen around 1900, and was patented by him in 1901. He called his machine the Telegraphone; it used a moving steel wire or tape passed under an electromagnet through which the varying current from a microphone and battery were passed. The machine worked,

From 1928 the Petersen-Poulsen system used a single film method, and was adopted by several European film companies

ABOVE LEFT In the early sound studios the camera was erected in a sound-proof booth

although not very well, and no progress was made with it, although it was on sale for a few years. In the absence of any means of amplifying the signal from the magnetic material its scope was very limited. A suggestion reported in *Machinery* in January 1917 was curiously prophetic. Writing of the Telegraphone, the author said,

> 'The talking picture has never been made a success because of the difficulty of obtaining perfect synchronism between the pictures thrown on the screen and the recording of the voice. With the telegraphone, perfect synchronisation is possible. This is accomplished by depositing a strip of pulverised iron filings directly on the film itself. The sound waves are thus carried directly on the same film as the pictures. In reproducing, an amplifier can be located behind the curtain and connected telephonically with the motion picture machine.'

In 1923 E. Petersen was granted a US patent for such a system, using a magnetic wire embedded in the edge of the film, but it was not commercially exploited. The Stille electromagnetic recorder was demonstrated in 1929 by Ludwig Blattner. It used 7mm-wide perforated steel tape, and was reported to have the capacity to record a wide tone range. It was demonstrated at Elstree studios but the film industry showed little interest in it, although the BBC experimented with the machine for some years. In 1928 Pfleumer, in Germany, patented the principle of coating paper or film with a magnetic material, and AEG and I. G. Farben developed the method which was incorporated in the Magnetophone recorder/reproducer in 1935. The sound quality was still imperfect, with a high level of background noise, but as a dictating machine it functioned well enough. Major improvements were made both in Germany, especially in the manufacture of magnetic tapes, and in America during the War and by 1948 magnetic recording had advanced far enough for RCA to develop a 35mm magnetic film studio recorder, using film made by Dupont and running at 18 inches (45.7cm) per second. At the same time, Western Electric developed a combined optical and magnetic recorder for studio use. By the next year, professional quality results were possible and by 1952 virtually

The Stille-Blattner Blattnerphone electromagnetic sound recorder used 7mm wide steel tape; it was demonstrated in 1929

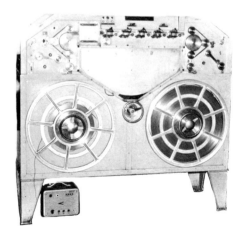

Ben Lyon and Jean Harlow (in her first major movie) starred in Howard Hughes' *Hell's Angels* (1930). In 1931, some road shows of this film were accompanied by a special 'binaural' sound track

all studio recording was done by magnetic machines, the sound tracks being converted to optical forms when the final prints were made. The introduction of methods of applying a magnetic stripe to a picture film, foreshadowed in the article of 1917, made possible the application of sound to amateur films and the use of several magnetic strips introduced the possibility of stereophonic multichannel sound.

The possibility of recording two sound tracks with separate microphones in order to present to the listener the illusion of a wide spread source of sound had been suggested for film use as long ago as 25 October 1911, when Rosenberg filed an English patent for a method of recording two sound tracks on a double width film, with signals from two separated microphones. The double sound film was run in synchronism with a picture film. Although not practical at the time, Rosenberg's idea was taken up later by the film industry. In 1931, some road-show presentations of the film *Hell's Angels* were accompanied by sound on a separate film with two tracks, enabling 'binaural' sound to be reproduced by speakers on either side of the screen and some sound effects could be played over speakers in the auditorium. In the Theatre Guild presentation of *The Miracle of Verdun* at the Martin Bell Theatre in New York in 1931, three sound reproducers were set up to feed 17 speakers, 11 backstage, two in the proscenium arch and four in the auditorium. They presented a 'third dimension in sound', and seven talking picture sequences were included in the stage production.

During the 1930s, Bell Telephone Laboratories carried out a detailed study into stereophonic sound systems. In April 1933 they demonstrated what they called 'auditory perspective', in which an orchestra performing in Philadelphia was relayed through three spaced microphones and separate transmitters to the Constitution Hall, Washington, where three amplifiers and speakers reproduced the sound in the auditorium. At the autumn 1937 Convention of the Society of Motion Picture Engineers Bell showed films of an orchestra, a ping-pong game, and played the sounds of men moving in a darkened room, using two stereophonic optical sound tracks. On 9 and 10 April 1940 they arranged a show at Carnegie Hall, New

York, playing stereophonic sound from a 35mm film carrying three separate tracks and a control track.

The first major film production to use stereophonic sound was Walt Disney's *Fantasia*. RCA engineers developed an eight-channel optical recording system. The *Journal of the Society of Motion Picture Engineers*, August 1941, reported on how the recordings were made:

'All the numbers, except *The Sorcerer's Apprentice* and the vocal portions of *Ave Maria*, were scored at the Philadelphia Academy of Music. Eight . . . recording channels were used . . . Separate channels recorded close pick-ups of violins, cellos and bases, violas, brass, woodwinds, and tympani. The seventh channel recorded a mixture of the first six channels and the eighth channel recorded a distant pick-up of the entire orchestra . . . The *Ave Maria* vocal numbers were recorded on three channels: two close channels separating male and female voices, with a distant overall channel for added reverberation.'

The multiple channels were mixed together, ending up on an optical sound film with three sound channels for left, centre and right of the screen, and a control track which was used to expand the sound levels in the auditorium. Notches in the edge of the film were used to work relays to bring in some of the sound to speakers at the sides and back of the auditorium, for example in the *Ave Maria* sequence. *Fantasia* had its premiere on 13 November 1940, but the full stereophonic sound presentations were only given on eight road-show performances, when the entire sound equipment had to be set up and dismantled in each theatre in turn. The stereophonic sound was an outstanding success, but the road shows had to be discontinued for reasons of cost and complication. Most people saw *Fantasia* presented with a conventional single optical sound track. However, it pioneered the use of multichannel stereophonic sound in the cinema, a technique which was exploited after the Second World War with the advent of the wide screen processes, as we shall see in chapter eight.

Cinema organs were first installed to provide musical and other sounds to accompany silent films. Later, they became a standard feature in all the larger cinemas

7

'In all the hues of Nature'

As with sound, it was realised that the addition of colour to the moving picture would greatly enhance its realism but when the cinema began there was no practical method of colour photography that could be applied to it. The easiest solution was to add colour by hand to each frame of the film. R. W. Paul's show at the Alhambra on 8 April 1896 included a hand-coloured film of an 'Eastern Dance . . . endowed with a brilliancy of colour that results in a very striking effect . . . [it] excited much enthusiasm', said *The Era*. Whether Paul was the first to present coloured films is not certain; a film of a very similar subject, the *Serpentine Dance*, coloured in red, blue and pale green, was in the first programme of the Vitascope, reported by the *New York Herald* on 3 May 1896. Whether this was the same film that Paul had shown we cannot say. It is likely that some films for the Kinetoscope had been coloured previously, but Paul seems to have been the first to project films in colour. Paul was certainly colouring films in April 1896; *The Era* of 2 May 1896 reported that the film of the 1895 Derby was now being shown in colour. The week before, it had described the method used:

'The colours have to be very carefully chosen, and then every photograph has to be painted, with the aid of a magnifying glass, in identical tints. The photographs are about the size of a postage stamp; and the work of colouring them occupies nearly three weeks – greatly increasing the cost of the exhibition, of course.'

By September 1896 the *British Journal of Photography* was able to report, 'The colouring of the pictures is almost a matter of course now, and the mingled effect of the many separately coloured positives makes every tint harmonious and pleasant'. Some of Paul's colouring was done by Mr Doubell, formerly a slide painter to the old Royal Polytechnic Institution, who, it was said, painted only two or three frames a day, under a powerful magnifier. Normally, however, the colouring was carried out by a team of painters, usually girls, each of whom applied one colour to the print before passing it to a colleague. For an important production, as many as six colours might be applied, although two or three were more usual. The colouring presented great problems, since the picture was only one inch by three-quarters in size. Henry Hopwood pointed out the problems in 1899:

'In an ordinary single lantern slide outline is of little moment, in a Living Picture it is everything. A spire of a church in the single view does not offend the eye if the colouring oversteps the proper outline, provided that the shape is rendered symmetrical. Far

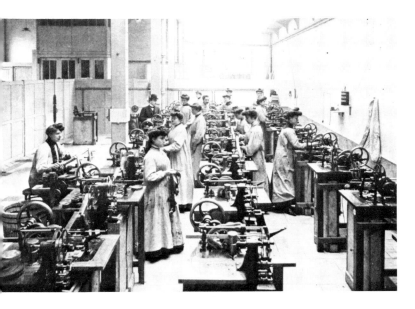

The Pathécolor printing room, where
colours were applied to prints through
stencil films

other in a Living Picture. The slightest variation between successive views gives rise to a continuous bulging and contraction which no respectable church would allow its steeple to indulge in. . . . Therefore, so far as regards the actual colouring, it should be of the nature of tinting rather than partaking in the gaudy display of the average lantern slide. Further, it should be done with extreme accuracy; better no colouring than a spoiled film . . .'

As the popularity of the new medium grew, so did the number of copies required from each film. The length of each subject grew from the minute or less of the first films to five, ten or even more minutes. To hand colour large numbers of long films became impossible, although it continued to be used for short sequences or for special effects – for example, the raising of the revolutionary flag in *The Battleship Potemkin* made by Sergei Eisenstein in 1925 was given extra dramatic impact by handcolouring the flag red. Here only a few dozen frames were involved.

To speed up the production of quantities of coloured films in 1905 the Pathé company adapted a method then in use for colouring postcards (see panel above). The Pathécolor stencil process started with the production of several positive copies of the film, from which, frame by frame, were cut those areas which were to be tinted in a particular colour. Up to six stencil films, one for each colour to be printed, were made. At first, the stencils were hand cut with fine knives like scalpels, but soon the process was mechanized. A master copy of the film was rear-projected onto a ground glass screen, one frame at a time. The operator moved a pointer over the screen, following the outline of the areas to be removed. A pantograph mechanism reduced the movement ten times, moving a vibrating cutting needle over another copy of the film, removing the relevant areas. The two films moved through the cutting machine in step with each other; it took about one hour to cut a metre of film. When the required number of stencils had been cut, the gelatin emulsion was stripped from them, and they were passed through a staining machine in registration with a positive print. A large toothed sprocket wheel ensured precise alignment of the two films, and the colour was applied by an endless loop of velvet ribbon, charged with dye by a rotating brush. The dye passing through the holes in the stencil coloured only those parts of the picture appropriate to it.

Hand-coloured film made with the 60mm Demeny-Gaumont Chronophotographe for a stage show, *La Biche au Bois* at the Chatelet Theatre, Paris in November 1896

Tinted and toned frames (below and bottom) from Herbert Ponting's film of the Scott Antarctic expedition, 1911-12, *The Great White Silence*

The film made several passes through as many machines as there were colours to be applied, and stencils prepared. The preparation of the stencils took a long time but once made, the stencils could be used to colour prints at high speed. About 300 women were employed by Pathé on the colouring work at their Vincennes factory. A minimum of 200 prints was normally necessary for each film, to make the process economic. The name of the process was changed to Pathé-chrome in 1929 but the principle remained the same. The stencil colouring method remained in use well into the 1930s.

A similar process was adopted by Gaumont around 1908. A 1912 advertisement for Gaumont coloured films claimed 'NO BRUSH-WORK – [they] reproduce all the hues of Nature in their true tonal values, and are entirely devoid of disturbing "rainbow" effects round rapidly moving parts of the picture'. (The latter reference is to characteristics of a rival photographic colour process, described on page 118.) Gaumont claimed that the colours were blended under the supervision of skilled artists, and were added to the film 'by the latest appliances'.

A process for the mechanical application of colour to a film strip was devised by Max Handschiegl in 1916, who, with Alvin Wyckoff, brought it to commercial application in America in the early 1920s. A separate print was made for each colour to be applied. Each frame was blocked out with opaque paint in the areas to which colour should be applied. A duplicate negative was made from the blocked out print, developed in a tanning developer which hardened the gelatin layer where it had been exposed and developed. Those areas corresponding to the blocked out areas on the print remained relatively soft, and capable of taking up dye. This dyed matrix film was brought into contact, in accurate register, with a positive print, to which the dye transferred in the appropriate areas. The print made several passes through the dye transfer machines, in contact with a separate matrix for each colour. Usually, three colours were applied. The process was used for, among other films, Cecil B. de Mille's *Joan, the Woman* (1917) (for which the process was developed), *Greed* (1924), *Volcano* (1926), *Phantom of the Opera* (1930), *The Merry Widow* (1925), *The Big Parade* (1925) and *The Lights of Broadway* (1925).

Rather less expensive but also less selective colouring methods were used to colour movie films. The black and white picture was given a wash of colour by bathing the film in a dye. The dye colours were chosen, at least in theory, to suit the content and mood of the story. Yellow was used for sunlit scenes and lamplit interiors; blue was chosen for night-time scenes. Blue-green or green was applied to seascapes and landscapes, fire scenes were given extra impact by red tinting and so on. The change from one colour to another might be used to heighten the effect of the story; for example, in a Pathé production of about 1910 an arsonist approached a factory at night. The scene was tinted blue but changed suddenly to red when the fire was started, producing a very effective impact.

An alternative to dyeing the film was to print it on stock made from coloured celluloid. The Belgian Gevaert company was the first to introduce coloured film bases, in 1912. Such films had the advantage of a much more even colouring than that given by dyeing the film. So widespread was the use of tinted films that in the mid-1920s it was very unusual to see a major production made entirely in black and white, the great majority of films being tinted at least in part, if not throughout.

Pathécolor

The Pathecolor stencil process was developed to mechanize the tinting of black and white prints. Introduced in 1905, it was operated up to the early 1930s. A print of the film to be coloured was projected one frame at a time onto a small screen. The operator moved a pointer over the enlarged picture, outlining all the areas to be tinted in a particular colour. A pantographic mechanical linkage connected to the pointer moved a cutter over another film strip, cutting out all these areas. As many as six stencil films might be prepared for as many different colours. The stencil films were run in contact with a new print through staining machines which applied dyes of suitable colours through the holes. The film ran through as many machines as there were colours.

Original film   *Red*   *Blue*   *Brown*   *Green*   *Yellow*

The Last Days of Pompeii, *1926, coloured by the Pathécolor stencil process*

The Life of Christ, *c. 1909, Pathécolor stencil process*   *Pathécolor stencil film, c. 1925*

The coming of sound films created a new problem: the dyes used to colour the film absorbed too much of the light by which the sound track was 'read' by the photocell. In 1929 the Eastman Kodak Company introduced a range of 16 Sonochrome film stocks on tinted celluloid, the colours of which did not interfere with the sound track. The colours were identified by exotic names: Inferno, Rose Dorée, Peach-blow, Fleur de Lys, Nocturne, Caprice and so on. Tinted films survived well into the era of the modern colour films, still being released in the 1960s.

Another method of producing a general colour effect was to tone the image. In this technique, the normal black and white silver image was converted to a coloured image, with the highlights – the lightest tones – remaining white. In the case of the tinted films, the image remained black and white, being overlaid by a wash of colour which coloured the highlights. Toning could be done in several ways. One method was to convert the silver image to another metallic form which was coloured. For example, toning with an iron compound produced a blue-green colour; uranium toning produced a reddish image and treatment with a sulphur compound converted the silver to silver sulphide, giving a warm brown, or sepia, tone. Alternatively, the silver image could be removed altogether and replaced by a transparent dye image. To produce more elaborate effects, tinting and toning could be combined. A sunset over the sea might be blue toned for the sea and sky, then dyed red or orange to tint the sun and clouds. These techniques would be used in suitable combinations. A typical film might be made up from mixed sequences of tinted, toned, stencil-coloured and black and white film. Although these techniques could be effective in their own way, the colours were not natural, and it was more by luck than by skill if the picture resembled the original colouring of the subject.

All practical methods of colour photography are based upon the principles proposed by James Clerk Maxwell in 1855 and demonstrated by him during a lecture at the Royal Institution in London in 1861. Maxwell showed that virtually all naturally occurring colours could be matched by an appropriate mixture of red, green and blue light. Using three lanterns, he projected three slides made from three negatives exposed through red, green and blue liquid filters. Each negative had recorded the proportions of one of those three colours present in the subject, a tartan ribbon. The positive transparencies made from the negatives were projected through similar filters to those used for exposure and the three coloured images were carefully superimposed upon the screen. There, they added together to reproduce the colour of the original. Although Maxwell's experiment gave only an imperfect rendering of the colour, due to deficiencies in the materials available to him, it worked well enough to demonstrate the principles on which colour photography is based. A successful application of those principles had to wait for the development of photographic materials which were sensitive to light of all colours.

In 1873 Dr Vogel discovered that by adding dyes to the sensitive material, its sensitivity could be extended, so that it would record green as well as blue. The new 'orthochromatic' plates were available commercially from 1882. The first really efficient dyes, extending the sensitivity of the photographic emulsion to all visible colours, were not available until the early years of this century, but by the late 1890s photographic materials could be made sensitive to orange and red-orange light, making colour photography practical.

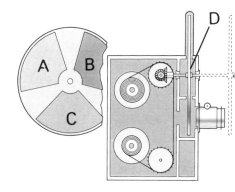

Lee and Turner's colour camera, 1899, had a rotating wheel fitted with red, green and blue filters (A, B, C). The wheel (D) could be placed behind or before the lens

The Lee and Turner projector, 1902, used 38mm wide film bearing successive colour separation exposures, projected through three lenses and rotating colour filters

The first attempt to apply Maxwell's experiment to cinematography was described in an English patent filed by F. Marshall Lee and Edward R. Turner on 22 March 1899. They proposed a camera fitted with a rotating wheel before the lens, carrying segments of red, green and blue filter. Thus, in succession on the film, three frames were exposed recording the proportions of these primary colours in the subject. The film was to be projected in a three-lens projector, in which a triple gate allowed three frames at a time to be shown and superimposed on the screen. As the film moved through the projector, each frame was projected three times, a rotating filter wheel with three concentric bands of coloured filters ensuring that on each projection the frame was shown in the colour appropriate to it.

A camera was built for Lee and Turner by A. Darling of Brighton in 1901. It used a film 1½in (38mm) wide, perforated between the frames. A working projector was built by April 1902. Turner died soon after. Charles Urban acquired the patent rights and contracted with George Albert Smith, a Brighton film maker, to continue the experiments. The process proved impractical to operate and Smith investigated other methods of making moving coloured pictures. Since the motion picture is based upon the principle that persistence of vision will permit a series of pictures to be added together to give the illusion of a continuous image, Smith investigated the possibility of making a colour photograph by projecting the component images in rapid succession. The idea had been patented by H. Isensee in Germany on 17 December 1897 but there is no evidence that he had made his method work. The problem was that if the three colour components were shown in succession at the normal rate of 16 pictures in a second a terrible effect of colour flickering was produced, which only became bearable at projection speeds of at least 48 pictures per second. Such high speeds made intolerable demands on both mechanism and film.

In 1906 Smith hit on an idea which for the first time made possible a practical colour movie film process. He found that by using only two of the primary colours, red and green, he could still produce a colour picture with an acceptably wide range of colours. He patented his two-colour method in November 1906. Smith used a camera, a modified Urban Bioscope, fitted with a rotating wheel bearing red and green filters, which passed between the lens and the film so that alternate frames were exposed to one of the two colours. The negative film was processed and printed and the black and white positive was shown in a projector also fitted with a filter wheel between the lamp and the gate. The film was threaded so that the red-exposed frame was projected by red light and the green-exposed frame by green light. The projector (and camera) operated at 32 pictures per second. At this speed, the alternate red and green frames combined to give a colour image with a surprisingly wide range of colour and only slight colour flickering. Flesh tints, a most critical subject, were particularly well rendered. The new process was named Kinemacolor, and was first demonstrated publicly at the Royal Society of Arts on 9 December 1908, although there had been a private show to the press at Charles Urban's headquarters, Urbanora House, on 1 May. From 26 February 1909 Kinemacolor was included as part of the regular programme at the Palace Theatre of Varieties in London. Kinemacolor films were shown in Paris at the Folies Bergères in April 1909, in Berlin at the Winter

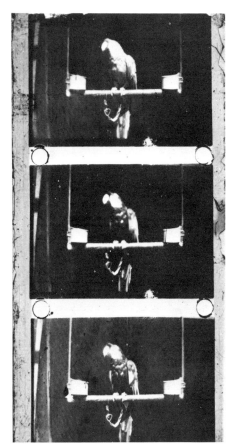

Lee and Turner colour film, c. 1902. The three frames represent records of red, green and blue

A Debrie Parvo camera fitted with a rotating two-colour filter wheel, for Kinemacolor filming

A pair of frames from the Kinemacolor film of the Delhi Durbar, 1912.

BELOW Interested spectator at the Delhi Durbar

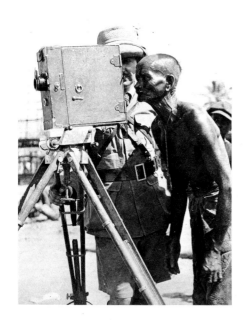

Garden in the autumn of 1909, while New Yorkers were able to see them in Madison Square Gardens on 11 December 1909. From 11 April 1911, Kinemacolor had a permanent home in London at the Scala Theatre.

One of the first major Kinemacolor productions was a comprehensive record of the Coronation procession of King George V and the Naval Review, shown on 28 June 1911 soon after the events had taken place. At the end of that year Charles Urban and seven of his best cameramen left for India to record in Kinemacolor the impressive ceremony of the Royal Durbar in Delhi, in honour of the new King-Emperor. A record lasting almost six hours was produced and was shown in two parts at the Scala from 2 February 1912. The theatre was crowded at every performance. A major documentary film on the making of the Panama canal was also completed and shown at the end of 1912. The *Pall Mall Gazette* said,

'Kinemacolor . . . passes from triumph to triumph. After an unparalleled success with the wonderful Durbar pictures, it enthralled a large audience last night with a no less astounding pictorial view of the making of the Panama Canal; it was followed with the intensest interest, and received with frequent outburst of irrepressible applause.'

The *Daily Telegraph* was equally enthusiastic:

'instructive as they are on the technical side, it is for their pictorial beauty probably that they will be most highly prized. No verbal description of what has been accomplished could possibly create, even approximately, the profound impression which these pictures by their vividness and perfect colouring produce on the mind of the spectator. To use a well-worn phrase, they must be seen to be believed.'

The Natural Color Kinematograph Company leased the rights to Kinemacolor on a regional basis, in which each operator had an exclusive franchise for his area, except in London where at the beginning of 1913 five theatres were showing regular Kinemacolor programmes, with others in the suburbs. Kinemacolor films were shown in twelve other countries and agents all over the world shot new subjects, which were released at the rate of several each week. This first practical method of colour cinematography was a great success, both technically and financially, from the moment it appeared. But it had its faults. Rapidly moving objects showed pronounced red and green fringes, since the two colour components were taken one after the other, and some colours, especially pure blues, were quite inadequately rendered. On the whole the quality was good, although the subjects were chosen so as to minimise these problems.

Inevitably, the success of Kinemacolor led to the appearance of imitations. One company, Friese Greene Patents Ltd had been formed in 1908 to exploit several patents, mostly impractical, filed by Friese Greene. From this came a new company, Biocolour Ltd, led by Colin Bennett, a former Kinemacolor cameraman. In Brighton in 1911 he began to present films made in a very similar way to those of Kinemacolor, except that instead of using a rotating filter wheel on the projector, the positive films were stained red and green on alternate frames. The Natural Color Kinematograph Company instituted proceedings for infringement of patent rights against Biocolour and for the next three years litigation dragged on. Biocolour, now renamed Bioschemes Ltd, on 18 December 1913 applied for the revocation of Smith's patent on the grounds of non-originality, insufficient description and prior public use before the patent was published, but the judge found the case not proven on all points, and the petition was dismissed.

In April 1914 Bioschemes appealed, and the Court of Appeal reversed the judgement and revoked Smith's patent. The Kinemacolor owners appealed to the House of Lords and in March 1915 their appeal was dismissed on the grounds that the patent had not specified the precise colours to be used, and that it had implied that a full colour reproduction was possible, instead of a pleasing compromise. There was, however, no question about the originality of the process. To protect the creditors of the Natural Color Kinematograph Company it went into voluntary liquidation in April 1914 and a new company, Kinemacolor Ltd, was formed to acquire the assets and property of the old company.

The Kinemacolor process continued to operate successfully well into the First World War, when another of its major productions, *Britain Prepared*, a film about the army and navy was shown in January 1916. The *Kinematograph Weekly* reviewed the film! 'Some of the pictures are so delicate, so artistic, and so remarkably vivid in their detail, so perfect in their composition, that they inevitably call to mind the work of Turner at his best.' During the next 20 years a number of revivals of the Kinemacolor principle of successive frame two-colour projection were demonstrated, although few got beyond this stage. They included Panchromotion (1913), Douglass Color (1916), early Prizma Color (1917), Biocolour – an improved version by Claude Friese Greene (1924), Vocolor (1932), Morgana Color –a 16mm film version for amateurs devised by Lady Williams of Pontyclud and demonstrated by Bell & Howell – (1932), and Omnicolor (1933).

Once Kinemacolor had shown that two-colour reproduction could give an adequate colour reproduction, other processes appeared in which pairs of red and green exposures were made simultaneously on the film and projected in superimposition. Usually, the two colour records were half the normal frame size, side by side in the normal frame area. To achieve this, either two small lenses were used, or a single lens fitted with a system of prisms which split

Biocolour film, 1911, a rival variant of the Kinemacolor process, had alternate frames stained red and green, so that no rotating filter was needed on the projector. However, the colour was less consistent than that of Kinemacolor

BELOW LEFT When the two frames of the Colcin film, 1913, were projected in superimposition through red and green filters they produced a colour picture. The two-colour records were fitted into the standard frame area (below)

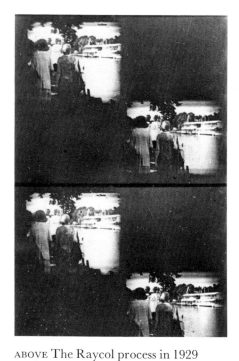

ABOVE The Raycol process in 1929 made two quarter-size colour records in opposite corners of the standard frame

ABOVE RIGHT Colin Bennett's Cinechrome film of the early 1920s used an extra wide film with the two full size colour records side by side

An improved version of Raycol, 1933, placed the two-colour records one above the other. This example is from the only Raycol feature film *The Skipper of the Osprey*

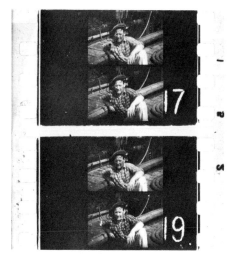

the light beam into two. The first two-colour additive method in which the two components were taken and projected simultaneously was the Colcin process, in 1913. The result of a Franco-Japanese collaboration, it was demonstrated at the International Kinematographic Exhibition in London in March 1913. Little more was heard of it. Cinechrome Ltd was formed in 1914 by Colin Bennett and for seven years he worked on various methods of obtaining two colour records on one film, using lens and prism devices. In the early 1920s Cinechrome used an extra wide film with two rows of normal sized frames, representing red and green exposures, side by side. The film, which was perforated down the centre as well as at the edges, was produced by Kodak Ltd. A Cinechrome film of the visit to India by the Prince of Wales was made by S. J. Cox in 1921. It was presented at the Royal Society of Arts in 1922 and later at the Stoll Theatre. After 1925 the process, renamed Cinecolor, reverted to the use of a normal film with two half-size pictures within the normal frame area, taken with a beam-splitting lens and prism device, but little commercial use was made of it.

In 1926 in Germany the Busch process was demonstrated; the film ran horizontally in the camera and a system of prisms split the beam from the lens into two, exposing two half-frame sized red and green records within the normal frame area. The projector ran the film conventionally, and a prism system rotated the two side by side images and superimposed them on the screen, through the appropriately coloured filters. The process was first used mainly for scientific cinematography but some advertising films were made with it around 1930.

The British Raycol process had some interesting features. Exploited by a company headed by the producer Maurice Elvey, in 1929 the Raycol process used a beam splitting optical system which produced a pair of quarter-sized pictures diagonally disposed within the normal frame – a rather wasteful arrangement, since half the available picture area was not used. To project the film, an ordinary projector was used, with the lens replaced by a special Raycol lens. The Raycol lens consisted of two D-shaped half lenses, one fitted with a red filter, and the other with no filter at all. The result of superimposing a red picture upon a black and white one might have been expected to produce only a washed-out reddish coloured image, but in fact a subjective impression of quite a wide range of colours was produced, albeit somewhat pale. This method was based upon an invention of Dr A. Barnadi patented in 1928. The advantage of this unusual projection arrangement was that the picture on the screen was rather brighter than it would have been with a green filter in use. The *Kinematograph Weekly* said there was an 'extraordinary range of colours almost certainly evoked by contrast'. A later report in the same journal said the results were 'pleasing . . . in some cases remarkable'.

In 1930 Albion Productions shot a short film, *The School for Scandal*, in Raycol, with Elvey directing. It was the first sound colour film to be made in England. By August 1932, it was claimed that 800 cinemas in the British Isles were equipped for Raycol projection, showing mostly short films. In 1933 the arrangement of the film was changed and the two small frames were placed one on top of the other in the centre of the frame. In July 1933, filming started on the first Raycol feature film, *The Skipper of the Osprey*. The trade press gave poor reviews to the film, criticising the poor definition, pastel shades and colour fringing. All additive processes involving the superimposition of two or more separate images produced some degree of colour fringing, due to the impossibility of exactly superimposing pictures projected through separate lenses. In the case of Raycol, the tiny images required considerable magnification, making registration that much more difficult and leading to poor definition and loss of screen brightness. After the release and failure of *The Skipper of the Osprey*, no more films were made in Raycol and nothing else was heard of the process.

Although the two-colour additive processes had the virtue of simplicity, they were limited in the range of colours they could reproduce. After the unsuccessful Lee and Turner process, the first practical three-colour process to be shown was developed by Léon Gaumont in France. In 1912 he patented a three-lens camera in which the three frames of film were exposed simultaneously through three filters, although successive exposures through a filter wheel were also proposed. To minimize the mechanical problems of moving long lengths of film intermittently, the height of each frame was reduced by a quarter. The projector used a triple lens unit, with the lenses sawn into oblong shapes to bring them close together, so as to reduce the fringing due to their separation. In fact, the registration in the Chronochrome process, as Gaumont christened it, was quite good, according to reports. The Chronochrome system was demonstrated first at the Société Français de Photographie on 15 November 1912. It was shown in London at the Coliseum, on a 20 × 12-foot (6.1 × 37 metre) screen on 16 January 1913. The *British Journal of Photography* said that it 'might well be more brilliant . . . [but was] admirable in all other respects'. The *Sheffield Daily Telegraph*, after the first provincial show in July 1913, said that it 'reproduces all vivid colours and delicate tints, brings a fullness and satisfaction that have not been attained before'. At its showing in New York in June 1913, at the 39th Street Theatre, the Chronochrome programme included some colour films with synchronised sound by the Gaumont Chronophone method. Chronochrome remained in limited use for some years; in 1919 a spectacular film record of the great victory parade in Paris was made.

At the cost of introducing some mechanical complication, the Chronochrome process achieved good quality by using three almost full-size component images. Most of the later processes using the same idea of simultaneous projection tried to pack the same information into the normal single frame area. The German Horst process of 1926, exposed the three colour records on a 60mm wide film in the camera, using a beamsplitting prism device behind the lens to give one picture above two others side by side. The developed negative film was printed by reduction onto a conventional 35mm film, so that the three small pictures ended up within a standard frame area. A triple projection lens arrangement superimposed them on the screen, through the appropriate filters. Several demon-

The Gaumont Chronochrome process, 1912, used a special three lens camera to record three almost full-size frames through red, green and blue filters. This example is from the Chronochrome record of the victory parade in Paris, 1919

The German Horst three-colour process, 1926, recorded three colour records on a special 60mm wide film, printed down to the standard film for projection

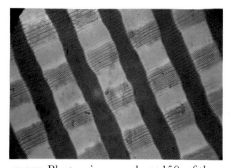

ABOVE Photomicrograph, ×150, of the colour reseau of the early Spicer-Dufay Dufaycolor reversal film

RIGHT Dufaycolor negative film, 1937, recorded the scene in complementary colours as well as reversed tones

BELOW RIGHT When printed onto Dufaycolor positive film the original colours and tones were restored

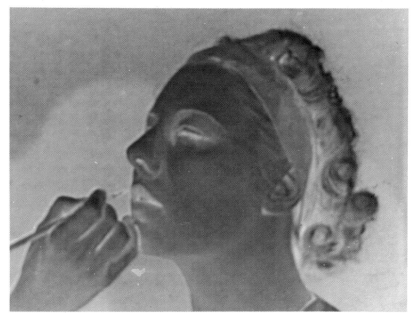

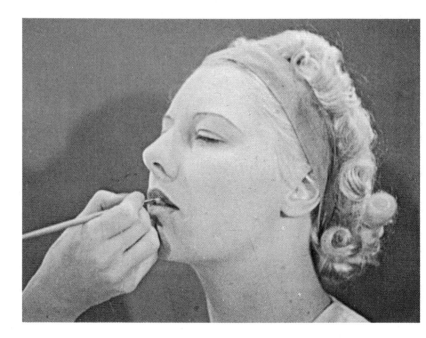

The French Franchita three-colour process was used to film the Coronation procession of King George VI in 1937

stration films were shown in 1930 in the Horst process: 'Flesh tints were admirable', said the *Kinematograph Weekly*, but little more was heard of it.

Another process using three separation images within the standard frame was invented by Maurice Velle in France and demonstrated there under the name Franchita, and as Opticolor in America and England. The first form of the process, shown in 1931, used an arrangement similar to the Horst process, with one small frame above two others, taken and projected by triple lens systems. By 1933, the method had altered to one in which two of the exposures were made one above the other, with the third to one side. A complicated mechanical and optical system was used in the camera to achieve this, but projection was straightforward, with a triple lens system. The new Franchita process was used to make a number of short films and a feature length production was shown in Paris in

1935. The Coronation procession in London in 1937, and the Changing of the Guard, were shot in the Franchita process. It was said to have been successful, within the inevitable limitations imposed upon it by the very small picture size, and the use of several lenses.

Several three-colour additive processes were proposed which used more complex methods of taking and projecting the pictures. One was devised by J. Szczepanik in 1924, and demonstrated by him the following year. He revived an idea that C. Francis Jenkins had tried at the very beginning of cinematography. The film was moved through the camera continuously, being exposed through a series of 18 lenses, carried on an endless belt moving in synchronism with the film. The lenses were fitted in sequence with red, green and blue filters, so that a succession of separation exposures was made on the film. The projector had a similar arrangement of lenses, so that at any given moment, the image on the screen was made up of super-imposed red, green and blue pictures, the combination of which constantly changed as the film and the lenses moved. Reports of the demonstrations said that the films showed inferior definition, flicker and poor colour balance. Although the optical company of Busch, in Germany, showed interest in the process, only a few cameras were made, and Szczepanik's process had no commercial use.

The Hérault Trichrome process was demonstrated in Paris on 1 October 1926, with three films made by A. Rodde – a fashion show, a documentary on Brittany and a tableau of the *Legend of the King of Ys*. Hérault Trichrome was an extension of the Kinemacolor principle to three-colour work, with successively exposed red, green and blue frames. The positive print was stained in these primary colours and projected at 24 frames per second. The colour flickering must have been almost intolerable.

The problem underlying all these additive processes was that the component images were produced and projected either by a separation in time through a single lens, or a separation in space through separate lenses. The former produced colour fringing on moving objects, the latter produced colour fringing over at least part of the screen. In addition, the use of smaller than normal frame sizes on

ABOVE The Spicer-Dufay reversal Dufaycolor film, 1931, was the first additive colour movie process to give a direct colour picture without additional optical devices

LEFT The Coronation Procession of King George VI, 1937, was filmed in the Dufaycolor negative-positive process

many of the processes led to poor definition. The problem was, how to record three images simultaneously through one lens on one film and how to superimpose those three images on a screen through one projection lens.

One solution was proposed by R. Berthon, a Frenchman, in 1909. He suggested the use of a film embossed with a series of minute lenses, or lenticles, on the celluloid base, shaped so as to produce on the film emulsion, an image of a three-colour banded filter fitted on the lens. The film was placed with the embossed base towards the lens. Each of the lenticles, acting like a miniature camera, split that part of the scene falling on it into three strips, exposed through the red, green and blue parts of the filter. The film, processed to a positive by reversal development, was projected through a lens fitted with a similar filter. The lenticles directed each strip of the picture behind them out through the appropriate filter band. The image on the screen was thus made up of very fine red, green and blue lines which, when viewed from a sufficient distance, could not be individually distinguished and added together to give a full colour image. Although the process was rather complicated in principle, it worked well in practice. Another Frenchman, A. Keller-Dorian, developed methods of embossing the film with round or cylindrical lenses, and the K.D.B. process (Keller-Dorian, Berthon) was publicly demonstrated on 17 December 1923 in the Hall of the Touring Club de France, after a number of private demonstrations during the previous year. The process was capable of results of high quality but there was considerable difficulty in printing copies of the film because of the complex nature of the optical arrangements needed and this virtually ruled it out as far as commercial use in the cinema was concerned. The major application of the principle came in 1928, when the Eastman Kodak Company launched a 16mm amateur film version. The Kodacolor film was the first colour process to be available to the amateur film maker and was very successful, despite some limitations. For example, the optical arrangements required that the lens be left at its maximum aperture of f/1.9 and exposure had to be controlled instead by the use of neutral density filters. Later, an ingenious ratio diaphragm was devised, acting like a pair of jaws, which reduced the exposure by masking down all three filters equally. The loss of light through absorbtion in the three-colour filter meant that only a small projected picture size was possible, although in the home this presented no great problem. The process was capable of very fine colour reproduction. It was finally discontinued in 1938, having been superceded by more efficient colour processes.

The lenticular film processes offered a greatly simplified method of taking and showing additive colour films as far as the user was concerned. The only modification to normal practice was the addition of the three-colour filter on the camera and projection lens. An even simpler process even did away with this by building the filters into the film itself. Since the 1890s there had been a number of still colour photographic processes in which a regular or irregular fine mosaic of microscopic colour filters was produced on the surface of a glass plate or film. Coated with emulsion, the plate or film was exposed through the base and filter mosaic, so that a single exposure made simultaneously three separate records on the same sensitive surface. Each part of the scene would record only behind those filters of a colour appropriate to it. When the emulsion was developed by reversal processing to a positive, the image would let more or

The lenticular film process invented by R. Berthon in 1909 was exploited commercially from 1928 with the introduction of 16mm Kodacolor film. The film base was embossed with cylindrical lenses, which, with a three-band colour filter placed in front of the lens, broke the image up into narrow vertical strips representing red, green and blue exposures. ABOVE A Kodacolor frame. BELOW An enlarged detail

less light through the tiny filters, depending on the colour of the original object recorded at that point. When seen from a sufficient distance, the pattern of red, green and blue dots merged to form a continuous coloured image. The mosaic colour processes were the only additive methods in which a colour image was given directly without the need for viewing lenses and filters. While the method worked well enough for still photography, where a relatively large plate or film was viewed directly, the huge magnifications involved in projecting cinema film at first ruled out the method for moving pictures, since the filter pattern was obtrusive on the screen. It took 20 years, after the general introduction of such processes in still photography, for a successful movie version to be produced.

The first public demonstration of the Spicer-Dufay mosaic colour processes was given in 1931. The film used a finely ruled, regular pattern of blue lines alternating with lines of red and green squares, giving about one million filter elements to the square inch. The process had originated in the Dufay Diopticolore and Dioptichrome processes of 1908 and 1909 – glass plate methods for still photography. Dufaycolor film was launched in 35mm size at the end of 1932, with an improved mosaic of red lines and green and blue squares. The trade press was impressed by the new process: 'Never before had such exquisite beauty been brought to the screen . . . [the] range and purity of the colours [are] unsurpassed by any existing system'. One report noted, however that 'a pure red seems so far elusive'. The film was manufactured for Spicer-Dufay by Ilford Ltd, who had devised a printing method for making positive copies from the positive originals. Dufaycolor was used at first for a number of short films, and sequences in the film *Radio Parade* of 1934 were shot in Dufaycolor when the process went into full production. There were mixed reviews of the film: the *Kinematograph Weekly* said that the Dufaycolor sequences were 'not up to the highest standards'. They had been shot in the studio, unlike the earlier demonstration films, and although the studio lighting had been quadrupled, it was still inadequate. For smaller scale studio use, and out of doors, the process worked very well. (See illustrations on previous page.)

The positive to positive process, however, had its drawbacks, and in due course a negative-positive process was developed, made possible by the creation of special developing and printing techniques. The camera film was given a single development to produce a colour negative in which not only was the tone range reversed but also the colours, which were reproduced as complementary to those of the original scene. Red was reproduced as blue-green, yellow as blue, green as magenta and so on. A mosaic print film was used for the prints, restoring the original tonal range and colours. The improved process was launched by the newly formed Dufay-Chromex company in 1937, when it was used to film King George VI's Coronation celebrations with great success, despite the poor weather.

Despite the convenience of the process, for which completely standard cameras and projectors were suitable, Dufaycolor was not widely used. Advertising, travel and documentary films were made but the only feature film was *Sons of the Sea*, made in 1939 and generally released in 1940. At its best, the colour could be very good, but the mosaic of colour filters, small though they were, was obtrusive on the screen, at least from the seats nearer the screen, since in a large cinema the frame was magnified in area 100,000 times or more. In addition, Dufaycolor suffered from a drawback inherent in all additive processes. The red, green and blue filters through which the pictures were projected by their very nature absorbed two thirds of the available projection light. Even in the brightest parts of the picture screen brightness was less than one third of that of a black and white film shown under the same conditions. If the colour filters were made lighter to increase the brightness of the projected pictures, then the depth of colour was correspondingly reduced.

An alternative method starts with white light, which is a mixture of all colours, and removes from it the colours which are not required, instead of building up all the colours by adding together several pictures in the primary colours red, green and blue. This can be done by using the complementary colours cyan (blue-green), magenta and yellow. Each of these absorbs one of the primary colours. For example, cyan absorbs red light; therefore, if a transparent cyan coloured image is made, the varying amount of this colour will remove in proportion red light from white light passed through it, acting therefore as did the black and white image and red filter of the additive process. Similarly, magenta will control green light and yellow will control blue. If three negative exposures are made to record the red, green and blue content of the scene, they may be printed to make three positives coloured cyan, magenta and yellow respectively, which if superimposed in exact register will combine to give a full colour reproduction of the original scenes. No complicated optical devices will be required to view the pictures, nor will they have an obtrusive line or mosaic structure. The subtractively coloured image will not absorb light strongly where there is no image, since all the projection light will be available to form the lightest parts of the picture on the screen. The principle of the subtractive colour process was described first by Louis Ducos du Hauron in 1868.

Although eminently suitable for colour motion pictures, the principle could not be applied until means were found of producing several colour images in exact registration on a single film. As with the additive processes, the first practical application was in the form of a two-colour method. Arturo Hernandez-Mejia described the first practical process in 1912. His Cinecolorgraph method used a camera fitted with a beam-splitting device which allowed two frames to be exposed at once through red and green filters. By using a special printer which printed every other negative frame, all the red-exposed negatives were printed on one side of a special film coated with emulsion on both sides. All the green exposures were printed on the other side of the same film, so that those frames exposed at the same time ended up on opposite sides of the same film strip, in exact registration. After processing, the black and white images were colour toned, blue-green for the red records and red-orange for the green records. Although the range of reproduced colours was limited, an adequate, commercially acceptable result was possible. The Colorgraph company did not progress beyond the stage of making demonstration films, but Hernandez-Mejia's method was adopted by many other companies, with various modifications, over the next 40 years.

The two-colour Kodachrome process was introduced for still photography in 1913, using two positive images on glass plates placed face to face. The first experimental movie version was developed in 1915. Two adjacent frames on the negative film were exposed in the camera simultaneously, through red and green filters. From the negative film a positive print was made and placed in a special printer with an optical system which permitted the pairs

The two-colour Kodachrome process, 1922, used double-coated film with red and green images on opposite sides, printed from separation negatives

of positive pictures to be printed simultaneously onto opposite sides of a double-coated film. This film was then processed in a special tanning developer which hardened the emulsion where development took place, and in proportion to it. Since the image was a negative, the unhardened areas formed a positive which would take up dye. After the silver negative image had been bleached away, the film was dyed red-orange on one side, blue-green on the other, the dyes taking up proportionally in the more or less hardened gelatin.

The first film made in the Kodachrome process was an experimental production shot in July 1916, called *Concerning $1,000* to a scenario written by Mrs Sylvia Newton. The entry of the United States into the First World War inhibited any further development for the time being, and the process was not brought to the stage of commercial exploitation until 1922. Several short films were made in the Kodachrome process, including one concerning haute couture featuring the actress-model Miss Hope Hampton in 1926. The Fox Film Corporation adopted the process in 1929, building a new $1,000,000 laboratory to exploit the renamed 'Nature Color' process. A few films were made in it by Fox, including *The London Revue* of 1930, but not much was heard of it after that.

William Van Doren Kelley, an American pioneer colour worker, had operated several variants of the Kinemacolor process from 1913, when he formed his first company, Panchromotion, later renamed Prizma Inc. His first, additive, film used a filter wheel on the projector, and was called *Our Navy*. It was shown at the 44th Street Theatre in New York in 1917. In 1918 he turned to subtractive colour photography and with Carroll H. Dunning developed the Kesdacolor process. The double coated film was printed on each side from negatives exposed through a fine screen of red and green lines. The first and only Kesdacolor film, *The American Flag*, lasted less than a minute, and was shown at the Roxy and Rialto theatres in New York on 12 September 1918. Soon after, Kelley reorganised the Prizma company and developed an improved two-colour subtractive process under the Prizma name. A one-reel travelogue, *Everywhere with Prizma*, was shown at the Rivoli theatre, New York in 1919. J. Stuart Blackton, a movie producer, was impressed, and

Fox 'Nature Color' was a version of the two-colour Kodachrome process, used for a short time around 1930

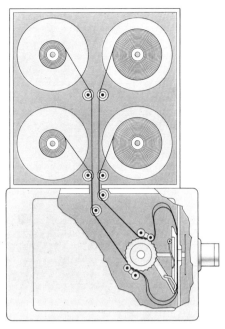

Cameras for bipack negatives were fitted with double magazines. The two films were run emulsion to emulsion together through the gate

Agfa bipack negatives provided colour records for printing on double-coated film. The poorer definition in the negative exposed behind the other (left) can be seen

contracted with Prizma to make a costume drama, *The Glorious Adventure*, released in April 1922. Other Prizma films made in 1923 included *Vanity Fair* and *The Virgin Queen*, as well as a number of shorts.

Aaron Hamburger's successful Polychromide process for still photography, operated in England from 1911, was adapted by him for cine work around 1918. It was demonstrated under the name Veracolor in 1924, but was better known under its original name. A special camera with a beamsplitter behind the lens exposed two negative films through red and green filters. As usual, the developed negatives were printed onto opposite sides of double coated film, which was exposed and processed to give a rather 'thin' black and white image. Each side of the film was dyed with a mixture of dyes – magenta and red on one side, malachite green and blue on the other. Treatment in a mordanting bath fixed the dyes in the film only where there was a silver image, and in proportion to it. Hamburger claimed that the use of mixtures of dyes gave a wider colour range. The Polychromide process was used into the middle 1930s, although only for short films.

One of the problems facing any colour film maker was how to obtain the pairs of negatives used to print the double coated positive film, without resorting to complicated and expensive optical systems. One solution was an adaptation of a method that had been used in still photography – the bipack, a pair of negative plates or films emulsion to emulsion, one exposed through the other. One of the first colour movie processes to use bipack negatives was the American Multicolor system, announced in 1928. A pair of negative films made and sold by Dupont under the name 'Rainbow Negative' were run emulsion to emulsion through a modified Mitchell camera. The upper film was orthochromatic, responding to blue and green light, and carried a filter layer which prevented those colours from passing through to the underlying panchromatic film, which responded to the orange and red light passing through the upper film. The negatives, exposed simultaneously in a single gate in the camera, were processed and printed onto double-coated film as usual. The print film was toned blue-green with iron on one side and red-orange with uranium on the other, the latter being also treated with a red dye to improve the colour. The Multicolor process was acquired by Howard Hughes in 1930 for a reputed $1,000,000. He had great hopes for the process, and built a $500,000 laboratory for it, with a capacity for producing three million feet of film per week. Despite all this Multicolor was little used. Multicolor sequences were included in *The Great Gaboo*, (1929), *Fox Movietone Follies of 1929* and other films, although mostly shorts were made. The last Multicolor film, *Dolores the Beautiful*, was reviewed in 1932 by the *Kinematograph Weekly*: 'The colour is good, though rather of the picture postcard variety'. In 1932 the process for which so much was anticipated was moribund, and the laboratories were taken over by another company, Cinecolor Inc. This company developed a process based on Multicolor, using a similar method of bipack negatives printed onto metal-toned double coated positive films. Cinecolor, announced in 1932, was used primarily for short films until 1940, when the first Cinecolor feature was produced – *The Gentleman from Arizona*. It was used extensively in the 1940s by many major Hollywood companies, particularly for costume dramas and Westerns; at its peak, the Cinecolor laboratories were producing 120 million feet (36,576 km) of colour prints in a year. After the ntroduction of the modern colour films in the early 1950s, the demand for Cinecolor dropped off and it was discontinued in 1954.

The American Magnacolor process was one of several descended from Kelley's Prizma process, and was introduced in 1931. Like Multicolor, it used bipack negatives and double-coated film, iron-toned blue-green on one side and dye-toned red-orange on the other. It was used for a number of films, mostly Westerns, including *Home on the Range, Rough Riders of Cheyenne, Man from Rainbow Valley* and *Last Frontier Uprising*. Other American two-colour processes demonstrated around 1930 included Photocolor (1930) which used a two-lens camera to produce the negatives, with a printing process similar to Polychromide; Vitacolor (1930) based on Prizma patents, and used for a few shorts; and Coloratura (1931) which used bipack negatives and double coated film specially treated so as to become selectively coloured on both sides after a single immersion in a bath of mixed blue toner and orange dye.

The great proliferation of these two-colour processes included several developed in Europe. The Dutch Sirius Color process (1929) used a camera with a beamsplitting system behind the lens to expose a single film, the film passing through two gates at right angles to each other. The double-coated print film was dye-toned. The process was demonstrated in London early in 1930 but was used only for a few shorts and advertising films. The German Ufacolor process used Agfa bipack negative films, and double coated film toned with iron and uranium. The process was demonstrated in 1930; it was used in England at that time under the name Chemicolor. The French Harmonicolor process, demonstrated in 1936, used Agfa bipack negative films. The double-coated film was stained on each side with a mixture of dyes, magenta and yellow-orange on one side, malachite green and blue-violet on the other. Treatment with a mordanting solution fixed the dyes to the silver image, the lighter densities being coloured yellow or green, the darker tones being coloured red-orange or blue-violet. After the removal of the silver image, the variation in the dye colours was supposed to give a wider colour range than that normally possible in a two-colour process. The first demonstration in London of Harmonicolor was the film *Talking Hands*, shown on 23 March 1936.

By the 1940s, most of the two-colour subtractive processes, apart from Cinecolor, were obsolete. The widespread use of the high-quality Technicolor process showed up the serious deficiencies in the simpler methods. The only significant new process using two-colour reproduction to appear after the Second World War was Consolidated Film Industries' Trucolor method, used in 1946 for *Out California Way* and for a number of other films, mostly second features. Bipack negatives were used to make prints on double-coated film, the emulsions of which contained colour couplers. These were substances which reacted with the products of the development process to form a coloured dye, in the position of, and in proportion to, the silver image. By development in a colour-forming developer, the two dye images were formed simultaneously, and the silver image was bleached away to leave transparent dye images. After 1950, Trucolor used the modern colour films, and by 1954 the two-colour process was obsolete and the last printing service was closed down.

While the two-colour processes provided a relatively simple means of producing colour movies, they were limited in the range of colours that they could produce. While full three-colour reproduction

RIGHT Multicolor, 1928-1932, was a two-colour process using double-coated film printed from bipack negatives

BELOW RIGHT Cinecolor was the most widely used of the two-colour processes in the 1940s

Mills' Zoechrome process, 1929, used a four-lens camera exposing alternate single black and white frames and three miniature colour separations. The film was printed by a complicated sequence of exposure, processing and resensitising

BOTTOM The final Zoechrome picture, the result of a sequence of printing and sensitizing operations (1929)

would be better, the problem was how to get three images onto one film. T. A. Mills patented a three-colour process in September 1921, which was demonstrated in 1929 under the name Zoechrome. Mills proposed a four-lens camera, one lens exposing a single, conventionally sized frame and the other three smaller lenses producing three small colour separation images in the space of the adjacent frame, the film being moved on two frames at a time. The alternate black and white full frame exposures were printed by a 'skip' printer in continuous sequence on a film, which was developed to give a conventional black and white print. This was varnished and recoated with emulsion and one of the smaller separation exposures was printed by enlargement in register with the existing image. The new print was dye-toned in the appropriate colour, varnished and recoated, and the second negative set was enlarged onto it, the print dye-toned and revarnished to receive yet another emulsion, and

ABOVE Ufacolor, 1930, a German two-colour process using Agfa bipack negatives and double-coated film

ABOVE LEFT *Pagliacci*, 1937, a film in Chemicolor, a two-colour process similar to Ufacolor

another printing and dye toning. This would seem to be doing things the hard way but the process worked adequately enough and reached the stage of trade demonstrations where it was described as a 'sound business proposition'. A reviewer said that the colour was 'as good as any I have seen'. It was claimed that £40,000 had been spent on the development of the process and in 1932 it was offered for sale. There were no takers.

The French Splendicolor process was shown to the Académie des Sciences early in 1929; it used a triple-lensed camera, the negatives from which were printed onto a film coated on one side with ordinary photographic emulsion and on the other with a clear gelatin layer. The gelatin layer was sensitized with a bichromate solution, and was then printed from a positive print made from the blue recording negative. The exposure selectively hardened the gelatin layer, which then took up yellow dye only in the unhardened, or less hardened areas. The film was coated with a second bichromated gelatin layer, which was exposed to a positive print from the green exposed negative and was dyed magenta. The conventional emulsion on the other side was printed from the red recording negatives, and dye-toned cyan. The process does not appear to have passed much beyond the stage of trade demonstrations.

The French Chimicolor process, developed by R. Valette from 1931 had a number of elements in common with Splendicolor. The specially designed camera produced three negative films, two of which were printed onto double-coated film, dye-toned cyan and magenta. One side was recoated with a bichromated gelatin layer and printed from a positive from the blue exposed negative. The selectively hardened gelatin layer was dyed yellow. The process had little use until after the Second World War, when it was employed for a time in the production of colour cartoons.

P. D. Brewster's first experiments in colour cinematography dated from before the First World War. On 12 April 1935 he demonstrated a three-colour subtractive process at the Royal Photographic Society in London, showing a film called *Let's Look at London*. He used a camera with rotating mirrors which directed the light from the lens in turn to three separate negative films. The prints were made on

A two-colour Technicolor camera used for productions in the early 1920s. A beam-splitter behind the lens (seen in the top picture) exposed two-colour separations at a time on a single film

Dr Kalmus with the improved two-colour Technicolor camera of the later 1920s

double-coated film on which the red and green exposures were printed and dye-toned to cyan and magenta images. The third, yellow, image was printed on one side of the film from a relief image made in bichromated gelatin, the thickness of which was proportional to the density of the image. The relief was dyed, and brought into contact with the final print film, to which the dye transferred. As with so many other processes, Brewster's did not pass beyond the stage of trade demonstrations.

The first entirely successful colour process used in the cinema was Technicolor. The company was formed in 1915 by Herbert Kalmus, Daniel Frost Comstock and W. A. Westcott. Their first process was a two-colour additive one, in which a camera with a beam splitter behind the lens exposed two frames at once. On the projector, a special optical system similar to that in the camera allowed the film to be projected through a single lens, registering the two images on the screen. The first Technicolor production was *The Gulf Between*, filmed in 1917. The processing was done in a mobile laboratory made from a converted railway carriage moved to Jacksonville, Florida, where the film was shot. The film was toured around the larger American cities but the precise adjustment required of the projection optical system proved to be a problem. Dr Kalmus said that it required an operator who was 'a cross between a college professor and an acrobat'.

This additive system was soon discarded in favour of a two-colour subtractive process. Negatives from the Technicolor camera were printed simultaneously onto two separate positive films made by the Eastman Kodak Company on specially thin film base. The exposed prints were processed so as to form relief images in the gelatin layer and the silver was removed. The two relief films were cemented back to back and the two gelatin layers were dyed red-orange and green to produce the final print. The first production in the new Technicolor process was *Toll of the Sea*, starring Anna May Wong. It was given its premiere at the Rialto Theatre on 26 November 1922 and was highly successful, grossing more than $250,000. The 'cemented positive' Technicolor process was used for colour sequences in several important films, including *The Ten Commandments* (1923), *Ben Hur* (1924) and *Cytherea* (1924). The next Technicolor feature film was *The Wanderer of the Wasteland* in 1924; this was also very successful, 175 copies being made for distribution throughout America. The biggest success of all for the early Technicolor process was Douglas Fairbanks' *The Black Pirate*, released in 1925. Dr Kalmus said,

'So far as audience reaction, press reviews, and box-office receipts were concerned, it was a triumph from the start, but for the Technicolor company it was a terrible headache.

Technicolor was still making the double-coated cemented together relief prints, so that the red and green images were not quite in the same plane, and the pictures didn't project too sharply on the screen. This double-coated film is considerably thicker than ordinary black-and-white film, with emulsion on both sides which tends to make it cup more readily and scratch more noticeably than black-and-white film. And the cupping could occur in either direction, more or less at random. Judging from the complaints, at each such change in the direction of cupping, the picture would jump out of focus. We sent new field men to the exchanges. We provided these men with a supply of new prints to replace the cupped ones in the theatres, in order that the latter might be shipped back to our laboratory in Boston for de-cupping. The newly decupped prints were temporarily satisfactory; the picture was a great success, but our troubles never ended.'

To overcome these problems, the Technicolor company perfected the technique of imbibition printing (see pages 134-5). The relief images produced on two print films were dyed and brought into contact with a blank gelatin coated film to which the dye transferred. The relief, or matrix, film could be redyed and used to print further copies. The transfer of the second coloured image from a second matrix film required an extremely precise printing machine in which the two films could be held in exact registration. The matrix films were produced from negatives from a greatly improved Technicolor camera developed in the mid-1920s. The imbibition process was introduced in 1928. It was used for sequences in *Broadway Melody* and *The Desert Song* in 1929, but the first major production was Warner Brothers' *On with the Show*, the first all-talking, all-Technicolor musical. *Gold Diggers of Broadway* was also shot in Technicolor in 1929, and was very successful, grossing $3,500,000. In 1930, Technicolor was contracted for 36 feature length productions. By now, the prints were made on a sensitized print film so that a silver image sound track could be printed on it.

In 1929, a three-colour camera was developed, taking three colour separation negatives in succession on one film, but this idea was soon discarded with the development of a new design, in which a prism beamsplitter behind the lens exposed three films running through two gates at right angles to each other. One gate took a bipack, with red and blue recording films, while the other took the green recording film. The first of the new 'three-strip' cameras was completed by May 1932, and Walt Disney was persuaded to use it for an experimental colour Silly Symphony cartoon called *Flowers and Trees*. This was so successful that Disney contracted with Technicolor for a whole series of films, finally adopting it for all Disney studios' productions (see pages 134-5).

The Technicolor process set the highest standards for colour in the cinema but suffered from the drawback that the three strip cameras were exceedingly expensive to produce, and were very large, even cumbersome, often presenting problems for location filming. The ideal material for colour cinematography was a single film, capable of use in any ordinary cine camera, which would be able in some way to make three simultaneous colour records. The concept of such a film, bearing three layers, each sensitized to one of the three primary colours and processed to yield three complementary coloured dye images, is derived from an idea which appeared quite early on in the development of colour photography. Louis Ducos du Hauron in 1895 proposed a multi-component pack of plates, films and filters which would make three separation negatives at one exposure and Dr J. H. Smith suggested a multilayer photographic plate for the same purpose in 1903. The principles behind the modern multilayer colour films were stated in a German patent by Rudolph Fischer in 1912. Manufacturing technology and chemistry were not able to produce working multilayer films until the 1930s, however.

A Hungarian chemist, Dr Bela Gaspar, worked on the development of a multilayer printing film: his Gasparcolor process was announced in 1933 and demonstrated in England the following year. The Gasparcolor film was coated with three layers, two on one

Two-colour Technicolor camera design, c. 1930. This example has been modified to expose three negatives in succession on a single film, an idea discarded in favour of the 'three-strip' camera

The 'three-strip' Technicolor camera, introduced in 1932 and used until the 1950s for three-colour Technicolor productions

In glorious Technicolor

The first successful Technicolor process was introduced in 1922. A two-colour camera with a beam splitter behind the lens recorded alternate images of the red and green content of the scene. A special printer printed the two sets of images simultaneously but separately onto two positive films on a specially thin film base produced by the Eastman Kodak Company. The exposed prints were processed to form relief images in the gelatin layer and the silver images were bleached away. The now transparent relief films were cemented back to back in register, and the reliefs were dyed red-orange and green to produce the final print. The 'cemented positive' process was used until 1928.

In 1928 an improved printing process was introduced in which the

Ben Hur, *1924, cemented-positive Technicolor*

Two-colour Technicolor imbibition print, 1929

Disney's Flowers and Trees, *1932, the first three-colour Technicolor film*

two relief images were produced as before, but the two films remained separate. They were dyed in appropriate colours and then brought in turn into close contact with a blank gelatin-coated film, to which the dye images were transferred with very precise registration. This method of imbibition or dye transfer printing formed the basis of the Technicolor process until the 1970s.

The imbibition printing process was extended to give three-colour prints in 1932, the relief or matrix films being derived from three negative films exposed in a newly designed 'three-strip' camera. Cyan, magenta and yellow dye images were transferred to the print film, which also carried a black and white 'key' image to improve definition and a silver soundtrack. The first three-colour Technicolor production was Walt Disney's cartoon *Flowers and Trees* (1932).

Three Little Pigs, *1933, cyan, magenta and yellow with a black and white key image*

The first live-action film shot in three-colour Technicolor was a short *La Cucharacha*, released in 1934. The first full-length feature to be shot entirely in three colour Technicolor was Pioneer Pictures' *Becky Sharp* (1935). This studio-shot production was very successful and was soon followed by an increasing number of colour feature films. The first Technicolor production made in England was *Wings of the Morning* (1936). This film was processed in America, but later in the year Technicolor established a laboratory at West Drayton, near London, to handle Technicolor productions in Europe. The large size and great weight of the 'three-strip' cameras complicated location filming but in 1937 *Trail of the Lonesome Pine* was shot entirely on location. In 1940

The first three-colour Technicolor feature, Becky Sharp, *1935*

Wings of the Morning, *1936, the first English Technicolor feature*

Henry V, *1944, colour by Technicolor*

The combined three-colour image made up of the frames opposite

Technicolor began development of a monopack film, based on the Eastman Kodak Kodachrome film. A single film exposed in the conventional cine camera was processed to give a direct colour positive. From this original, three black and white separation negatives were produced by printing through red, green and blue filters and these were used to produce the printing matrices as before. At first, Technicolor Monopack was used for

location filming sequences, the first use being in *Lassie Come Home* (1942). The first film to be shot entirely in Monopack was *Thunderhead – Son of Flicka* in 1944. After the introduction of Eastman Colour Negative in 1950, the three-strip cameras became obsolete, although the imbibition printing process remained in use until the 1970s, when the reduced demand for quantities of release prints made it uneconomic to continue to manufacture them.

side, one on the other. The three emulsions contained dyes, cyan on one side and magenta and yellow on the other, and were sensitized to red, green and blue light respectively. The film was printed in turn from three positive films made from separation negatives, through filters of the appropriate colour. As the exposed film was processed, the dyes in the three layers were destroyed in proportion to the development taking place. After the silver image had been bleached away, three positive dye images were left. Since the process required sets of separation negatives, its use was in the main limited to animated films. The three negatives could be made in succession on a single film when photographing still drawings or models. The colour was potentially very good, with strongly saturated colours. It continued in use until the outbreak of the Second World War, notably for George Pal's Puppetoon films.

The Gasparcolor process started with all the dyes present in the film, the process destroying them where they were not needed. Another method was to create the dyes during the processing operation, putting them in where they were needed. The first successful process of this kind, and the first of the modern colour films, came about as the result of the work of two young American professional musicians and amateur chemists, Leopold Mannes and Leo Godowsky. During the 1920s they had worked on a number of two-colour subtractive processes using two-layer coatings on glass. After some help from the Eastman Kodak Director of Research, Dr C. E. K. Mees, the two were invited to join the Research Laboratory, where they worked on methods of processing multilayer films, while their colleagues tackled the problems of manufacturing such materials. The product of this collaboration was Kodachrome film, introduced in 1935. The film was coated with three emulsion layers – the top one sensitive only to blue light, the middle to blue and green, and the bottom layer to blue and red. To deal with the unwanted sensitivity of the two lower layers to blue light, a yellow filter was placed under the top layer and above the bottom two. By a single exposure the three layers simultaneously recorded the proportions of the three primary colours. The exposed film was first developed to a black and white negative. Then the film was re-exposed to light, and developed in a cyan colour-forming developer containing colour couplers which reacted with the chemical products of development to form a dye in the same position as and in the same proportion as the silver image. The cyan dye formed in the top two layers was then bleached out by a controlled penetration bleach the action of which was stopped before it reached the bottom layer. The top two layers were redeveloped in a magenta dye-forming developer, and then the top layer was bleached. Finally, this layer was re-developed in a yellow dye-forming developer and all the silver images were bleached out, leaving three dye images only. Kodachrome film was introduced in April 1935 in 16mm film size for amateur use, followed by 8mm amateur film in May 1936. A simplified and improved processing procedure was introduced in 1938, in which the successive developments and bleaches were replaced by a method of selective re-exposure and colour development of each layer in turn. The process has remained substantially the same ever since.

In 1940 Dr Kalmus of Technicolor reported that they were working with the Eastman Kodak Company on the development of a 'monopack' film – a version of the Kodachrome film producing a direct colour positive after exposure in a conventional camera. The

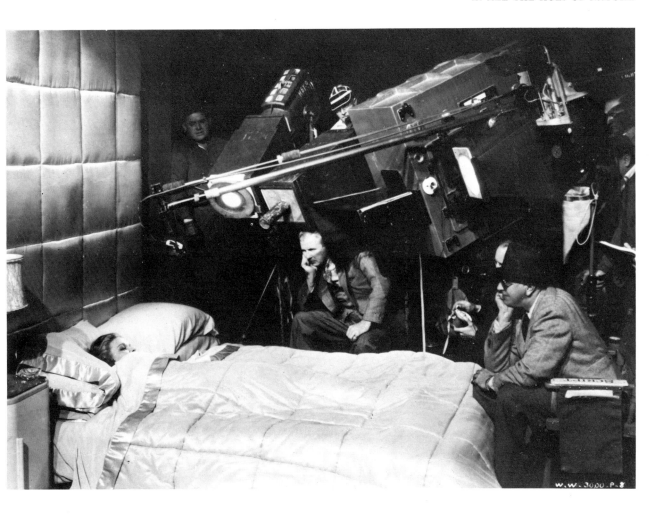

A sound-proofed Technicolor camera filming *Vogues of 1938*

positive film was to be printed through red, green and blue filters onto negative films, which were then used to make the printing matrices. Technicolor Monopack was used first for the location filming in *Lassie Come Home* in 1942, and subsequently in many other films. The first film to be shot entirely in Monopack was *Thunderhead – Son of Flicka* in 1944. The 16mm Kodachrome film was also used as the basis for a number of Technicolor productions. Notable uses included several documentaries of the war in the Pacific, Walt Disney's 'True-Life Adventure' series, and *The Conquest of Everest* in 1953.

The Agfa company in Germany also launched a multilayer colour film process, at the end of 1936. This film, Agfacolor, first available in 16mm film size, had a similar construction to Kodachrome film, but the colour-forming substances were incorporated in the three emulsion layers instead of being carried in the colour developers. Therefore, after a negative development, a single colour development produced the three colour images simultaneously in all three layers. In 1939 Agfa began experimental production of a colour negative material for use by professional film makers. The exposed multilayer colour film was given a single colour development producing a colour negative with reversed tone and colour values. This was to be printed onto a multilayer positive film to make the release prints. The new process was operational in 1940, and after use in a number of short films was used for a feature, *Frauern sind doch bessere Diplomaten*, in 1941, Subsequently a number of Agfacolor feature films were produced in wartime Germany, including *Die*

TOP LEFT The Agfacolor negative process was developed during the Second World War. The three-layer colour negative was printed onto a similar positive film to restore the original colours

TOP RIGHT The introduction of Eastman Color materials in 1950 soon led to the almost universal adoption of colour in the cinema

ABOVE LEFT *Othello*, 1956, shot in Sovcolor, a Russian development of the Agfacolor process

RIGHT *The Wild North*, 1952, was filmed in Anscocolor, a variant of the Agfacolor process

Goldene Stadt (1942), *Immensee* (1943), and *Baron Munchausen* (1945). After the war, with the release of Agfa's patents and manufacturing procedures a number of motion picture colour processes appeared based on the Agfa principles. They included Gevacolor (Belgium, 1947), Ferrania Color (Italy, 1952) and Ansco Color (America, 1953). The latter process was used widely in Hollywood for about two years; the first feature in Ansco Color was *The Wild North* (1953). Other films included *Seven Brides for Seven Brothers* (1954), *Kiss Me Kate* (1953), *The Student Prince* (1954) and *Brigadoon* (1954). As a reversal positive to positive process, Ansco Color had been in use since the end of the war, the first Ansco Color film being *Climbing the Matterhorn*, made in 1946. It had also been used for several feature productions, including *16 Fathoms Deep* (1947), *Alice in Wonderland* (1949) and *The Man on the Eiffel Tower* (1948). The Russian film industry adopted Sovcolor – a version of Agfacolor, a process which had first been used in Russia for a sequence in Eisenstein's film *Ivan the Terrible* (1943–46). Among the notable early Sovcolor films were *Romeo and Juliet* (1955) and *Othello* (1956).

A major contribution to the development of the colour motion picture was made with the introduction of Eastman Color materials. They were used on an experimental basis in 1949 and became commercially available in 1950. The Eastman Color negative film incorporated a principle known as coloured coupler masking, which had been used in the very successful Kodacolor film for colour prints

in still photography. By making the colour forming couplers, carried in the layers of the film, themselves coloured, the film automatically compensated for some of the dye deficiencies which would otherwise reduce the clarity and brilliance of some colours in the final print. The improved colour rendering of the Eastman Color materials led to their widespread use throughout the world within a few years. Eastman Color negatives were used to make the printing matrices for the Technicolor process, thus making the three strip cameras obsolete. Eastman Color materials formed the basis of a number of other 'processes' such as Warnercolor, Color by de Luxe, Color by Consolidated, Metrocolor, Pathecolor, and so on.

The Japanese Fujicolor negative-positive motion picture process was introduced in 1955 in Japan and was later launched in America in 1967. Fuji print film was used for a number of American productions in the 1960s, including *The Golden Voyage of Sinbad, Tora! Tora! Tora!* and *The Last American Hero*, the negatives for which were made on Eastman Color film. During the last decade or so, the colour materials supplied by a number of manufacturers have become compatible with each other, so that it is no longer possible to identify a film as produced by a specific process, as it used to be in earlier times. Today, the production of a black and white film by the cinema industry is very rare. Colour materials can now be used under lighting conditions in which black and white work would not have been possible a decade or two ago and colour film is now almost the universal medium for the cinema.

LEFT The Eastman Color negative. RIGHT Eastman Color positive. Both were introduced in 1950. The negative film incorporated coloured coupler masking, a technique which produced improved colour rendering

8

Wider still and deeper

One of the factors which reduced the realism of the early moving pictures was the limited size of the projected picture. The action might be life-like, but it was seen, as it were, through a small window. It had been appreciated since the days of the Panoramas that by filling the entire field of vision of the observer with a picture, a remarkable sense of realism was introduced. In the 1890s several panoramic lantern entertainments were introduced, providing an optical equivalent to the paintings of the Panorama but with the possibility of additional effects. Charles A. Chase in America designed and patented the Electric Cyclorama which was demonstrated in 1894 and shown subsequently throughout the rest of the decade. The *British Journal of Photography* described an improved version shown in 1895:

'The apparatus consists of a huge lantern installation suspended from the ceiling like a chandelier. This contrivance holds the operator and eight lanterns, each lighted by an electric arc, and throwing a combined picture on a screen of cylindrical section, ninety metres in circumference and ten high. Extremely accurate registration is required, that in the junction of the views no awkward overlapping takes place. This is brought about by the accurate placing of the chandelier-like lanterns and lanternist stand. The pictures once arranged and planned for continuing in series, a further improvement is carried out by introducing kineto-

Chase's Electric Cyclorama of 1895 used eight pairs of magic lanterns to project panoramic dissolving views onto a cylindrical screen 90 metres in circumference. The lanterns and their operator were suspended from the ceiling like a chandelier

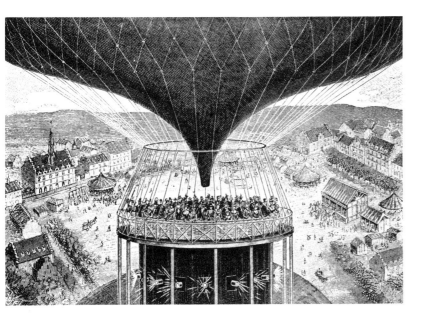

The projection of Grimoin-Sanson's Cinéorama took place in the Decogonal Hall at the Paris Exposition of 1900. Ten synchronised projectors presented a 360 degree moving picture panorama on a screen 100 metres in circumference.

scope pictures in motion, thrown upon the screen in the usual manner from a second lantern system. The apparatus is as ingenious as it must be costly, but we much doubt the commercial success of the scheme, especially at the present time, when, judging from provincial and other accounts, the public seems to be surfeited with lantern shows.'

The reference to projected animated pictures must have been speculative, since, as we have seen, no efficient film projection system existed in America at that time. The Electrorama, patented by Thomas W. Barber in 1894, was shown by C. W. Locke in London in May and June 1898, at 'Niagara', St James's. A cylindrical screen 40 feet (12.2m) high and 400 feet (122m) in circumference surrounded the audience. Ten radially arranged lanterns were set on the top of a tower, giving a continuous panorama from slides $7\frac{1}{4} \times 6\frac{1}{2}$in ($184 \times 165$mm) in size. The light source for all ten lanterns was a single lime cylinder lit by ten oxy-hydrogen jets.

The first practical attempt to create a moving picture version of the Panorama was made by the Frenchman Raoul Grimoin Sanson, who patented his Cinéorama on 25 November 1897. Sanson arranged ten cinecameras facing radially outwards so as to cover the entire horizon. The cameras were operated by a single winch handle in the centre, requiring the efforts of two or three men to keep it turning. The ten films were to be projected in a cylindrical building fitted with a decagonal screen, using ten projectors mechanically linked to maintain synchronism. The Cinéorama was to be a feature of the great Paris Exposition of 1900. In the last week of April, 1900, the camera outfit was fitted into the basket of a large balloon,

'managed in the ascent by the Count de la Vaulx and M. Mallet, two well-known aeronauts. After various incidents, rather of an alarming kind, as the machine showed a disposition to cast its moorings before its gear had been properly adjusted, the balloon, at a few minutes past five, amid the cheers of an enormous crowd, with which the Tuileries terraces were densely packed, was let off, and rose swiftly, bearing at once to the south-east. Immediately on the word "Go!" the machinery revolving the camera films was set moving with a wild whirring sound, so that the first scene which visitors to the cinéorama show will view on their balloon journey over Paris will be in the foreground the friends of the aeronauts and many members of the Tero and Automobile Clubs waving their hats and handkerchiefs, and on rising a little higher the surging crowds round the terraces, with the Place de la Concorde equally thronged, and the Exhibition beyond.'

The results from this dramatic flight were hand-coloured and presented in the Decagonal Hall at the Exposition, on a screen 100 metres in circumference. In the centre of the hall stood a simulated balloon basket, in which the audience stood and under which was the projection box with the ten linked projectors. The first few shows were reported as being an 'undeniable success', but the Préfecture of Police closed it down due to the severe fire risk from the unventilated projection booth in which ten 40-amp electric arcs were running and on top of which the audience were standing.

In the Galerie des Machines at the same Exposition, the Lumières demonstrated a wide film projection system developed in 1898, using apparatus manufactured by Carpentier. The film was 75mm wide – the widest ever to be used in conventional cinematography – and the picture size was 45×60mm, well over six times the area of the standard 35mm frame. It was shown on a screen 65 feet (20 metres) wide in the Salle des Fêtes, before audiences of 25,000 people, throughout the Exposition. Although it was the widest, the Lumière film was only one of several wide films in use at the time. The Edison 35mm film gauge, although the most widely used, was not yet accepted as a universal standard and the virtues of a larger film format were considerable at a time when the inadequacies of the photographic material used showed up only too well with the considerable magnifications involved in film projection. We have already considered the 60mm-wide film introduced in the Demeny-Gaumont machine of 1896; this size was also taken up by Prestwich in England. The Viventoscope machine made by A. S. Newman for Blair in England used film 48mm wide and the 68mm-wide Biograph film remained in use well into this century.

An animated film entertainment which involved the creation of a considerable degree of realism for the audience was Hale's World Tours. A mock-up of a Pullman railway carriage was built, set on a platform which could be rocked and vibrated to simulate the movement of a train, while fans created the effect of the passage of air. The moving scenery was seen through the end window of the carriage, using projected films taken from moving trains. The show opened in London in Oxford Street in 1906, and was initially very popular but the company overstretched itself, opening other Hale's Tours in too many places with long leases and high rentals and by the end of 1908 the business was in liquidation. As with the ascending balloon effect of the Cinéorama, the object of these entertainments was to involve the audience by giving the illusion of participation in an actual experience, but both systems involved mechanisms too complex to permit the shows to be widely used.

The Widescope process, demonstrated in 1922 by the American John D. Elms, used a simpler arrangement more easily adapted to use in an ordinary cinema. The special camera took a pair of 35mm films side by side, each recording half of a panoramic scene. The two films were projected side by side on a wide screen from two projectors linked by a universal joint connector. The Widescope system never passed beyond the stage of trade demonstrations, however. J. H. Powrie, who had pioneered several processes for still colour

Alberini's panoramic picture process, 1924, used horizontally running 35mm film. The large 24 x 40mm frames were recorded through a rotating lens covering a 65 degree angle

photography, in 1924 proposed the use of a film $1\frac{7}{8}$in (48mm) wide running horizontally in the camera, giving a frame size of about $2 \times 1\frac{1}{2}$in (50×38mm). These large negatives were to be printed by reduction onto a standard 35mm film, the object being to give a better quality image with finer detail, which would permit projection on much larger screens. Nothing much came of Powrie's suggestion at the time but, as we shall see, the principle did come into commercial use in more recent times. The Alberini panoramic picture process of 1924 (a busy year for wide screen inventors) adopted an idea used in panoramic cameras for still photography. The lens was mounted on a rotating drum and during each revolution scanned an angle of about 65°, rather wider than usual, recording it on a 35mm film running horizontally through a curved gate. The large negative size, 24×40mm, was reduced during printing onto a standard film. Elms adopted a similar idea for his improved Widescope process in 1927, using a rotating lens to record a 60° angle of view on a $2\frac{1}{4}$-in (57mm) wide film.

Lorenzo del Riccio devised his Magnascope system to increase the dramatic impact of sequences in conventional films. A screen much larger than usual was fitted to fill the entire proscenium arch of the cinema and was masked down at the sides and top to give the then conventional, rather small screen size. Operators backstage received advanced warning about two minutes before the changeover to a special sequence using film run on a Simplex projector of high light output and fitted with a lens giving a much larger picture. The operators withdrew the black masks uncovering the larger screen, four times the area of the conventional one. As the special sequence began, the picture thus seemed to enlarge. Magnascope was used first for the naval battle sequence in *Old Ironsides* at the Rivoli Theatre in New York in 1926. Later, the elephant stampede in *Chang*, the battle scenes in *The Big Parade* and the aerial sequences in *Wings* were all given increased dramatic effect by projection in Magnascope. Although the process was simple, expanding the screen at suitable moments was extremely effective and was used for a number of years in larger cinemas. The chief projectionist at London's Marble Arch cinema devised a variation on the idea using a variable focus projection lens which could enlarge the picture continuously, while the screen was manually unmasked. The Giant Expanding Pictures were demonstrated by George Palmer on 7 July 1930 but this method suffered from a severe diminution of brightness as the picture was enlarged, whereas in Magnascope screen brightness was maintained by changing to a more powerful projector. Nonetheless, by the summer of 1930 nine cinemas in Britain had installed the G. P. Giant Expanding Picture system and 35 more were proposing to introduce it.

For some sequences in his film *Napoléon*, the French producer Abel Gance adopted the multiple picture approach. The system was designed and patented by André Debrie in 1926. A triple screen was constructed on which at certain points in the film three mechanically linked projectors could show either a triptych of a central picture flanked by different images, or a panoramic scene across the screen. The latter was made by three cameras driven by a single electric motor. The film was shown first on 7 April 1927 at L'Opéra in Paris. Gance's 'Triple Écran' system aroused considerable interest in the film world and was said to have been the stimulus behind the development of other wide screen processes that appeared in America during the years that followed.

A development of major importance to the growth of wide screen methods was described by the French Professor Henri Chrétien to the Société Français de Physique in 1927. He had refined a principle employed in 1897 by E. Abbé, who had designed a cylindrical lens system in which the image produced was compressed laterally, but not vertically, to give a distorted image. A circle photographed with such a lens would be reproduced as an ellipse. Chrétien produced a lens suitable for photography called the Hypergonar, which, when attached to a standard camera lens, compressed twice the normal lateral angle of view into the standard frame. He proposed that the films should be projected on a machine also fitted with the Hypergonar lens, so that the distortion would be corrected giving a picture of twice the normal width on the screen. The Hypergonar lenses went into commercial production in 1928. They were demonstrated in America but no-one seemed interested in them at the time. Claude Autant-Lara, a French producer, used Hypergona lenses in the making of his film *Pour Contruire un Feu*. The film not only included sequences of wide screen projection but also used variable masking of the screen to alter the picture shape, while sometimes the screen was split into two pictures. The film ran for several months in Paris in 1929. Chrétien used Hypergonar lenses for a presentation at the International Exposition in Paris in 1937, using two interlocked projectors projecting two pictures side by side onto a screen 197×33 feet (60×10 metres) in size, fitted on the outside facade of the Palace of Light. The join between the two pictures was made less obvious by two fixed saw-tooth shutters which blended the edges of the two beams. The film trade still showed no interest in the possibilities of the anamorphotic, or 'squeeze' lens.

In 1929 there was a sudden flowering of interest in wide screen presentations in America. George K. Spoor and P. John Berggren had been working on a wide film process using film $2\frac{1}{2}$in (63.5mm) wide for some years. The Spoor-Berggren 'Natural Vision' process was demonstrated in May 1929 in *Lady Fingers*, shown on a 52×30 foot (15.8×9.1 metre) screen (see panel on page 145). By March 1930, *Dixiana*, with Bebe Daniels, was in production by RKO, who also that year shot *Danger Lights* in 'Natural Vision'. *Danger Lights* opened on 1 November 1930 at the State Lake Theatre in Chicago, whence, after a month's run, it moved to the Mayfair Theatre, New York for seven weeks. The process had its drawbacks: the projector was very noisy – like a 'machine gun or riveting machine' said one report – and a three-quarter horse-power compressor was needed to provide air to cool it. The sound track was carried on a separate

Early wide films

Although almost from the beginning the 35mm film width had been adopted as the standard for movie film, in the early days a variety of larger film formats were in use. Among them were the 48mm Viventoscope of Blair, the 60mm Demeny-Gaumont and Prestwich, the 68mm Biograph and the 75mm Lumière film created especially for the Paris Exposition of 1900. The undoubted advantages of the larger formats which gave brighter and sharper pictures on the screen were offset by the increased cost of the film and the mechanical complications of building larger projectors. After the early years of this century the smaller 35mm format was universally employed by professional film makers.

A growth of interest in large screen presentations in the later 1920s led to a revival of wide films. The Spoor-Berggren 'Natural Vision' process, demonstrated in May 1929 used a film $2\frac{1}{2}$ in (63.5mm) wide, which, it was claimed, was capable of filling a 70-foot wide (21.3m) screen. The first 'Natural Vision' feature was *Campus Sweethearts* (1929). The process had its problems. The projector was very noisy, and the sound track was carried on a separate film, running at 24 frames per second, while the picture film ran at 20 frames per second. This led to synchronisation problems if either film broke.

The Fox Grandeur system used a $2\frac{3}{4}$ in (70mm) film, with an integral sound track. The first presentation, a full programme of wide film newsreel and the feature *Fox Movietone Follies of 1929*, was shown in September 1929. Fox Grandeur gave a high quality of both picture and sound, and several features, including Raoul Walsh's *The Big Trail* (1930) were produced in it.

Paramount's wide film process, Magnafilm, was based on a smaller film 56mm wide. The first presentation, of a short musical feature *You're in the Army Now*, was

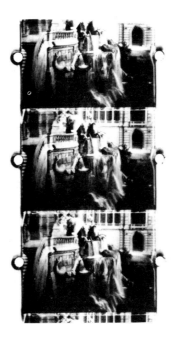

ABOVE *48mm-wide film used in Blair's Viventoscope, 1897*

BELOW *70mm Fox Grandeur film, 1929 showing a tennis match featuring Bill Tilden*

BOTTOM *56mm Paramount Magnafilm process, 1929, from* You're in the Army Now

given on a 40 x 20-foot (12.2m x 6.1m) screen in July 1929. Magnafilm had no great success.

Warner Brothers' Vitascope system employed a 65mm film, which could be run on standard projectors after a simple conversion. The first Vitascope feature, *Kismet*, was premiered in October 1930. Warners proposed that the 65mm original should be reduced to 35mm in printing to make the productions available to cinemas not equipped for wide film presentation. The same 65mm format was adopted by United Artists, who shot their feature *The Bat Whispers* (1930) simultaneously in 35mm and 65mm. Metro-Goldwyn-Meyer's Realife process also used 65mm film. The first MGM feature in 65mm was *Billy the Kid* (1930). Generally the film was shown as a 35mm reduction print from the original.

The wide film processes had no great success at this time. The cost of conversion to wide screen presentation coming on top of the recent expensive installations of sound film equipment could not be borne by most cinemas. After a year or two wide films were dropped, until their revival in the 1950s.

film, running at 24 frames per second, while the film ran at 20 frames per second. This caused considerable problems with resynchronisation if either film broke.

The Fox Grandeur system went one better by adopting a $2\frac{3}{4}$ in (70mm) wide film, with a frame size of 48×22.5mm, and a 10mm wide sound track (see panel). The process was shown first at the Gaiety Theatre, New York on 17 September 1929, with a sound newsreel and a feature shown on a 40-foot (12 metre) screen. The newsreel included a tennis match featuring Bill Tilden, a baseball game, the Tiller Girl dancers, drill by West Point Cadets and a duck farm! The feature was a 70mm version of *Fox Movietone Follies of 1929*, which had been shot also in 35mm. In 1929, Fox produced *Happy Days* in Grandeur, and *The Big Trail* in 1930, shooting both in 35mm as well. Both the picture and sound quality were excellent, due in large part to the special Mitchell cameras and Super Simplex projectors designed for Grandeur.

Paramount adopted a smaller film system, developed by Lorenzo del Riccio and built by André Debrie, which they called Magnafilm. The film was 56mm wide; the first demonstration was at New York's Rivoli Theatre on 25 July 1929, on a 40×20 foot (12×6 metre) screen. A short musical feature film *You're in the Army Now* was shown. It was reported as being 'only moderately satisfactory', and little more was heard of it. The following year Warner Brothers entered the wide screen field with their Vitascope system, using a 65mm negative film (see panel). A conversion was available for a standard projector, taking 30 minutes to install; the machine could then be changed from 35mm to 65mm use at the turn of a knob. Most Vitascope productions, however, were to be reduced to 35mm print size for normal showing. United Artists also adopted 65mm film, shooting in 1930 the feature *The Bat Whispers* in the large film size as well as 35mm. The third company to take up 65mm film was Metro-Goldwyn-Mayer. They called their method 'Realife', the first film in which was *Billy the Kid*, shown in October 1930. The film was shown as a reduction print onto standard 35mm film from the larger negative. *Billy the Kid* made no impact on the public, and after a second film, *Great Meadow* in 1931, MGM dropped the 'Realife' process.

The wide film 'revolution' was over almost before it had begun. The reasons were given in an article in *The Bioscope* in May 1930, under the title 'Wide Film Wobbling'. It described the opposition of the cinema trade to the extra cost of the projection apparatus, at a time just after most cinemas had had to re-equip to install sound systems and discussed the problems for the film producers of trebled production costs and increased distribution difficulties. It concluded, 'This novelty, therefore, is to be tucked away to be brought forward when the industry needs a fresh stimulant'. Only George Spoor soldiered on, showing his wide films in the Spoor Spec-tac-culum in the Century of Progress exhibition in Chicago in 1933. He was preparing to make two dramatic films 'of distinction', and to build five theatres to house the wide screens. By August 1933 it was announced that his theatre was to close through lack of support, and it 'appears to have definitely sounded the knell of wide film'.

However, there were other ways of making wide screen pictures without using wide films. Chrétien's Hypergonar lens had shown one way. The idea of anamorphotic lens attachments to squeeze a wide image onto a standard film was taken up by the English engineer George Ford working with F. W. Watson Baker of Watson

The Fulvue process, 1930, used an anamorphic lens on the camera to squeeze the picture horizontally (left). A similar lens on the projector restored the picture to its original wide angle proportions (right)

and Sons. Their Fulvue process was announced in March 1930; an anamorphotic lens squeezed twice the normal lateral field of view into a standard frame. The film could be projected on any conventional machine, the lens of which had to be fitted with a Fulvue attachment costing around £20. A reviewer of a trade demonstration pointed out in January 1931 that Fulvue would do everything that the American wide films could do but with minimal extra cost over conventional projection. The trade show on 15 June was reported as 'striking, novel and eloquent'. *The Bioscope* said 'Results already achieved appear to put the process beyond criticism on practical grounds'. Despite its being considered a commercial proposition, it was not taken up by the trade at a time of general economic depression. A similar system, proposed by the Victor Talking Machine Company in America in January 1930 was also not accepted by the trade. A cylindrical lens attachment designed by Sidney H. Newcomber and manufactured by the C. P. Goerz American Optical Company in 1930 under the name Ciné-Panor was sold for a short time for 16mm film making, but had no large scale application.

The 'fresh stimulant' referred to by *The Bioscope* in 1930 was made necessary in the years after the Second World War, as with the rise in popularity of television in America and elsewhere cinema audiences began to decline. By producing bigger and, it was hoped, better pictures, audiences might be lured back to the big screen. The first and the most spectacular of the postwar wide screen processes was invented by Fred Waller, whose experiments in wide screen presentation had begun before the war. In 1939 he demonstrated a multi-projector show on a spherical screen – the Perisphere – at the New York World's Fair, but no further sponsorship was forthcoming. During the war he adapted his system for gunnery training. He worked on the principle that for distances beyond 20 feet (6.1 metres) peripheral vision – the view from the corner of the eye – was a more important factor in suggesting depth and realism than binocular vision. Waller's 'Flexible Gunnery Trainer' used a curved screen covering 150° horizontally and 75° vertically, on which five projectors in synchronism projected pictures of aircraft, shot from five synchronised cameras carried in aircraft, on land or at sea, depending on the type of gunnery training required. The trainee gunner sat at the controls of a dummy gun, receiving the same view of the scene that he would have in real life. As the aircraft, or other subject, moved on the screen, the gunner followed it with his 'gun'. When the 'gun' was 'fired', a complex linkage recorded the aiming position on a 'hit scoring' machine running in synchronism with the projectors. At the same time, the trigger handle was vibrated to give the correct 'feel' of a gun firing. The 'hit scoring' film was analysed through a photoelectric system which recorded the number of 'hits', feeding back information to the gunner when his aim was correct. The Waller trainer was a very elaborate device. An Eastman Kodak engineer, James Reddig, when asked what it looked like, said,

> 'Oh, that's easy. You take the end off the Triborough Bridge, put four men on it with their feet dangling in the air, a console like a church organ, and behind that photocells, amplifiers, levers, scanners and a lot of other things that I cannot understand. Then, take the Perisphere from the World's Fair, cut it into four pieces, push the end of the Triborough Bridge into one of the pieces, and you have a Waller Gunnery Trainer. It's as simple as that.'

Four gunners at a time could use the Trainer and its near perfect simulation of actual combat conditions was invaluable in training gunners rapidly and efficiently.

After the war, Waller worked to adapt his system for use in the cinema. By 1948 he had made and demonstrated a working system which he called Cinerama. The first public show opened on 30 September 1952 at the Broadway Theatre, New York. A deeply curved screen 50 × 25 feet (18.3 × 7.6 metres) carried a picture covering a visual field of 145° horizontally and 55° vertically which when seen from the best seats virtually filled the visual field of the spectator. The picture was produced by three projectors in three separate booths, running in synchronism, each providing one third of the scene. Where the pictures met on the screen, the edges were blended by vibrating sawtooth devices in the projectors which

Waller's Cinerama process, 1952, used three films photographed in three synchronised cameras. Each frame was half as high again as usual. Three synchronised projectors projected the film onto a deeply curved screen to reconstruct the panorama (below). A fourth film carried seven stereophonic sound tracks

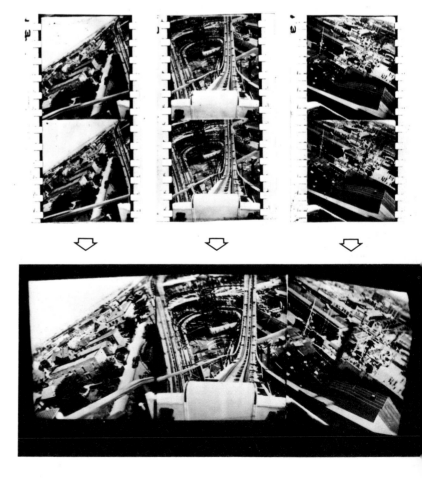

softened the edges of the pictures to make the joins less obtrusive. Standard 35mm film was used but each frame was half as high again as on standard film, to give extra height to the picture. A fourth magnetic film carried seven stereophonic sound tracks, six played from loudspeakers behind the screen and one feeding effects to speakers arranged around the auditorium. The synchronism of the three projectors and the sound track, together with focusing, adjustment of sound levels and so on, were all controlled by an operator seated at a console at the front of the theatre. The films were shot using three linked cameras fixed as a single unit. The impact of the first Cinerama presentations on audiences used to seeing films on the small, almost square screens then in use was tremendous. The first Cinerama film, *This is Cinerama*, opened with a roller coaster ride which was so realistic that audiences imagined many of the physical effects of such an experience, crying out as the roller coaster dipped down the track. Some people experienced nausea or dizziness.

Despite some of its defects – the still noticeable joins and the mismatching of brightness and colour between the three prints – Cinerama was very popular for a number of years. Clearly, the very special and expensive installation was a restriction, limiting its use to a relatively small number of theatres in large cities. By 1961 there were 11 installations in America and 30 in the rest of the world. After the first programmes – *Cinerama Holiday, Seven Wonders of the World, Search for Paradise* and *South Seas Adventure*, all of which were travelogues, two feature fiction films were made by Metro-Goldwyn-Meyer: *How the West was Won* (1962) and *The Wonderful World of the Brothers Grimm* (1962). By this time, however, the novelty had worn off the wide screen show, and Cinerama was facing competition from a variety of other processes, most of them involving far less complex methods of presentation. In 1963 Cinerama adopted a single 70mm wide film method for the next production, *It's a Mad, Mad, Mad, Mad World* and by 1966 all three-picture Cinerama installations had been replaced by single film systems.

The tremendous initial success of Cinerama started a rush to develop rival systems. The first in the field was Twentieth-Century

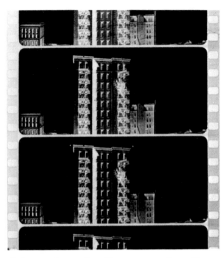

A frame from the 65mm negative of *It's a Mad, Mad, Mad, Mad World*, 1963. It was the first single-film Cinerama production

Poster for the Technicolor CinemaScope production of *A Star is Born*

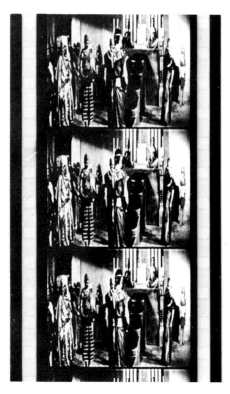

The CinemaScope process, 1953, used anamorphic lenses to squeeze the picture horizontally, with a similar lens on the projector. Four magnetic sound tracks were placed on either side of the perforations, which were reduced in size.

Fox, who took up Henri Chrétien's anamorphotic Hypergonar lens method. The CinemaScope process was demonstrated at the Spring Convention of the Society of Motion Picture and Television Engineers in Los Angeles on 27 April 1953. The 'squeezed' picture, with twice the normal horizontal field of view, was accompanied by four-track stereophonic sound carried on four magnetic sound tracks, placed on each side of the film perforations, which were reduced in size to make room for them. The first CinemaScope feature film was *The Robe*, which opened at the Roxy Theatre, New York, on 16 September 1953. While the CinemaScope picture with its aspect ratio (of width to height) of 2.55 to 1 did not have the full visual impact of Cinerama, it could be more easily installed in the average cinema, which needed only to enlarge the screen. By 1955 it was estimated that over 31,500 cinemas throughout the world were equipped for CinemaScope films, with more converting every week. In that year 35 feature films were shot in anamorphotic processes in America alone. To reduce the cost of installation for smaller cinemas, CinemaScope prints with a single optical sound track were produced, with some small loss of the edge of the picture to make way for the track, reducing the aspect ratio to 2.31 to 1.

Paramount adopted a different approach. The limitation on the enlargement of the very small picture on the movie film was set more by the negative image than by the print film, since to achieve an adequate sensitivity, the grain structure of the negative emulsion had to be relatively large. The print film could be made with much finer grain. By using a large negative image reduced to a smaller size during printing, a more detailed image could be produced, capable of enlargement to a much larger size. Paramount's Vista-Vision process used a 35mm film running horizontally in the camera, exposing a negative 36 × 24mm, double the normal frame size. For normal use this film was printed by reduction onto a standard 35mm film with a 24 × 18mm frame size, but for special presentations, a contact print from the larger negative film could be run in special projectors. The first VistaVision production was *White Christmas*, shot at the end of 1953 and shown first at the Radio City Music Hall on 27 April 1954, on a 55 × 30 foot (16.75 × 9 metre) screen. The improved quality given by using larger negatives was immediately obvious and exhibitors were happy since VistaVision prints could be shown on standard projectors. Vista-Vision films were normally provided with a single optical sound track, but a method called Perspecta sound gave, if the projectors were suitably equipped, a pseudo-stereophonic sound reproduction. Inaudible signals carried in the sound track were detected by the sound equipment and switched the sound to left, right or centre of screen loudspeakers as required. Ordinary projectors ran the sound track as normal. The VistaVision process was used very successfully for a number of years, being finally discontinued after the making of *One Eyed Jacks* in 1961.

For his Todd-AO system, Michael Todd, with Dr Brian O'Brien of the American Optical Company, adopted the 65mm negative size discarded in the early 1930s. A 'bug-eye' extra wide angle camera lens was developed, recording an angle of view of 120° on the film, with an aspect ratio of 2 to 1. The film ran at 30 frames per second and was printed onto a 70mm wide film, the extra width allowing the use of six magnetic sound tracks for stereophonic sound. The film was projected onto a deeply curved screen, typically about 50 by 25 feet (15.25 × 7.6 metres) in size. The first Todd-AO

The Todd-AO process, 1954, used a 65mm wide negative film (above) printed onto a 75mm wide print film, with six magnetic sound tracks (below). This example is from *Oklahoma*

Paramount's VistaVision process, 1953, used a horizontally running film in the camera (top). The double size image was reduced in printing to a standard size (middle). For special shows, a same-size print (bottom) could be made from the original negative

production was *Oklahoma*, filmed in 1954 and released the following year, shown first at the Rivoli Theatre, New York on 13 October. The second Todd-AO film, *Around the World in 80 Days*, was shown in the spring of 1957 and *South Pacific* appeared early in 1958, by which time over 50 theatres were equipped for the wide film with the special screens. Todd-AO could give much of the visual effect of Cinerama, without the obtrusive joins and complex projection arrangements, although when the very wide angle camera lenses were used there was serious distortion of vertical lines at the edges of the picture. After a few years, the deep screen installations and wide angle lenses were discarded in favour of more conventional methods, and the 65mm negative, 70mm print combination was widely adopted by other major producers, as we shall see.

By the mid 1950s the wide screen pattern had been set. Four methods were in use: the multiple projector arrangement of Cinerama, the 'squeezed' image system of CinemaScope, the wide film approach of Todd-AO and the quality print produced by reduction from a larger negative used in VistaVision. During the next few years there was a proliferation of processes based on these ideas. The Walt Disney organisation developed Circarama, installed in Disneyland in July 1955. Eleven Cine-Kodak Special 16mm cameras were interlocked and used to produce 11 films covering the entire 360° horizon – shades of Grimoin Sanson's Cinéorama! These films were shown by 11 synchronised projectors on a 40-foot (12 metre) diameter cylindrical screen, eight feet (2.4 metres) high. No attempt was made to conceal the joins between the pictures and in fact each projector was set up to project through the gap between two pictures onto the screen opposite. The Circarama show was presented at the Brussels World Fair in 1958. A similar system, Kinopanorama, was developed in Russia in 1959. It used 22 screens in two tiers of 11, with nine-channel stereophonic sound. The lower screen was 13 feet 4 inches (4 metres) high and 93 feet 6 inches (28.5 metres) in diameter and showed the main scene, while the upper screen, a truncated cone, carried the sky with aerial scenes and so on. By 1963, the Disney Circarama process had been simplified to take nine films instead of 11.

The Cinemiracle process was very similar to Cinerama, using three interlocked cameras and projectors. The projection layout was simplified by the use of a single projection box with all three projectors, mirrors being used to deflect the left and right hand images onto the screen. The first and only Cinemiracle production was Louis de Rochemont's *Windjammer* which opened at Grauman's Chinese Theatre in Hollywood on 9 April 1958. A deeply curved screen, 63×26 feet (19×8 metres) was installed. After a few demonstrations in America and elsewhere, the Cinemiracle process was bought by Cinerama Inc. in 1960.

To reduce the complication to the exhibitor of having to have three projectors working at once, Tom Smith and Rowe E. Carney devised in 1958 a method using a special optical system on the camera which divided a panoramic view into three sections. A 90° centre section was recorded on the bottom half of a standard frame, while the top of the frame was occupied by two left and right sections covering 45° angles each. An entire 180° scene was thus recorded on one film, within one standard frame. A similar optical system on the projector reconstructed the complete image on a semi-cylindrical screen. At the trade demonstration in December 1958 it was stated that the system could bring big screens shows to small communities, but nothing seems to have come of the process.

The idea of combining several wide-screen image components on one film also occurred to L. Bronesby and V. Wells, who devised the Wonderama-ARC 120 process. Starting from an existing wide film or 'squeezed' negative, a special printer divided the image into two, rotating the halves vertically so as to lie on end within the normal frame. Two-channel magnetic sound tracks could be applied to the film outside the perforations. A similar optical device fitted to the projector presented the two halves as one picture, a vibrating shutter device blending the edges so as to minimise the join between them. The first Wonderama film, *Honeymoon*, was shown in August 1960 in Blackpool, England; the second, *Parisian Ballet* was shown at the Lutetia cinema in Paris. A later Wonderama production, *Mediterranean Holiday*, was released in a wide film Cinerama version in 1965. It is difficult to see what possible advantage the process had over, say, the use of a single 'squeezed' picture method.

After the great initial success of CinemaScope, a number of companies adopted the same principle of anamorphotic optical systems, mostly compatible with each other and with CinemaScope. There were too many variants to mention in detail; most of them could be distinguished by the use of the -Scope suffix in their names. One or two involved small differences of principle. Superscope, introduced in 1955 used ordinary cameras and lenses to film the essential action restricted to an area of 2 to 1 aspect ratio in the centre of the frame. In the laboratory, prints were made by expanding the centre of the image vertically, enlarging it to fill the standard frame. The distorted image could be corrected by projecting it with a standard 'scope projection lens. The Techniscope system, devised by Technicolor Italiana in 1963, used a similar principle, exposing a frame of half the normal height, with conventional lenses, stretching the image vertically during the printing process to produce a standard frame with an anamorphotic image. Both Superscope and Techniscope did not suffer from some of the distortions produced in images shot through anamorphotic lenses. Techniscope was particularly attractive to producers, since only half the normal amount of negative film stock was used.

The Techniscope process recorded half height, unsqueezed images on 35mm film. During printing, anamorphic optics expanded the pictures vertically to give a standard 'scope print (below).

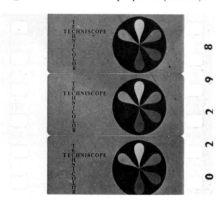

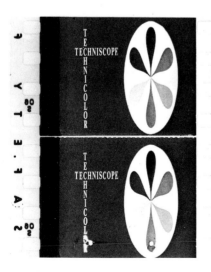

During 1955 Twentieth Century Fox developed the CinemaScope 55 process, taking a leaf out of the VistaVision book. A wide film negative was made on 55mm film (actually 55.625mm wide) using anamorphotic lenses to record a 'squeezed' image. This was printed by reduction onto a standard 35mm film, with six stereophonic magnetic sound tracks. The first film in CinemaScope 55 was *Carousel*, given its first showing on 16 February 1956. The second and last production, *The King and I*, was shown on 28 June 1956. A few 'road-shows' of the latter film were given using special projectors taking 56mm wide film prints. The improved quality produced from the wide film negatives did not offset the increased production costs and the CinemaScope process reverted to its original form.

Faced with a growing demand for prints in various 'squeezed' and 'unsqueezed' formats, in 1956 the Technicolor Motion Picture Corporation developed a system of its own, called Technirama. Standard 35mm colour negative film was run horizontally through the camera, as in VistaVision. A degree of anamorphotic compression of the image was given at this stage, using the Delrama optical system which employed prisms instead of lenses to 'squeeze' the image, a system developed by the Dutch Delft Optical Company. From this master negative prints could be made in 35mm or 16mm film sizes, 'squeezed' by introducing further compression in the printing, or 'unsqueezed' by removing the compression introduced in the camera. Optical or magnetic sound tracks could be provided to suit almost any requirement. For special shows, a double-frame horizontal projector could run contact prints from the original negative. The first Technirama production was *Monte Carlo*, given its premiere at the Rivoli Theatre in December 1956. The improved Technirama 70 process permitted 'unsqueezed' 70mm prints to be

CinemaScope 55 films were shot with anamorphic lenses on 55mm wide negative film (above) and reduced in printing to standard CinemaScope prints. This example is from *Carousel*

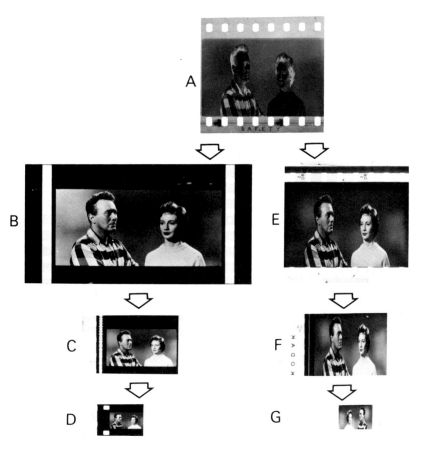

Technirama (1956) used a double frame negative (A), with partial 'squeezing'. This could be used to produce an unsqueezed print on 70mm film (B) or 35mm film (C) or 16mm film (D). A same-size print could be made on 35mm film (E). With further squeezing, 'scope prints could be made on 35mm film (F) or 16mm film (G)

An elaborate decor typical of many of the 'super' cinemas of the thirties. Such designs created problems in the installation of ultra-wide screens

made from the horizontal negatives; it was first used by Walt Disney for *The Sleeping Beauty* in 1959. A further improved version, Super Technirama 70, was used for *Solomon and Sheba* (whose world premiere was at the London Astoria Theatre late in 1969) and subsequently for many other productions.

Following the lead of Todd-AO, several companies adopted wide film methods. Metro-Goldwyn-Mayer's Camera 65 process used a 65mm-wide negative film in the camera, just as the company's Realife method had done a quarter of a century before. The film was shot with anamorphotic lenses, squeezing a 3 to 1 aspect ratio into the frame. Release prints were made on 35mm film with a further 'squeeze' to give the normal 'scope-type print with four magnetic sound tracks. The first MGM Camera 65 film was *Raintree County* (1957). For large scale shows, 70mm prints were made, with six magnetic sound tracks. The 70mm projector was fitted with a suitable anamorphotic lens. Panavision-70, introduced in 1957, was for all practical purposes identical to MGM Camera 65. The first Panavision production was *The Big Fisherman* (1959). Ultra-Panavision used a 90° wide angle lens to produce panoramas; it was used for a number of films, including *Ben Hur* (1959); *How the West was Won* (1962) – the three Cinerama prints being 'extracted' from the wide film negative – and *Mutiny on the Bounty*. Since 1971, virtually all wide screen productions have been shot on 65mm negative film and printed as 70mm 'unsqueezed' prints.

A Technirama 70 print

An idea for producing a completely hemispherical image was devised by Adalbert Baltes of Hamburg and was demonstrated by him in the Cinetarium at the Photokina photographic trade fair in Cologne in 1958. A single film camera was pointed vertically at a hemispherical mirror, recording a circular image in which a 360° horizontal and 180° vertical view was reproduced. The film was projected upwards onto another hemispherical mirror at the top of a domed auditorium 40 feet (12 metres) in diameter. The chief problem with such a system is that the brightness of the projected image is limited by being spread over a very large area. The same principle was used in the Spacearium at the Seattle World Exhibition in 1962. A 70mm film allowed a large hemispherical screen, 78 feet (23.8 metres) in diameter to be used. The picture covered a 360° horizontal and 160° vertical angle. The first film, *Journey to the Stars*, was shown in April 1962.

One of the latest wide screen methods, the IMAX system, uses a 65mm film running horizontally in the camera, using wide angle lenses to record a large frame size of 70×50mm. The prints are made on horizontally running 70mm film, with six magnetic sound tracks. Three tracks feed speakers at left, centre and right of the screen, two supply sound to speakers at left and right at the rear of the auditorium and the sixth feeds a speaker in the ceiling. In the Cinesphere theatre the IMAX films are shown on a dished screen about 90 feet (27.4 metres) in diameter with a radius of about 80 feet (24.4 metres). From the seats at the front, the top of the screen is actually over the heads of the audience. The IMAX system was shown first with the film *Tiger Child* in the Fuji Pavilion at EXPO '70 in Japan, the film being used for the most part for multiple image effects, the full frame being used for only about 20% of the shots. The second production *North of Superior* (1971) and subsequent films have concentrated on the wide screen possibilities of this very large format.

The original shape of the movie picture had been set rather arbitrarily by W. K. L. Dickson when he developed the 1×0.75in (24×18mm) frame size for the Edison Kinetoscope, thus establishing the aspect ratio of 1.33 to 1, which remained almost unchanged until the coming of the widescreen processes. In the early days of the wide screen revolution after the Second World War, many owners of small cinemas, unable to afford the extra apparatus, went 'wide screen' by the simple expedient of masking off the top and/or bottom of the projector gate. The fact that this often cut off the heads or feet of the actors on the screen was a matter of indifference – as it is today when wide screen films are shown on television with half the picture missing on the small screen. In cropping the picture, the exhibitors were following a suggestion made many years before in the *Kinematograph Weekly*, in February 1913:

'A more artistic screen – If you mask the gate of your projector, so that while the width remains as before, the height is decreased, the result is a better shaped picture – more artistic. The portion masked off will never be missed.'

Artistic or not, after 1953 most films were shot with the new shape in mind, the essential action being contained within an area with an aspect ratio of around 1.6 or 1.85 to one. There is no reason, however, why some shape other than a horizontal rectangle should not be used for the picture if the producer required it. Silent film producers, notably D. W. Griffith, masked pictures down to different shapes to enhance the dramatic or pictorial content. Narrow vertical and horizontal rectangles, squares, and circles were used. Claude Autant-Lara's use of a changing screen shape has already been mentioned. In 1955 Glenn H. Alvey Junior, sponsored by the British Film Institute, developed his Dynamic Frame process, which was demonstrated in the short film *The Door in the Wall*, shown in 1956. The film was shot in VistaVision and during the printing stage continuously variable masking was used to alter the size, shape and position of the image on the film, the masking being set to enhance the action and dramatic content of the scene. For example,

Glen Alvey's Dynamic Frame film *The Door in the Wall*, shot in VistaVision, used continuously variable masking in printing to alter the picture size and shape. For example, the picture having closed down to a small frame at one corner (above), opened up suddenly to full screen size (below)

as a character came out of a narrow alleyway, the picture, which had closed down to a narrow vertical rectangle, opened out to its full horizontal width. In another sequence, as the boy hero sits down in a strange garden, he is gradually enclosed in a tiny square in one corner of the screen; with a clap of thunder, the screen suddenly opens up to its full size, showing him at the foot of a huge dinosaur. Although the Dynamic Frame process produced effects which could be quite dramatic, no further productions were made in this process.

The wide screen systems, especially those using peripheral vision effects, such as Cinerama and Todd-AO, enhanced the realism of the scene by, as it were, placing the audience in it. Another way to do this was to use stereoscopy to provide an image in depth. In chapter two we saw how this was based on the use of a 'left eye' and 'right eye' image presented to the appropriate eye by optical devices, so that they fused in the brain to create an illusion of three dimensions in the picture. The moving picture had hardly been born when the first attempts were made to add depth to the moving picture. The first recorded demonstration of projected stereoscopic still images was made by J. C. d'Almeida at the Académie des Sciences in 1856. He showed two stereoscopic images coloured red and green in rapid succession in the lantern, viewing the screen through spectacles fitted with red and green lenses. The red lens 'saw' only the green picture and the green lens, the red. By persistence of vision, the two fused to give the illusion of a single picture in depth. In 1891 Ducos du Hauron patented a refinement of this 'anaglyph' method, in which the two stereoscopic images, coloured red and blue, were superimposed on each other, and viewed through red and blue glasses. This method was used by C. Grivolas in 1897 to project stereoscopic moving pictures. Two negative films were taken with a double camera, with lenses separated by the distance apart of the human eyes. Twin projectors, mechanically linked, projected the two films onto the same screen through red and blue filters. The audience were able to see the films in depth by viewing the screen through red and blue glasses. Not much more was heard of stereoscopic films until the early 1920s, when there was a sudden revival of interest.

The Fairall process used the anaglyph principle, with stereo

The anaglyph method of magic lanterns projection used in the 1890s superimposed a pair of stereo pictures through red and green filters. The audience viewed the screen through red and green spectacles, showing the scene in depth

pairs of·films in linked projectors, shown through red and blue-green filters. *The Power of Love*, the first, and probably the only, film by Henry H. Fairall was shown on 9 September 1922 at the Ambassador Hotel Theatre in Los Angeles. W. V. D. Kelley, of Prizma Color fame, printed his red and green coloured stereoscopic images on opposite sides of double coated film. The negatives were taken in a camera exposing two frames of film at once, with prisms to give the necessary separation of the left and right points of view. The first demonstration of Kelley's 'Plasticon' pictures *Movies of the Future* was given in Christmas week 1922 at the Rivoli Theatre in New York, the audience wearing spectacles with coloured Cellophane filters. The similar 'Plastigram' process of Frederic E. Ives and Jacob E. Leventhal was given its first public showing in 1923 at the Cameo Theatre, New York. The films included *A Runaway Taxi*, *Luna City*, *Ouch* and *Zowie*. These films were re-run in 1925 by the Pathé company under the name Stereoscopiks.

The 'Teleview' stereoscopic process, shown at the Selwyn Theatre in New York at Christmas 1922 used a different method of viewing. The back of each seat was fitted with a mechanical shutter, synchronised with the projectors. The shutter covered each eye in turn, so that the left eye saw only the left eye pictures, and the right eye, right eye pictures. As might be expected, the multitude of shutters made some noise in operation. The film, a space travel subject, *M.A.R.S.*, 'did not prove very impressive as a dramatic composition'. This method was virtually identical to one shown by C. Dupuis in Paris in 1903. Neither demonstration led to any true commercial realisation.

After this brief flurry of activity in the early 1920s, nothing much happened for over ten years. In late 1935 J. F. Lebenthal revived his 'Plastigrams' under a new name – 'Audioscopiks'. With a producer, Pete Smith, Leventhal made a series of short films, with the stereoscopic anaglyph pairs printed on one film by Technicolor. The series was bought in 1936 by Metro-Goldwyn-Mayer, who showed them in America, France, England, Spain, Italy and North Africa. Pete Smith produced a short comedy thriller, *Third Dimension Murder*, in the process in 1940.

While the anaglyph method could give good stereoscopic synthesis, it had its drawbacks. Some spectators complained of visual fatigue and the system permitted only monochrome images. An alternative viewing method used the properties of polarised light. Light emitted from most light sources consists of waves undulating in all planes. Certain substances have the property of passing or reflecting only those light waves undulating in the same plane. By using two such polarising filters, with their planes of polarisation at right angles to each other, on two projectors showing stereoscopic pairs, a stereo image is seen when the screen is viewed through spectacles fitted with similar polarisers, each one of which will pass only one of the two images. The first suggestion of the use of polarised light in this way was by J. Anderton in an English patent of 7 July 1891. He proposed using polarisers made from bundles of thin plates of glass, projecting stereoscopic pairs of still pictures onto a calico screen covered with matt silver paper, necessary to preserve the polarisation of the reflected images. Dr. G. R. Wilson adapted this method to cine projection in his patent of 1896, using two interconnected cameras and projectors, with the results viewed through polarising analysers. While the principle was sound enough, the cumbersome and inefficient polarisers made the method impractical.

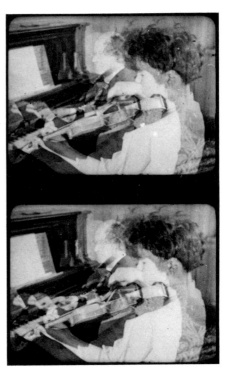

Audioscopik stereo movies of the 1930s used the anaglyph principle. The red and blue images were printed on one film in superimposition, and the audience wore spectacles with red and blue filters

By a coincidence, a simple, cheap and efficient polarising material was developed almost simultaneously by Dr E. H. Land in America and Bernauer of Zeiss-Ikon and Käseman in Germany. Dr Land in his patent of 1932 suggested a method of depositing crystals of Herapathite in a thin film, which was then stretched or rolled to align all the needle-like crystals in one direction. The sheet of Polaroid, as Dr Land called his material, on a microscopic scale, resembled a grating which allowed only those light waves undulating in the plane of the spaces of the grating to pass through. The first demonstrations of projected stereoscopic films using polarising materials were given in June 1936 at the Haus der Technik in Berlin. The stereoscopic images recorded side by side on a single film were projected through Zeiss polarising filters onto a metallised screen. The film *Zum Greifen Nah* (*You can nearly touch it*) was made on a fairground, using a two-colour process using Agfa materials. It was shown to the public on 12 December 1937 at the Ufa Palast am Zoo in Berlin. A second production, *Sechs Madel Rollen in Wochenland* was made in an improved system using a horizontally running film in 1939.

Polarised light stereoscopic movies were shown at the New York World's Fair from 4 May 1939. The Chrysler Motors exhibit showed a black and white film of the assembly of the Plymouth car. The following year Chrysler ran a Technicolor stereoscopic film, *New Dimensions*, on their exhibition stand and the Pennsylvania Railroad exhibit presented a stereo film, *Thrills for You*, in black and white, with polarising projection. All three films were made by the Loucks and Norling studios; it was estimated that the three films were seen by over four million people.

At about the same time the Russian engineer Semyon Pavlovich Ivanov was perfecting a stereoscopic process which did not require the audience to wear special spectacles. It was based upon several methods for still photography patented and demonstrated at the beginning of the century, notably by A. Berthier, E. Estenave and F. E. Ives. The principle of the parallax stereogram involved placing a regular line screen or grid just in front of the sensitive surface. When exposed in a twin lens camera, the lines of the grid, seen from each lens, covered part of the plate. Matters were so arranged that the images produced by one lens fell on those parts of the plate shielded from the other lens. Thus, on the same plate, two interlaced images were recorded. A positive print from the double negative could be viewed through a grid adjusted so as to conceal from each eye those parts of the image belonging to the other. A single picture in depth could then be seen. Ivanov adapted this idea for the cinema. His first patent was filed in 1935 and using a glass grating he demonstrated his process in 1937. In 1940 he replaced the glass grating with a fine wire screen. The system was installed in the Moskva cinema in Moscow in 1941; 112 miles (180km) of wire were used to make a grid over a screen of about 14 by 19 feet (4.25 × 5.8 metres). The films were shot with a conventional camera with a beam splitting device on the lens, producing two vertical format pictures side by side in the standard frame area. The sound track ran between the two pictures on the print. The film was back-projected, with a grid on the projector side of the screen to divide the two pictures into interlaced line images. A similar grid on the audience side created the correct viewing conditions for 200 seats laid out in a fan-shaped area. This was necessary for in some places in the auditorium no true stereoscopic image was presented. The process underwent several changes;

Most 3D movie systems require that the audience wear polarising or colour filter spectacles

a lenticular ribbed glass screen replaced the wires and, by limiting the size of the perforations, the format was changed to a square. This improved process, developed in 1946, was used to make the stereofilm *Robinson Crusoe*, shown in February of the following year on a 16½-foot (5 metre) square screen at the Vostok Cinema, Moscow. Later still, in 1952, the picture was changed to one of standard format, the stereo pictures being recorded one above the other through a prism system. By 1955 12 cinemas in the USSR were showing stereoscopic films. At its best, the system worked very well but the viewer had to keep his or her head still, as quite small sideways movements could produce a temporary loss of the stereoscopic image. However, each seat had several positions in which the true image could be seen. The line screen was not visible at normal viewing distances.

The only application of the parallax stereogram process for moving films outside the USSR was the Cyclostereoscope, developed by Francois Savoye. In this system the two pictures were projected on a grid screen which rotated rapidly to remove the line effect. It was shown at the Luna Park, Paris, in 1949.

As a special attraction for the great postwar exhibition at the Festival of Britain, held in London in 1951, a cinema was built on the site to show the latest techniques in film and television. A series of stereoscopic films were commissioned for the Telekinema. The first test film made in the London Zoo was very effective. Two Technicolor 'three-strip' cameras were strapped together to make a stereoscopic film, *The Distant Thames*, later expanded and re-named *Royal River*, shown with a three-track stereophonic sound track. The Scots-Canadian animator Norman McLaren was commissioned to make two stereoscopic animated films, *Now is the time – to put your glasses on* and *Around is Around*, and the ballet *The Black Swan* was filmed. The first programme was shown to the international press on 30 April 1951, using polarised light projection with Polaroid spectacles for the audience. The Telekinema was a great success, with long queues for each performance.

It was responsible for arousing interest in stereoscopic films throughout the world film industry and was followed by a wave of stereoscopic productions in America the following year. The first to be shown was *Bwana Devil* shot in 'Natural Vision' (not to be confused with the earlier wide film process) by Arch Obler, and was first

A poster for Warner's most successful
3D movie *The House Of Wax*, 1953

shown on 26 November 1952 at the Paramount Theatres in Hollywood and Los Angles. It was a phenomenal success with the public.
The film was shot in Ansco Color, and was projected using Polaroid
analysers. The American film business plunged into the production
of '3D' films. Metro-Goldwyn-Mayer dusted off their old anaglyph
Audioscopiks and ran them again, renamed 'Metroscopix', in
America and Europe. The second 3D production was Warner
Brothers' *The House of Wax*, shown first on 10 April 1953, accompanied by six-track stereophonic sound. It was a record success.
More than 60 feature films were shot in 3D in 1953 and some 20 or
more were in production in Hollywood in 1954. However, by the
end of 1953 the interest of the public was waning. Audiences complained of eye strain and headaches, probably caused by badly
aligned projectors. Many of the later productions were released in
'flat' versions only, and within a year 3D was dead. There have been
only spasmodic attempts to reintroduce stereoscopic films since
then. Space Vision, shown in Chicago in 1966 in *The Bubble* used a
pair of 2.66 to 1 aspect ratio half-frame images one above the other
on the film; the process was used by Carlo Ponti and Andy Warhol
for the film *Flesh for Frankenstein* in 1974. Most of the other applications of stereoscopy in the 1960s and 1970s have been for sex films
and 'soft pornographic' productions.

The Space Vision stereo process
recorded a stereo pair of wide screen
format images one above the other in a
normal frame area, obviating the need
for two projectors. The film was
projected through polarising filters, and
the audience wore polarising spectacles

Before leaving the processes which have broadened and deepened
the horizons of the cinemagoer, we should look briefly at the use of
another dimension – smell! The association of odours with movie
presentations has been around for some time. S. L. Rothafel added
the scent of roses to the atmosphere in his theatre in Forest City,
Pennsylvania in 1906, during the showing of the film of the Pasadena
Rose Bowl game. A similar experiment was carried out by A. E.
Fowler of the Boston Fenway theatre, when showing the film *Lilac
Time* in 1929. Lilac scented perfume was added to the air conditioning just before the film started; the audience were moved to applaud
as the scent spread throughout the theatre. Low Brook tried more
elaborate experiments in shows at Hollywood, Santa Barbara and
elsewhere in 1934. Operators released a variety of more or less

appropriate odours into the air conditioning ducts to synchronize with particular moments in the film. The problem was, of course, the time taken for an odour to reach the whole theatre, and the time taken for it to be removed and replaced by another. Michael Todd Jr overcame these problems to some extent with his Smell-O-Vision system, demonstrated in the feature film *Scent of Mystery* premiered on 12 January 1960 at the Cinestage theatre in Chicago. An odour dispenser, installed at a cost of about $30,000, passed the smells through a network of pipes to ducts in the back of each seat, ensuring that almost every member of the audience received the smell at the same time and at the right moment in relation to the film. The smells were released by electrical signals derived from the sound-track on the 70mm colour print. *British Kinematography* reported,

> 'Some of the odours used in this film are roses, peach, wood shavings, baking bread, bananas, boot polish, tobacco, perfume, ocean breeze, oil paint, wine, garlic, gun smoke, clover, coffee, brandy, lavender, carnation, train smoke, incense and last but not least, fresh air!'

Competing with Todd's Smell-O-Vision was the Aromarama, conceived by Charles Weiss. Less sophisticated than its rival, Aromarama released its repertoire of 72 smells into the theatre air conditioning. The feature film *The Great Wall of China* was accompanied by smells when shown at the De Mille Theatre from 2 December 1959. It was generally well received:

> 'Here the audience's nose is assailed by the odours of Hong Kong streets, "honky tonks", cormorants, incense, sour wine, floral processions, fireworks, construction work, tigers, horses etc'

reported *British Kinematography*. Critics were mixed in their reactions. Some were highly complimentary, but the *New York Post* critic said, 'The great green outdoors upon one occasion came through as celery tonic . . . Ideally you have the impression of being surrounded when the scent strikes you as right but, when it is wrong, half-wrong, or unimpressive, it can be a distraction.' Neither process was used for another film. Smell-O-Vision's Bill Roos was quoted as saying 'We're scared to death that on opening night the competition will come to the theatre armed with Air-Wick'. With sight, hearing and smell catered for, only the sense of touch is left unstimulated. In *Brave New World*, written in 1932, Aldous Huxley postulated the Feelies:

> 'I hear the new one at the Alhambra is first rate. There's a love scene on a bearskin rug; they say it's marvellous. Every hair of the bear reproduced. The most amazing tactual effects.'

How long shall we have to wait?

Movies in the home

When cinematography first arrived in the mid-1890s, there was no distinction between amateur and professional equipment, but manufacturers soon began to produce apparatus aimed at the domestic market, where large scale projection was not required. The first specifically amateur apparatus appears to have been the Amateur-Kinetograph produced by the German manufacturer Oskar Messter in 1897. It used 35mm film, and the camera could be converted into a projector for showing the film. Since the standard film was used, it did not offer any economy in running costs.

Birt Acres' Birtac camera, 1899, with its film

The first low-cost amateur apparatus to reach the general market was designed by Birt Acres.

He demonstrated his Birtac camera, which he had patented on 9 June 1898, to the Croydon Camera Club on 25 January 1899, and put it on the market in England in May of that year. The Birtac used a half width film, 17.5mm wide, produced by splitting the standard film down the middle. The camera was a compact wooden box, which could be carried in a leather case fitted with pivoted flaps covering the lens and the viewfinder so that it could be used unobtrusively in its case, in the manner of the 'detective' still cameras of the time. The Birtac took 50 feet (15.2 metres) of film on daylight loading spools; the mechanism was hand turned, a beater movement providing the intermittent motion. The exposed and printed film was projected by the same machine by attaching a lamphouse and reversing the lens. The Birtac system was very economical, since each frame was a quarter of the area of the standard frame. The outfit cost 10 guineas, including a lantern lamphouse. A further 2 guineas would buy a developing and printing outfit.

'Photographs anything in Motion, from a Toy Terrier to an Ocean Greyhound.'

The Biokam. REGISTERED

A Combined Cinematograph & Snap-Shot Camera, Printer, Projector, Reverser, and Enlarger.

FITTED WITH TWO SPECIAL VOIGTLANDER LENSES.
Finished in Polished Ebony. Size 5 × 5½ × 9¾ inches.
PRICE COMPLETE **£6 6 0**

Advertisement for the Biokam

The Biokam projector and film, 1899

The Birtac was closely followed by the Biokam, demonstrated by T. C. Hepworth at the London Camera Club on 24 March 1899. It was advertised as 'a combined Cinematograph & Snapshot camera, Printer, Projector, Reverser and Enlarger'. The outfit consisted of a basic mechanism unit with a claw intermittent, taking a film 17.5mm wide, perforated with narrow slots in the centre of the film between the frames. To this unit could be attached a metal film box, containing 25 feet (7.6 metres) of negative film, which, after exposure, was fed into a 'film receptacle' – a wooden light-tight box attached to the back of the mechanism, into which the film was fed loosely, without being wound up. The box had two separate compartments, so that two rolls of film could be exposed in succession. The mechanism unit could be converted in turn into a printer, to expose a positive film through the negative, and, with the addition of a light source, into a projector to show the films. One frame at a time could be exposed, so that the Biokam could be used for a large number of still photographs, which could be enlarged onto photographic paper by using the same mechanism. The basic Biokam outfit cost six guineas; for 11 guineas a full outfit was supplied, including developing apparatus and a special projection lantern. The film cost 3/6d for about 45 seconds running time, or 700 single snapshots. Developing and printing cost 14/- per roll, and professionally produced film subjects could be bought for 10/- each. The Warwick Trading Company marketed the Biokam, claiming that it 'Photographs anything in motion from a Toy Terrier to an Ocean Greyhound . . . Truly a fearful weapon to place in the hands of the already dangerous amateur photographer, says the pessimist!'

Another machine for the home was designed by J. A. Prestwich early in 1899. The 'Junior Prestwich' used a daylight loading film half an inch (13mm) wide, with a frame size of $\frac{1}{2}$ inch $\times \frac{3}{8}$ inch (13mm $\times$ 9.5mm). It was reported to be 'in course of manufacture in bulk', but does not seem to have come to anything. The next amateur apparatus to appear was Gaumont's 'Chrono de Poche' camera sold from the end of 1900. The film was 15mm wide, with a centre perforation, and was driven by a clockwork motor – the first use of this feature in an amateur camera. The intermittent movement was produced by a beater, with which the larger Gaumont machines had been fitted. Once again, the same mechanism served for projection.

L. U. Kamm's Kammatograph outfit of 1900 used a different principle, based on his patent of 17 March 1898. His machine took a 12-inch (30.5cm) circular glass plate on which 600 exposures could be made as the plate rotated intermittently and slowly traversed behind the lens. The idea of an optical equivalent to the gramophone record had been

The Kamm Kammatograph, 1900

suggested by several inventors, and was to be revived periodically, as we shall see. 1900 was a year of some activity in the amateur field, with the appearance of La Petite Cinematographe, a combined camera and projector using centre-perforated 17.5mm film, and the Mirographe, introduced by Reulos and Goudeau of Paris, using a 21mm film with the edges notched in lieu of perforations.

The Ernemann Kino camera, 1904

The Vita home cinematograph, sold in Vienna in 1902-3, used the glass disc principle; the outside casing resembled a large book. It made little impression on the public. The German Ernemann company, well known for its still cameras, entered the amateur movie field in 1903 with its Kino camera. The first version used a claw intermittent to drive a centre-perforated 17.5mm film, taking pictures 16mm $\times$ 10mm.

An improved model, introduced in 1904, used an eight-armed Maltese Cross mechanism to drive an intermittent sprocket wheel. The apparatus was made with the customary quality and efficiency of all Ernemann apparatus. The separate mechanism unit had various attachments to allow it to be used for taking, printing and projecting the film. Alternative versions took 50 or 100 feet (15.2 or 30.4 metres) of film in detachable magazines.

The Kinora camera, 1908

An English Company, Kinora Ltd, revived the flip-book idea introduced in the earlier Lumière apparatus of the same name, in a form particularly suited to the home. The Kinora system won a silver medal on its introduction at the Franco-British Exhibition at the White City in London in 1908. As well as providing flip-book reels printed from professionally shot films, Kinora Ltd supplied a camera in which rolls of 1-inch (25.4mm) paper or celluloid film could be exposed by the amateur. The exposed negative films were processed and printed by Kinora and made up into reels for the Kinora viewers, which were available in a number of forms from very cheap, basic hand-turned models to elaborate versions mounted on ornate pedestals and driven by clockwork. The Kinora system remained on the market for some years and enjoyed a modest success.

The Société des Cinéma-Plaques of Paris produced a variation on the glass-plate movie camera with its Olikos camera of 1912. A rectangular glass plate was used in the camera, which exposed on it 12

about 6mm × 4mm in size, with two rows of perforations between them. The film was a safety film, on a base of cellulose acetate, rather than the highly inflammable cellulose nitrate used for standard film and was produced by the Eastman Kodak company. In a letter to Edison of 4 June 1912, Eastman said,

> 'Concerning the cellulose acetate film which we are furnishing you for your Home Kinetoscope, we beg to say that we believe the article to be a perfectly safe one for use in such an apparatus or we would not consent to supply it. In our opinion, the furnishing of cellulose nitrate for such a purpose would be wholly indefensible and reprehensible.'

The Pathé Kok Home Cinematograph, 1912

The Duoscope, 1912, was another combined camera and projector, using 17.5mm film

rows of seven frames in sequence, the frame size being 7mm × 8mm. The camera could hold up to 18 plates which could be exposed in turn. The camera was converted for projection by attaching it to a lantern. Like most of the glass plate systems, it did not prove popular. The Duoscope apparatus, also introduced in 1912, used 17.5mm film, with two perforations on the line between the frames. An electric lamp was built into the camera body, so that by connecting it to a battery the camera could be used as a projector.

The Edison Home Kinetoscope, 1912

Until this time, all amateur cinema apparatus had used the very dangerous nitrate film, which represented a severe fire hazard in the home. The Edison Home Kinetoscope could project, it was claimed, pictures from 16 inches × 12 inches (40.6cm × 30.5cm) to 64 inches × 48 inches (162.5cm × 122cm) in size. The projector cost from £14 to £19, and the film subjects, all printed from professional productions cost from 10/- to £4.

In the same year, 1912, the French Pathé company launched their Pathéscope Home Cinematograph, known also as the Pathé Kok (from the Pathé trademark, a crowing cockerel). As with the Edison machine, the emphasis was on safety. The Pathé film was 28mm wide, on cellulose acetate safety film. The film had three perforations on one side and one perforation on the other side of

Film for Edison's Home Kinetoscope

Edison also entered the home cinema field in 1912, with his Home Kinetoscope. The film was 22mm wide, with three rows of pictures of

each frame, so that it was quite impossible to run conventional film in the projector. The light was provided by a small electric lamp run from a dynamo driven from the film transport mechanism, so that if the film stopped moving, the dynamo stopped turning and the light went out. Although a Pathéscope 28mm film camera was available, the principle use of the projector was to show prints made from professional productions. Such films were sold for 2d a foot and a library service was available, supplying 12 subjects a week for a subscription of 10 guineas a year. The machine was capable of projecting a 3-foot × 2-foot (91cm × 60cm) picture; it cost £15, including two films, a screen, carrying case and a cleaning outfit. For an extra 35/- a battery was available so that single pictures could be shown. It was a very popular machine; by 1918 over 10,000 had been sold and it was estimated that 25,000,000 feet of printed positive film had been produced. Because of its large frame size – 19mm × 14mm, not much smaller than that on the standard film – the quality of the projected image was very good.

In 1917, A. F. Victor, an American, designed a Safety Cinema projector to take 28mm film, which he modified to carry three perforations on each side of the frame. He tried to persuade other film producers to supply reduction prints for his projectors, but with only limited success. He did persuade the newly formed Society of Motion Picture Engineers to adopt his 28mm film format as a standard for safety film. The Victor films could be run on a Pathéscope machine, although the reverse was not possible. Several new models of both Victor and Pathéscope projectors appeared during the next few years.

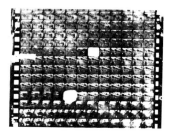

Proszynski's Oko machine, 1914, took a 12cm wide perforated film

The inventor of the Aeroscope camera, Kasimir Proszynski, demonstrated to the Royal Photographic Society on 20 January 1914 an unusual camera-projector based on a design he had patented in 1912. He had first worked with, but then discarded, methods of sequence photography on glass plates. Instead, his new design used a film 12cm wide, perforated on both edges. The camera exposed horizontal rows of 15 pictures, 7mm × 5mm in size, across the film, which then moved on a step, taking a further row of pictures back in the other direction. Proszynski claimed that the Oko camera could take up to 30 feet (9.1 metres) of film, giving a record lasting almost an hour, at a running speed of 10 pictures a second. The running costs were therefore very

low. The same mechanism, with the addition of a special electric lamp, also designed by Proszynski, served to project the film. The Oko machine was manufactured for a time in London by the Warwick Trading Company and later, in the early 1920s, about 100 were made in Warsaw.

The Movette, 'A system of Motion Photography for the Home', was introduced in 1917, by Movette Inc. of Rochester, New York. It had several novel features. The film was 17.5mm wide, with two circular perforations on each side of the frame. The negative film, on nitrate base and made by the Eastman Kodak company, was enclosed in a metal box, from which a loop was drawn out for threading in the camera – the first application of magazine loading in an amateur camera. The developed negative was printed onto Eastman safety positive film, which was loaded into a magazine for use in the projector. Up to 200 feet (61 metres), equivalent to four camera films, could be loaded in one projection magazine. The camera, tripod and projector outfit cost about $150 and negative film, developing and printing cost $5.25 for 50 feet (15 metres). Each 50-foot reel lasted one minute and 40 seconds. The Movette system represented the first real attempt to simplify film-making for the non-

The Movette system, 1917, used cameras loaded with chargers of 17.5mm film with circular edge perforations

expert, with its magazine loading camera and projector, fixed focus and fixed aperture lens which required no adjustment, and reasonably economic film costs. In its day, it did not make a big impression, but it introduced features which were to be successfully exploited by others.

In 1918, the American Wilart Instrument company, producers of a widely used professional cinecamera, developed an amateur movie system which they called the Actograph. It used a 17.5mm safety film, with one perforation to each side of the frame. The film was carried in a detachable external double magazine rather like a miniature version of that used on the Bell & Howell professional camera. Like the Movette, the camera was simple to operate, and was very small, being barely 9 inches long by 7 inches high (23cm × 18cm). A suitcase-sized projector was available to show the films.

The Urban Spirograph disc

In 1923 Charles Urban reintroduced the idea of the disc cinematograph in his Spirograph projector, which had been designed ten years earlier, but not much exploited at the time. The Spirograph took a 10½-inch (26.7cm) disc of Eastman safety film carrying 1,200 frames 0.22 inches × 0.16 inches (5.6mm × 4.1mm) in size, in a spiral of 12 rows. The edge of the disc was perforated for accurate transport. The discs were printed from 35mm professional film subjects via an intermediate glass disc negative. The Spirograph was intended only as a home cinema apparatus, and no camera was available for amateur use.

The Urban Spirograph projector, 1923

In 1922 the first of what was to be one of the most popular, and still surviving, amateur film systems appeared. The French Pathé company developed an alternative to their earlier Pathéscope 28mm film projector, which was bulky and cumbersome. They decided upon a film 9.5mm wide, with a slot perforation between the frames, similar to that used on a number of the earlier 17.5mm films. The Pathé company launched the new film with a home cinema projector, the Pathé-Baby, on 4 November 1922. The films, reduction prints from professionally made 35mm originals on 9.5mm safety film, were carried in small circular magazines carrying about 28 feet (8.5 metres) of film.

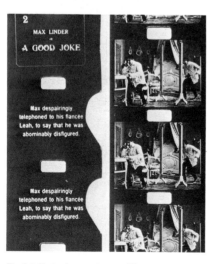

Pathé-Baby home cinema film

The Pathé-Baby home projector, 1922

The film was easily loaded, being automatically taken up in a chamber below the mechanism, from which it was rewound back into the magazine after projection. The projector was hand-turned, although later bolt-on electric motor drives were available. To achieve an economy in film, Pathé developed an ingenious mechanism in the projector which sensed the presence of notches in the edges of the film, holding it stationary for three or four seconds, when it then moved on normally. Thus, titles needed to be printed on only three or four notched frames at most, and did not take up a significant part of the short length of film. The Pathé-Baby projector cost 275 francs, and film subjects cost five or six francs each. A large library of films was available for hire as well as for sale.

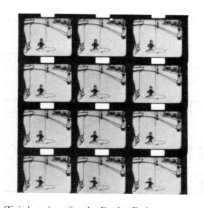

Triple prints for the Pathé-Baby

The prints were made three at a time on a special 35mm film stock, which after printing and processing was perforated and slit into the 9.5mm widths.

In January 1923 the Eastman Kodak Company announced the culmination of several years of research into a new system of amateur film making based on a new 16mm film size. Work had begun as long ago as 1914, when J. G. Capstaff of the Kodak Research Laboratory saw an experimental camera built some years before by F. W. Barnes, manager of the Hawkeye camera works of the Eastman Kodak company. The Barnes camera used 35mm film run twice through the camera to expose two rows of pictures. When the film was processed and printed, Barnes proposed to project it by attaching a lamphouse to the same mechanism. At the time, the project had come to nothing. Capstaff used the camera to work out a satisfactory method of processing the film exposed in the camera to give a positive image directly, without the need to print on another film. Capstaff considered that such a reversal process would reduce the cost of amateur cinematography to a reasonable level by eliminating the need for two separate films. By 1916 a suitable process had been worked out, giving good quality, fine-grained, positive images. Various subdivisions of the standard 35mm frame size were tried out in the Barnes camera, until Capstaff decided that a frame size of one-sixth of the standard frame represented the best compromise between economy and quality. This picture area was 10mm × 7.5mm in size, and adding an extra 3mm on either side for perforations, gave a film width of 16mm. Since this was not a convenient subdivision of 35mm film, it greatly reduced the risk that others might supply dangerous nitrate-based films, instead of what Eastman saw as the obligatory safety film.

After a break in development work after America's entry into the First World War, work was taken up again in 1919. A prototype 16mm camera was completed by May 1920, and a projector was designed soon after. The 16mm film's perforations

Bolt-on electric motor drive

The Cine-Kodak camera, 1923, introduced the 16mm film format

apparatus was announced to the trade on 12 August 1923; both camera and projector were hand turned. Victor also produced a few electrically driven cameras, but, like Eastman, also had trouble with the Willard batteries and they were soon discontinued.

Bell & Howell were next in the field, with the Filmo camera and projector. The design was based on a 17.5mm Filmo system, using the same film as the Actograph, which had been launched in October 1922, but had hardly reached the market before the Eastman Kodak 16mm film appeared. The redesigned apparatus appeared towards the end of 1923 as the Bell & Howell Filmo 70 camera and projector. The Filmo camera was the first 16mm camera to have clockwork motor drive. Victor followed with a spring driven camera in May 1925, and the Ciné-Kodak Model B camera, with an integral clockwork motor, appeared in July of that year.

option of a direct or reflected image as required and the motor units were supplied without a reflecting finder. The batteries for the motors gave some trouble and they were discontinued in November 1923, although an improved electric drive attachment was reintroduced in May 1924. The Ciné-Kodak outfits – camera, tripod, projector, splicer and screen – sold in America for $335. The reversal film cost $6 inclusive of processing and return postage. Although the apparatus was not cheap, the running costs were very much lower than in other systems; for example, 16mm cost about one fifth of the cost of the equivalent running time on 35mm negative-positive film.

The Pathé-Baby camera, 1923

were arranged one on either side of the line between the frames. The new format was demonstrated to various technical societies early in 1923, and the new 16mm film, the Ciné-Kodak camera and the Kodascope projector were announced to the photographic trade in June 1923.

The camera was solidly made, with a diecast metal body and capacity for 100 feet (30.5 metres) of film, enough for four minutes, on daylight loading spools. A claw mechanism provided the intermittent movement. The camera was hand turned, although a motor drive unit was available, containing a Mastercraft Corporation electric motor driven from a Willard battery. The bolt-on motor drive unit also incorporated a reflecting viewfinder to supplement the direct vision viewfinder on the camera. After the first 200 had been made (from serial number 701) the cameras were modified to incorporate a pivoting mirror in the viewfinder to give the

The Kodascope projector, 1923

Alexander Victor set to work to design a camera and projector for the new film gauge as soon as it was announced in January 1923. His

Meanwhile, the Pathé company had been working on a camera for their 9.5mm film, and the first experimental models were designed

and built by Continsouza, and tested in January 1923. The Pathé-Baby cinecamera was announced on 4 November 1923, and was on sale in December. Pathé had also decided upon a reversal process for the film, which was loaded in a metal charger containing about 30 feet (9 metres) of film. To load the camera, the charger was simply dropped in and a loop of film drawn from it was slotted into the gate – the simplest loading system so far. The camera was hand turned, each revolution exposing seven frames and it was very small and compact. A bolt-on clockwork motor drive was available from 1926 and in 1928 the Pathé Motocamera, with an integral clockwork motor, was introduced.

Curiously enough, the arrival of the first really practical and economic home movie systems using small film sizes coincided with a proliferation of compact 35mm cinecameras designed to attract the amateur. We have already considered, in chapter five, the Sept camera, a combined camera, projector and printer for both movie and still photography which had been introduced in 1921. The Bol Cinegraph camera, designed by the creator of the later, famous Bolex 16mm camera, appeared in the same year. It too acted as camera, printer and projector for 35mm film. It held about 76 feet (23 metres) of film in a double charger, and was hand turned. It had a very ingenious frame viewfinder incorporating the focusing scale and a pendulum level. The Ica Kinamo camera, introduced around the same time, took 50 feet (15.2

The Ica Kinamo camera, c. 1922

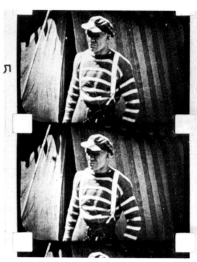

Pathé Rural 17.5mm film

Campro 35mm paper film

metres) of 35mm film in a daylight-loading double charger. The first model was hand turned, but by October 1925 a new model with an attached clockwork motor was available. The Campro combined camera and projector, shown at the Royal Photographic Society on 15 November 1927 was different, offering the option of making the films on paper instead of celluloid, although the latter could be used. Perforated 35mm paper rolls were used, and the prints on paper were shown by illuminating them with two lamps which attached to the front of the camera. The idea was novel, but the camera was not well made and did not prove to be a success commercially.

The Pathé company attempted to produce a rival to 16mm by launching a new 17.5mm film in 1926. The new film, called Pathé Rural, was shown first at the Société Français de Photographie on 10 February 1926. The films were produced by printing in pairs by reduction on a 35mm safety film from standard originals. The print stock was appropriately perforated

with one perforation on each side of the frame line, as in 16mm, and after printing the film was slit to give two prints, 17.5mm wide, with a frame size about 60% larger than the area of a 16mm frame. This advantage was not sufficient to overcome the disadvantage of its noncompatability with the growing range of 16mm equipment. Pathé had conceived the gauge as specially suitable for small cinema use in country districts – hence the name – but it was little used outside France. A 17.5mm camera, the Rex Motocamera, a scaled-up version of the 9.5mm model, was available in the early 1930s, but it made little impression.

The Homovie camera, 1929

While the 16mm and 9.5mm films had proved popular because of the great economy they offered over the standard 35mm film, attempts were continuously made to reduce the costs of home movies even further. In

The Bol Cinégraphe, 1921

The Homovie camera gate

The Cine-Kodak Eight-20 camera, 1932

The Univex Straight 8 camera, c. 1936

Film for the Homovie

1929 the Kodel Electrical and Mfg Company in America introduced their Homovie system. The camera used ordinary 16mm film, but produced four small pictures within the normal 16mm frame area. The gate of the camera oscillated from side to side while the camera was running, and the film was pulled through the gate half the normal length at a time. This produced a picture sequence in which the second picture was taken next to the first, the third was taken above the second, the fourth was taken next to the third and above the first, and so on. The projector, with a built-in rear projection screen, operated in the same way. Four times the normal running time, a total of sixteen minutes, was possible from a standard 100-foot (30.5 metre) reel, but the oscillating gate made the camera very noisy in operation.

A similar economy was the aim of a new film gauge introduced in August 1932 by the Eastman Kodak Company. The new Ciné-Kodak Eight-20 camera took a 25-foot (7.6 metre) roll of 16mm wide film

with twice the usual number of perforations. The film was run once through the camera, exposing quarter-size images down one half of the width of the film. It was then reloaded and run back onto the original spool, taking a second set of pictures on the other half of the film.

The new 8mm film gauge

After processing, the reversal developed film was slit down the middle to make two lengths of 8mm wide film, which were joined together to make a 50-foot (15.2 metre) length which would last for four minutes in the projector. Despite the very small frame size, the image quality was very good, certainly adequate for domestic use, achieved through the use of specially developed high resolution emulsions. In an effort to reduce even further the already small size of the camera, in September 1935 Bell & Howell announced the Filmo Straight Eight camera, in which a 50-foot (15.2 metre) roll of 8mm wide film was run once through the camera. The

Universal Camera Company followed with the Univex Straight 8 camera using the same film loading method. Other single-run 8mm cameras appeared in following years, but the system had its drawbacks and it never achieved the wide popularity of the 'double-run' 8mm system.

While the economies of the new 8mm film attracted many new recruits to home moviemaking, in the 1930s the real battle, for the European enthusiasts, was between 16mm and 9.5mm. In America 16mm was favoured, 9.5mm film having never gained a significant following there. The 'nine-fiver' pointed to the economy of his gauge, the frame size being virtually equal to that of 16mm film, but with no wasted area for perforations, The 9.5mm cameras and projectors were very cheap, were simple to load and to use and there was a very wide range of library films available. The 'sixteen-mil' user pointed to the real risk of film damage posed by the centre perforation of 9.5mm, if the film jumped in the projector. As far as equipment was concerned, 9.5mm did offer a wider choice of inexpensive apparatus.

Several combined camera-projector models were introduced in the 1930s, representing the ultimate economy in equipment. The Midas camera was shown at the British Industries Fair in February and March 1934. For seven guineas the purchaser acquired a solidly built camera which took 30 feet (9.1 metres) of 9.5mm film in circular

169

The Midas 9.5mm camera, 1934

magazines. A small electric motor, powered by two dry cells held in a detachable battery compartment, operated the mechanism when it was used as a camera. The processed films could be projected by the same mechanism, but this time turned by hand, and a built-in electric lamp provided the light when the machine was connected to a battery. The original models were not entirely satisfactory, and much improved versions were sold in the autumn of 1938: the Improved Midas, Super Midas and Midas de Luxe. The latter two models had more powerful lamps, giving a bigger picture. An adaptor outfit permitted the Midas to project films of up to 400 feet (122 metres) in length, with a resistance which allowed the lamp to be run from the main electricity supply. The 9.5mm Campro camera-projector,

The Campro 9.5mm camera/projector

shown at the British Industries Fair in February 1935 was less well engineered and designed. It used a clockwork motor to drive the film and a small electric lamp was built into the camera to project the processed film. It was capable only of projecting a picture a few inches across if anything like adequate brightness was needed.

Several important technical innovations appeared first in the 9.5mm medium. The Eumig C-2 camera, introduced in 1935, incorporated a photoelectric cell, connected to a meter, the needle of which was visible in the viewfinder. An iris diaphragm over the cell was connected with that of the lens, so that as the needle was aligned in the viewfinder, the lens was automatically set to the correct exposure. This principle was extended to Eumig's 8mm C-3 camera in 1937. The 8mm Eumig C-4 camera, introduced in 1938, was driven by an integral electric motor; the Midas camera, as we have seen, had this feature in 1934, in which year the 16mm Amigo Electra camera was first sold, also with a built in electric motor. While the 9.5mm gauge competed very effectively at the lower end of the range of prices, when it came to advanced and specialised equipment it could not compete with 16mm.

The Cine-Kodak Special camera, 1933

The first camera to offer professional facilities to the amateur user was the Ciné-Kodak Special camera, launched in April 1933. This precision-built camera offered a range of filming speeds from eight to 64 frames per second, a two-lens turret, a variable and totally closing

shutter for fade and dissolve effects, backwinding facilities, single frame exposures for animation, a critical reflex focusing device, masks for special effects, split screen shots and so on, clockwork or hand drive, interchangeable film magazines, a very wide range of lenses and special accessories for scientific or technical filming. The Swiss-made Paillard-Bolex 16mm camera was introduced in 1935. While it did not have quite the range of facilities offered by the Ciné-Kodak Special camera, it was versatile enough for most film makers. Both cameras came into increasing use by professional photographers in educational, scientific and industrial cinematography. The French Emel C-82 camera brought some of the facilities of these advanced cameras to 8mm filming in 1938.

One of the advantages of 9.5mm filming over 16mm was in the simplicity that it had in camera loading. The Pathé charger could be loaded with a roll of film in the dark, a very simple operation. The loaded charger was easily fitted in the camera in daylight. On the other hand, 16mm and 8mm cameras used spools of film from which a length had to be drawn and threaded through the mechanism onto a take-up spool. While this could be done in daylight, care had to be taken that light did not reach the rest of the film on the spools during this operation. The Agfa Movex camera, demonstrated on 10 December 1928, overcame this problem by using a charger not unlike that for 9.5mm cameras, loaded with about 40 feet (12 metres) of 16mm film. The loaded charger dropped into the camera, with the minimum amount of threading to be done. The Simplex Pockette camera, introduced in 1931, used a magazine containing 50 feet (15.2 metres) of 16mm film; the magazine located directly into the camera with no need to thread the film. Ensign, in England, introduced an improved version of the Simplex Pockette in 1935. The Bell & Howell Filmo 121 camera (1934) used a magazine with a similar principle, also containing 50 feet of 16mm film. The Ciné-Kodak Magazine camera, launched in 1936, used a magazine containing 50 feet of 16mm film and equipped with an integral footage counter and continuous film-driving sprocket. The claw mechanism, in the body of the camera, drove the film through a slot in the magazine. A safety shutter on the magazine closed automatically as it was withdrawn from the camera, so that a partly exposed magazine could be removed without fogging the film. The Bell & Howell Filmo 141 model of 1938 used the same magazine, as did a number of other cameras during the next 20 years. The Siemens and Halske Kino C8 camera, shown at the Leipzig Spring Fair in 1936, used cassettes preloaded with ordinary daylight loading 8mm film spools, permitting the easy and safe reloading of the camera. The Agfa Movex 8 camera used an 8mm wide film loaded in a 33-foot (10-metre) cassette for easy loading. The Ciné-Kodak Magazine Eight camera, model 90, sold from 1940, used a magazine loaded with double-run 8mm film.

Sound came to several of the small film gauges in the 1930s. The earliest models used synchronised discs, like the professional Vitaphone system. The DeVry Cinetone projector was one of the first: a 16mm machine synchronised to a disc player, giving $3\frac{1}{2}$ minutes of sound film at a playing. It was demonstrated to the Royal Photographic Society on 22 April 1929. The Victor Animatophone of 1930 was novel in having the turntable placed vertically, with a counter-balanced 'floating' pickup arm. The Bell-Western Electric portable 16mm sound projector of 1932 used a conventional disc arrangement, as did the English Ensign Home Talkie outfit of the same year. The latter employed a Silent-Sixteen 250 projector synchronised with a record player operating at 78 or $33\frac{1}{3}$ rpm. The Paillard-Bolex Talkie projector was unusual in being a dual gauge machine, capable of running 16mm or 9.5mm films synchronised with a turntable. It was demonstrated to the Royal Photographic Society on 19 April 1932. By this time, however, the sound-on-disc principle was obsolete in the cinema.

The British-Thompson-Houston 16mm sound projector appears to have been the first 16mm sound-on-

Dr C. E. K. Mees on 16mm sound film

film projector to be marketed. Its first public demonstration was given in September 1931 at the Imperial Institute in London. The sound track was placed inside the perforations, to one side of the picture, as on 35mm film, and the picture was reduced in size to make room for it. It was the American RCA-Victor sound projector however which set the pattern for 16mm sound film apparatus. The film was perforated down one edge only, the sound track being placed along the other edge. It was introduced in January 1932. The following year, the RCA-Victor sound camera was announced, for direct sound recording while filming. The sound track was recorded on the edge of the film by a beam of light from a small battery operated lamp, reflected from a small mirror attached to a diaphragm vibrated by speech from the camera operator. The

The RCA Sound camera, 1935

'microphone' grille came close to the mouth when the camera was held in the normal operating position. The cameraman could speak commentary which was recorded as a variable area sound track along the edge of the film. The camera was not generally available until the autumn of 1935. Late in 1933 Westinghouse introduced their 16mm sound-on-film projector, and the next year there was a veritable flood of sound projectors from, among others, Agfa, British Acoustic Company, Gaumont British, Bell & Howell, Debrie and Siemens. Pathé launched a sound version of their 17.5mm Rural film with the Pathéscope Home Talkie projector in 1934. Like 16mm, the 17.5mm sound film used single perforated film with the sound track on the opposite edge. In the same year the

9.5mm variable density and variable area sound tracks (above left and right) and Pathe Rural 17.5mm sound film

Donelli sound projector introduced yet another format – 17.5mm film perforated in the centre like 9.5mm film, and with the sound track along one edge. Not surprisingly, it did not succeed. The Pathéscope Vox projector brought sound to 9.5mm films, at the end of 1937. The variable area or variable density sound tracks were run along one edge of the film.

We have seen already how colour came to amateur cinematography. In fact, the first coloured home movies were Pathé 9.5mm library films in the 1920s, some of which were coloured by the stencil colouring process. The lenticular Kodacolor film process of 1928 made colour film-making available to the amateur for the first time; a similar film was available from Agfa in 1932. Dufaycolor film in 16mm size was on the market in the summer of 1934 and in 9.5mm size in the late summer of 1937. The first of the modern integral tripack colour films, Kodachrome, was available in 16mm form in America from April 1935 and 8mm Kodachrome film followed in May 1936. Agfacolor 16mm film was announced in late 1936 and was generally available from the spring of 1937.

After the end of the Second World War there was a shift in popularity of the gauges. The quality of the 8mm film, especially the colour materials, was improving all the time, and the technical innovations and improvements were mostly applied to 16mm and 8mm equipment. The 9.5mm gauge struggled on, owing its survival mainly to the large quantity of second-hand equipment which remained in Europe after the War. It could no longer compete on the grounds of economy with the cheaper 8mm system, which had a much wider range of equipment. In a last, rather desperate attempt to win back an economical share of the market, the Pathéscope company introduced a new format – Pathé-Duplex 9.5mm film – in 1955. The new film had two perforations on the frame line instead of one. This film could be used in conventional 9.5mm cameras with a modified claw mechanism. Alternatively, a

Pathé Duplex, Monoplex and Classic formats

special camera was developed in which the film ran horizontally, passing twice through the mechanism, rather in the fashion of 8mm film. On each pass, half the width of the film was exposed, the 'wide screen' format pictures running side by side. After processing, the film was slit into two 4.75mm strips, becoming Monoplex film. The new system was advertised in May 1955, but remained almost unobtainable for some time. New Pathéscope Lido cameras, in versions for the 'classic' 9.5mm, for Duplex film, and for both formats appeared in 1956, but did not sell in large numbers. By 1959 the *Amateur Cine World* reported that the new format 'does not seem to have caught on . . . one never hears of it nowadays'. From that time, new 9.5mm equipment appeared less often and although at the time of writing 9.5mm film is still alive, it is only just so. The 1950s saw the rapid development of 8mm cine apparatus. The widespread introduction of automatic or semi-automatic exposure control and the use of electric motor drive were important developments in that period. The 16mm gauge became progressively more professional in its uses, and by the mid 1960s was used only by a relatively small number of advanced amateurs, the general amateur market being almost exclusively catered for by 8mm systems.

An important development in postwar sound films for amateurs was the introduction of magnetic sound recording. The RCA-1000 sound projector, shown first in October 1951 in Hollywood, was probably the first to be equipped to record and play back magnetically striped 16mm film as well as conventional optical sound tracks. The Pathé Marignan 9.5mm projector recorded and replayed magnetic tracks only; it was introduced in 1953. In 1960 the Fairchild Ciné Eight sound camera, with a fully transistorised recording amplifier built in, used 8mm film pre-striped with a magnetic sound recording track, for direct sound recording while filming. In the same year the Kodak Sound 8 projector was one of several introduced to record and replay sound tracks on magnetically striped film. John A.

Maurer demonstrated his 8mm optical sound film method in May 1961; for some years it was on the verge of commercial exploitation, but finally the superior sound quality of magnetic sound won the day.

The Kodak Super 8 camera, 1965

The most recent change in amateur film-making came in 1965 with the introduction of a new film format – Super 8 film. The new film had been proposed by the Eastman Kodak Company in 1962. The standard 8mm film had been derived by dividing 16mm film in half. The result was that in proportion to the small frame size, an inordinate amount of the film's area was non-picture – perforations, frame lines and so on. The new format was designed to make more efficient use of the film, by reducing the size of the perforations, and moving them nearer the edge of the film. By this means, the picture area was increased by 50%. Space down the edge opposite to the perforations was available for a sound track. The new film was launched in May 1965 in the form of a cartridge containing 50 feet (15.2 metres) of the new 8mm wide film. To load the camera, the cartridge was simply inserted, with no threading. A range of Kodak Instamatic Movie cameras was introduced at the same time, and soon a wide variety of apparatus was available from other manufacturers. At the same time, the Japanese Fuji company introduced their Single 8 film. The film width, perforation size and disposition and picture size were identical to those of Super 8, but the cartridge was different, with the feed and take-up compartments one above the other, whereas in the Super 8 cartridge they were side by side. Within a few years, manufacturers of amateur cine equipment had turned over almost exclusively to Super 8 apparatus.

There have been a number of technical advances incorporated in the design of Super 8 apparatus in recent years. The 'existing light' cameras use special wide aperture lenses, long exposure shutters and high speed films to permit films to be shot in ordinary levels of artificial light. The first of these high-speed cameras were the Kodak XL33 and XL55 cameras introduced in 1971. The rapid development of transistorised electronics has led to the development of Super 8 sound recording cameras, recording sound simultaneously with the pictures of

Kodak Sound 8 projector, 1960

pre-striped film in sound cartridges. The first of these 'single system' sound cameras were the Kodak Ektasound cameras (1973).

Today, for a relatively modest

outlay, the amateur film-maker has at his disposal a sophisticated system for recording movement, sound and colour of which the pioneers could only have dreamed. Wordsworth Donisthorpe's hope of talking, moving pictures in colour, expressed in 1878, has in a hundred years become available for anyone with a little money to invest and a bare modicum of technical knowledge. Rapid access to the pictures made in the camera, as in the Polaroid-Land Polavision system, where the film in a cartridge is available for viewing 90 seconds after being removed from the camera, and especially with home videotape apparatus becoming more and more portable and versatile with the advance of electronics, will further extend the scope of the amateur film maker. Making and replaying home movies will be almost as simple as watching TV.

Bibliography
General books:
Barnes, John, *The Beginnings of the Cinema in England*, David and Charles, Newton Abbot, 1976
Cook, Olive, *Movement in Two Dimensions*, Hutchinson, London, 1963
Deslandes, Jacques, *Histoire Comparée du Cinéma, Vol. 1*, Casterman, 1966
Fielding, Raymond, (ed.), *A Technological History of Motion Pictures and Television*, University of California Press, 1967
The Focal Encyclopaedia of Film and Television Techniques, Focal Press, London and New York, 1969
Souto, H. M., *The Technique of the Motion Picture Camera*, Focal Press, London and New York, 1967
Thomas, Dr D. B., *The Origins of the Motion Picture*, HMSO, London, 1964
Vivie, Jean, *Traité Général de Technique du Cinéma*, 1945
Individual inventors:
Coe, Brian, *W. Friese Greene and the Origins of Kinematography*, *The Photographic Journal*, March-April 1962
Hendricks, Gordon, *Beginnings of the Biograph* (The Beginnings of the American Film), 1964
Hendricks, Gordon, *Eadweard Muybridge, the Father of the Motion Picture*, Secker and Warburg, London, 1975
Hendricks, Gordon, *The Edison Motion Picture Myth*, University of California Press, 1961
Hendricks, Gordon, *The Kinetoscope* (The Beginnings of the American Film), 1966
Stanford University, *Eadweard Muybridge – The Stanford Years*, Stanford, 1972
Sound history:
Cameron, J. R., *Sound Motion Pictures*, Cameron Publishing Company, 1959
History of colour:
Coe, Brian, *Colour Photography*, Ash & Grant, London, 1978
Cornwell-Clyne, A., *Colour Cinematography*, Chapman and Hall, London, 1951

The International Encyclopaedia of Film, Michael Joseph, London, 1972
Ryan, R. T., *A History of Motion Picture Colour Technology*, Focal Press, London and New York, 1977
Thomas, Dr. D. B., *The First Colour Motion Pictures*, HMSO, London, 1969
Wide screen and 3D:
Cornwell-Clyne, A., *3-D Kinematography*, Hutchinson, London, 1954
Dewhurst, H., *Introduction to 3-D*, Chapman and Hall, London, 1954
Spottiswoode, R. and N., *The Theory of Stereoscopic Transmission*, University of California Press, 1953
Wysotsky, M. Z., *Wide Screen and Stereophonic Sound*, Focal Press, London and New York, 1971

Picture credits
The author and publishers wish to thank the following individuals and institutions for the use of the illustrations listed below. The new diagrams are by Les Smith. All unlisted illustrations are from the collection of the Kodak Museum, Harrow, Middlesex.
Mrs A. S. Acres, 72-3
Barnes Museum of Photography, 35 (below left), 81 (bottom right)
Howarth-Loomes collection, 27 (bottom), 28 (right)
Narodni Technische Muzeum, Prague, 36 (below), 49 (above), 70 (above rt.), 71 (above left), 109 (bottom rt.)
National Film Archive, 5, 6 (above right), 65 (bottom right), 80 (above), 83 (centre), 84 (above right), 85 (centre, above right), 99, 100 (top right, bottom left), 106 (rt.), 110-1, 149 (below), 154 (above), 159, 160 (above)
Science Museum, 4, 9 (below, below left), 13, 16 (below), 29-30, 36 (top), 37, 41, 44-5 (bottom), 46, 47 (right), 48 (above), 49 (below), 52 (below), 55 (centre), 57 (below), 61, 65 (top left), 74, 93, 116 (bottom rt.), 141
Technicolor Inc, 132, 137

Index